# Psychoanalytic Education at t

Training in psychoanalysis is a long and demanding process. However, the quality of education available is hugely variable across the world. The structure of psychoanalytic education, centered on the hierarchical "training analysis" system, reflected a concerted effort to maintain a stable and high quality educational process. However, throughout time this system has become a major source of institutional contradictions that affect the training of candidates, the scientific developments within psychoanalysis, and the nexus of psychoanalytic theory and practice with the surrounding scientific, social and cultural world. *Psychoanalytic Education at the Crossroads* examines the ways in which group processes, the hierarchal culture in institutes, the influence of individual personalities, the lack of research and the faults in supervision can all stifle creativity and hinder candidates' progress. In this compelling work, Otto Kernberg sets out clear suggestions for how these issues can be addressed, and how he sees the future of psychoanalytic education across all psychoanalytic settings and schools of thought.

The first part of this volume is focused primarily on the analysis of the nature of these problems and their effects on the personal analysis and supervision of candidates; on theoretical and clinical seminars; on selection, progression, and graduation; on educational principles and requirements, developments of theory and technique and, in particular, limitation versus expansion of the realm of interests and applications of psychoanalysis. The second part of this volume deals with proposals of solutions to the problems encountered, and major suggestions for innovation in psychoanalytic education.

The author's work in this area has been hugely influential. Kernberg has made a substantive difference in the development of psychoanalytic institutes and education, and continues to do so. *Psychoanalytic Education at the Crossroads* is essential reading to anyone involved in psychoanalytic education, whether as a psychoanalyst, psychoanalytic psychotherapist, trainee, trainer, or supervisor.

**Otto Friedmann Kernberg** is a psychoanalyst and professor of psychiatry at Weill Cornell Medical College, USA.

"The vitality of psychoanalysis depends on its ability to train creative and committed practitioners and contributors. In this volume Otto Kernberg incisively, passionately, and at times humorously dissects the ills that plague psychoanalytic education, offering thoughtful suggestions for constructive change. The result is a book that not only addresses crucial issues of institute training but that offers a provocative meditation on the place of psychoanalysis within the broader society. Kernberg's ideas are essential reading for anybody interested in the current state of psychoanalysis, and for anybody who cares about its future prospects." Jay Greenberg, PhD, Editor, *The Psychoanalytic Quarterly*.

"*Psychoanalytic Education at the Crossroads* is a wonderful and indispensable critique and reflection, based on extensive and intensive personal experience and careful observation of what happens internationally in this realm of our discipline. The present and the future of psychoanalysis are closely connected to the way we teach it and help our young colleagues to develop their own independent thinking. Its author is one of the leading psychoanalytic thinkers and clinicians of our time, Otto Kernberg. His passion, his tireless dedication, his creativity and his concerned critique, as well as his brilliant capacity to present and to systematize his views are all reasons that lead me to enthusiastically recommend the reading of Psychoanalytic Education at the Crossroads to analysts, analysts in training and all those who are interested in this fascinating work in progress that is psychoanalysis." Cláudio Laks Eizirik, Past President of the IPA.

"In a highly organized and comprehensive manner that is his trademark, Otto Kernberg addresses the intricacies of psychoanalytic education in this book. He deconstructs the challenges inherent in a process that simultaneously seeks to inculcate a historical group identification, immersion in a wide-ranging body of theory, mastery of an elusive craft, and the development of a lasting professional identity. Kernberg elucidates the regressive group processes that often undergird and undermine psychoanalytic education and delineates innovative strategies to solve the problems rampant in this enterprise. At a time when the discipline is facing threats from many directions, his book is a powerful wake-up call for the international psychoanalytic community!" Salman Akhtar, MD, Training and Supervising Analyst, Psychoanalytic Center of Philadelphia.

"This book is a wonderful summary of opinions about psychoanalytic education, published in the recent past. Plus conclusions and practical recommendations. And as such an important contribution to help the psychoanalytic community to work on the revival of interest in psychoanalysis. The book is a survival-kit for those institutions and societies that are aware of the necessity to change and a wake-up call for those that do not. A must for continuing the discussions and a guideline for implementation of change." Henk Jan Dalewijk, Psychiatrist and Psychoanalyst in Private Practice.

"Otto Kernberg's ideas and efforts to secure the future of psychoanalysis are most impressive. In this book he provides a comprehensive examination of the problems in psychoanalytic education and supervision and shares his thoughts on how to preserve the psychoanalytic identity. Significant proposals are offered for maintaining the dignity and the prestige of psychoanalysis and psychoanalysts in the scientific environment and in the rapidly changing world. This book should be read by anyone who is interested in individual and societal mental health." Vamık Volkan, Emeritus Professor of Psychiatry; author of *Enemies On The Couch: A Psychopolitical Journey Through War and Peace*.

"Otto Kernberg, one of the most distinguished psychoanalysts in the world, traces the current crises in psychoanalysis to its educational structure, its failure to develop a research basis, and the dysfunctional organization of psychoanalytic institutes and societies, with the training analyst system at the core. His goal is to catalyze the transformation of psychoanalytic institutes from their current role—a mixture of trade school and theological seminary—to a new role, a synthesis of art academy and university college. Some will agree, while others might challenge his prescription, but any serious discussion of psychoanalytic education must begin here." Robert Michels, MD, Walsh McDermott University Professor of Medicine and Psychiatry, Weill Medical College of Cornell University.

# THE NEW LIBRARY OF PSYCHOANALYSIS
General Editor: Alessandra Lemma

The New Library of Psychoanalysis was launched in 1987 in association with the Institute of Psychoanalysis, London. It took over from the International Psychoanalytical Library which published many of the early translations of the works of Freud and the writings of most of the leading British and Continental psychoanalysts.

The purpose of the New Library of Psychoanalysis is to facilitate a greater and more widespread appreciation of psychoanalysis and to provide a forum for increasing mutual understanding between psychoanalysts and those working in other disciplines such as the social sciences, medicine, philosophy, history, linguistics, literature and the arts. It aims to represent different trends both in British psychoanalysis and in psychoanalysis generally. The New Library of Psychoanalysis is well placed to make available to the English-speaking world psychoanalytic writings from other European countries and to increase the interchange of ideas between British and American psychoanalysts. Through the *Teaching Series*, the New Library of Psychoanalysis now also publishes books that provide comprehensive, yet accessible, overviews of selected subject areas aimed at those studying psychoanalysis and related fields such as the social sciences, philosophy, literature and the arts.

The Institute, together with the British Psychoanalytical Society, runs a low-fee psychoanalytic clinic, organizes lectures and scientific events concerned with psychoanalysis and publishes the *International Journal of Psychoanalysis*. It runs a training course in psychoanalysis which leads to membership of the International Psychoanalytical Association – the body which preserves internationally agreed standards of training, of professional entry, and of professional ethics and practice for psychoanalysis as initiated and developed by Sigmund Freud. Distinguished members of the Institute have included Michael Balint, Wilfred Bion, Ronald Fairbairn, Anna Freud, Ernest Jones, Melanie Klein, John Rickman and Donald Winnicott.

Previous general editors have included David Tuckett, who played a very active role in the establishment of the New Library. He was followed as general editor by Elizabeth Bott Spillius, who was in turn followed by Susan Budd and then by Dana Birksted-Breen.

Current members of the Advisory Board include Liz Allison, Giovanna di Ceglie, Rosemary Davies and Richard Rusbridger.

Previous members of the Advisory Board include Christopher Bollas, Ronald Britton, Catalina Bronstein, Donald Campbell, Sara Flanders, Stephen Grosz, John Keene, Eglé Laufer, Alessandra Lemma, Juliet Mitchell, Michael Parsons, Rosine Jozef Perelberg, Mary Target and David Taylor.

## TITLES IN THIS SERIES

## TITLES IN THE NEW LIBRARY OF PSYCHOANALYSIS "BEYOND THE COUCH" SERIES

THE NEW LIBRARY OF PSYCHOANALYSIS

General Editor: Alessandra Lemma

# Psychoanalytic Education at the Crossroads

## Reformation, change and the future of psychoanalytic training

Otto Friedmann Kernberg

Routledge
Taylor & Francis Group

LONDON AND NEW YORK

First published 2016
by Routledge
2 Park Square, Milton Park, Abingdon, OX14 4RN

and by Routledge
711 Third Avenue, New York, NY 10017

*Routledge is an imprint of the Taylor & Francis Group, an informa business*

*British Library Cataloguing in Publication Data*
A catalogue record for this book is available from the British Library

*Library of Congress Cataloging in Publication Data*
Names: Kernberg, Otto F., 1928– , author.
Title: Psychoanalytic education at the crossroads : reformation, change and the future
    of psychoanalytic training / Otto Friedmann Kernberg.
Other titles: New library of psychoanalysis (Unnumbered)
Description: Hove, East Sussex ; New York, NY : Routledge, 2016. | Series: The new
    library of psychoanalysis | Includes bibliographical references.
Identifiers: LCCN 2016005910| ISBN 9781138928701 (hardback : alk. paper) |
    ISBN 9781138928718 (pbk.        ) | ISBN 9781315681405 (e-book)
Subjects: | MESH: Psychoanalysis—education | Collected Works
Classification: LCC RC502 | NLM WM 18 | DDC 616.89/170076—dc23
LC record available at http://lccn.loc.gov/2016005910

ISBN: 978-1-138-92870-1 (hbk)
ISBN: 978-1-138-92871-8 (pbk)
ISBN: 978-1-315-68140-5 (ebk)

Typeset in Bembo
by Swales & Willis Ltd, Exeter, Devon, UK

Dedicated to the memory of
Robert Wallerstein
teacher and friend

# Contents

# Contents

# Acknowledgments

While, of course, assuming full responsibility for all critique and proposals in this volume, I wish to acknowledge the influence of those teachers and colleagues who have inspired me with their thoughts and contributions, whose council and recommendations have influenced my thinking and writing, and to whom I acknowledge my profound gratitude.

My earliest experiences with functional leadership and the delicate balance of relations between leadership and followership, their influence on group morale, enthusiasm and productivity, came from my adolescent experiences as a member of a Jewish youth group in Valparaiso, Chile, guided by Hans Aufrichtig, a Zionist youth leader in Germany who gathered immigrant Jewish children in Valparaiso to form an organization modeled after the tradition of the romantic, early twentieth-century tradition of German youth groups. There, a spirit of shared relations to nature and art was fostered, and a corresponding ideology of democratic solidarity built up. In a completely different context, this awareness of the impact of leadership on organizational functioning was fostered by Dr Jorge Romano, the director of a Mental Health Unit working with slum populations in Santiago, Chile, of which I became a member as a medical student. Dr Romano managed an organizational structure that fostered, despite long hours and minimal pay, an ongoing spirit of enthusiasm for our joint work over a number of years.

Dr Ignacio Matte Blanco, Professor and Chairman of the Department of Psychiatry of the Medical School of the University of Chile, the founder of the Chilean Psychoanalytic Association, and the developer of a path-breaking psychodynamic psychiatry department, both determined my choice of career within medicine, and provided an exemplar of brilliant, functional, non–authoritarian leadership that obtained its strength from the communication of the professional ideals that inspired him. The breadth of his intellectual realm, his profound knowledge of neurobiology, mathematics and philosophy, together with the influence of his training in the British Psychoanalytic Society left profound traces in my future development. At his Department of Psychiatry I also obtained my basic training in psychoanalytic group psychotherapy under the leadership of Dr Ramon Ganzarain, who, in later years, transferred his teaching to the Menninger Clinic in Topeka, Kansas.

A Rockefeller Foundation Fellowship at the Henry Phipps Clinic and the Department of Psychiatry of Johns Hopkins Medical School in Baltimore, Maryland gave me the opportunity to deepen my learning of group psychotherapy, as well as the general application of research methodology to study psychotherapy process and outcome with Dr Jerome Frank. Also at this time, I had the opportunity, through my friendship with Dr Lawrence Kubie, to engage in critical thinking about psychoanalytic theory from an ego psychological viewpoint, and to contrast, unafraid, the traditional tenets already provided through my mentorship with Dr Ignacio Matte Blanco.

But the most important influence on my psychoanalytic thinking, as well as on my development regarding group psychology and the theory of organizational functioning came as a result of my time at the Menninger Foundation, in Topeka, Kansas. There, under the leadership and personal guidance of Dr Robert Wallerstein, to whom this book is dedicated, a distinguished leader of American and international psychoanalysis, one of the most innovative presidents of the International Psychoanalytic Association, and the Director of the Menninger Foundation Psychotherapy Research Project, I obtained my training in research on the psychoanalytic and psychotherapeutic process, and obtained knowledge and experience regarding the tasks and constraints, frustrations and creativity of functional leadership.

It was Dr Wallerstein who had facilitated my tenure in the United States, and throughout many years remained an inspiring mentor and loyal friend. The practical learning in the context of our relationship was powerfully reinforced by the theoretical learning provided by Dr John Sutherland, former editor of the International Journal of Psychoanalysis and Director of the Tavistock Clinic, who helped me significantly in further advancing my knowledge in psychoanalytic group psychotherapy and more importantly, brought about my acquaintance in depth with the British Independent psychoanalytic tradition. This helped me to complement and integrate my previous training influenced by the Kleinian orientation of the Chilean Institute of Psychoanalysis, and the Ego Psychological Orientation of the Topeka Psychoanalytic Institute, where I became training and supervising analyst.

It was through frequent visits to Topeka by Dr John Sutherland, and those of Drs. Edith Jacobson and Margaret Mahler that I became initially acquainted, and then profoundly influenced by their work, particularly by the developmental and meta-psychological studies of Edith Jacobson.

Dr Harry Levinson, the Director of the Department of Industrial Psychology of the Menninger Foundation provided me with early learning about organizational leadership, which then was reinforced by my experiences as a student and then staff member of the A. K. Rice Institute. Dr Margaret Rioch, distinguished leader of that Institute, and Dr Roger Shapiro, together with the teachings of Dr Pierre Turquet, and Dr Didier Anzieu further enhanced my understanding of small and large group psychology. Later on, the seminal work of Dr Vamik Volkan at the GAP Committee on International Relations further contributed to enriching this area.

My intimate working relationships throughout my twelve years at the Menninger Foundation with Dr Robert Wallerstein, first, and then with three leading international psychoanalysts, Drs Herman van der Waals and Ernst and Gertrude Ticho, all of whom had been directors of the Topeka Institute and provided major leadership at the Menninger Clinic and its psychotherapy department, provided me with an enormous background of information regarding the history of psychoanalytic institutions in Austria, the Netherlands, Brazil, as well as the American Psychoanalytic Association, my first orientation toward the international psychoanalytic scene, and the problems being debated in administrative psychoanalytic circles.

It was in New York, where I have resided since 1973, that I have had the opportunity of joint work and personal relationships with psychoanalytic colleagues at the Columbia University Center for Psychoanalytic Training and Research, and as part of my functions as Director of the Westchester Division of The New York

Hospital and Professor of Psychiatry at the Weill Cornell Medical College under the Chairmanship of Dr Robert Michels at first, and currently under the Chairmanship of Dr Jack Barchas, that I have become acquainted with the nature of creative leadership of large psychiatric organizations. Under the inspired leadership of Dr Robert Michels, distinguished leader of the American and the International Psychoanalytic Community, and Dr Jack Barchas, an internationally renowned leading neurobiological scientist, my views have been fundamentally influenced and expanded about the boundary functions of psychoanalysis with its surrounding scientific and academic world.

Within the American and, particularly the New York psychoanalytic community I am most grateful for the ideas, stimulation, and encouragement I have received from Drs Martin Bergmann, Harold Blum, and the late Dr William Grossman. Dr Robert Tyson, Secretary of the International Psychoanalytic Association during my presidency, was of extraordinary help in learning from his political skills, tactfulness, and wisdom. In Germany I received knowledge, inspiration, and tactful criticism from Drs Peter Buchheim, Horst Kächele, the late Dr Irmhild Kohte-Meyer, Dr Rainer Krause, Dr Ernst Lürssen, Dr Gerhard Roth, and Dr Almuth Sellschopp; and in Austria, from Drs Stephan Doering and Peter Schuster.

Several former Presidents of the International Psychoanalytic Association have been of enormous help and inspiration: they include Drs Serge Lebovici, Joseph and Anne-Marie Sandler, Daniel Widlocher, and Cláudio Eizirik. I learned from major collaborators and influential leaders during the time of my presidency of the IPA, Drs David Sachs, André Lussier, and Sara Zac de Filc. The late Dr Arnold Cooper, colleague and friend at the Columbia Center and former President of the American Psychoanalytic Association influenced me profoundly in my critical examination of the conflicts in psychoanalytic education, as did Dr César Garza Guerrero in Mexico. The late Dr André Green, a major contributor to contemporary psychoanalysis, opened for me significant horizons regarding psychoanalytic thinking, and his open and deep criticism of "chaos and petrification" in psychoanalytic education helped me to formulate my own views.

A particular gratitude goes toward the recently deceased former Director of the Columbia University Center for Psychoanalytic Training and Research, Dr Ethel Person, who, in addition to her original contributions to gender identity and sexuality was an original, path-breaking director at the Columbia Institute. She gave me proof of how an inspired, functional leadership may change an organization rapidly, increase its productivity and decrease whatever paranoiagenic features may be latent in the institution.

Throughout all the years in New York, and particularly since I assumed Directorship of the Personality Disorders Institute (PDI) of the Weill Cornell Medical College at the completion of my term as Director at the Westchester Division of the New York Hospital, I have been privileged to have the enthusiastic encouragement and loyal collaboration of a number of colleagues, all of whom have contributed significantly to the fields of psychoanalysis and psychodynamic psychiatry. They include, first of all, Dr John Clarkin, Associate Director of the Personality Disorders Institute at Cornell, and Dr Frank Yeomans, Director of Training of the PDI and Director of the Personality Studies Institute in New York, and our colleagues, Drs Eve Caligor, Monica Carsky, Diana Diamond, Kay Haran, Mark Lenzenweger, Kenneth Levy, Armand Loranger, and Michael Stone. I particularly wish to mention Ms Jill Delaney, who has been teaching psychiatric residents and post–residency fellows with me over many years, and who has been particularly helpful in carefully editing all my scientific papers. Her help in the editing of this volume has been invaluable.

And then I need to mention, not without sadness, the extraordinary, pioneering contributions regarding the personality disorders of childhood and adolescence and the psychotherapy of adolescence, of the late Dr Paulina Kernberg, my first wife, whose death has been not only a terrible personal loss but a great loss for our field. However, we are fortunate that under the leadership of Dr Lina Normandin, and the collaboration of Dr Karin Ensink, from Quebec, Paulina's work is being continued and developed further at this point. She was an encouraging presence all through good and bad moments of life during the years of our life together and helped me to deal with the difficult early times of my critical analysis of psychoanalytic education. And I have been very privileged by the presence and support, in recent years, of my present wife, Dr Kay Haran, another senior therapist and supervisor of our Personality Disorders Institute, who has given me a second lease of life, and powerfully stimulated the completion of the present work. And this leads me, finally, to my deep gratitude to the indefatigable work of Ms Louise Taitt, the Administrative Secretary of the Personality Disorders Institute, at Cornell, the watchdog over the efficiency, appropriateness, order and work responsibility of the Institute, and the patient reviewer, organizer, and integrating force that has pulled all the chapters of this book together and carried it on to its publication. To all of them my deepest gratitude and, once again, I do not make any of them responsible for the ideas that I am proposing in this volume.

# INTRODUCTION

The present volume is a result of fifty years of experience and concern with the nature of psychoanalytic education. I trained as a psychoanalyst at the Psychoanalytic Institute of the Chilean Psychoanalytic Association, in Santiago, Chile, under the inspired, charismatic, and creative leadership of Ignacio Matte Blanco, from 1951 to 1961. I joined the Topeka Psychoanalytic Institute at the Menninger Foundation in Topeka, Kansas, in 1961, where I followed advanced psychoanalytic studies and eventually became a training and supervising psychoanalyst in 1966. I then experienced still a new psychoanalytic environment and culture, upon moving to New York in 1973. At that point, I joined the New York Psychoanalytic Institute and Society, and the Psychoanalytic Center for Training and Research at the Department of Psychiatry of the College of Physicians and Surgeons of Columbia University. By the time I finally settled, as a Training and Supervising Psychoanalyst at the Columbia University Psychoanalytic Center for Training and Research, I had experienced three or four significantly different centers of psychoanalytic education. This experience evolved further when, as part of my professional and research activities in psychoanalysis as well as in psychiatry, and as part of my interest in the study and research on personality disorders, I was privileged to obtain views of psychoanalytic institutions in Europe, North and South America.

It was a profoundly educative, stimulating and inspiring universe of experiences, but also the source of growing concern over problems with psychoanalytic education and the destiny of psychoanalysis in our time, that originated my interest in studying these problems and in attempting to contribute to the solutions of some of them.

1

Gradually, deep concerns for the future of psychoanalysis as a science and a profession became central in these efforts. Psychoanalysis as a fundamental contribution to the culture of the twentieth century seemed to have an assured, stable place, but I felt that this could not be said for psychoanalytic science and profession in the new, twenty-first century that we were entering.

Beginning in 1984, I expressed my concerns and the results of my exploration of problems in psychoanalytic education in a series of papers published over the years, represented in the chapters of the present volume in roughly historical order. They illustrate my path from reflections on the nature of psychoanalytic identity, to the impact of the surrounding culture on particular idiosyncrasies of psychoanalytic institutions in different countries, and to the impressive, largely unrecognized and yet overwhelming influence of regressive group processes on the vicissitudes of psychoanalytic education. I attempted to apply both psychoanalytic theory of group processes and general theories of organizational leadership to the analysis of conflicts and difficulties in psychoanalytic institutes. I gradually reached the conclusion that the structure of psychoanalytic education, centered on the hierarchical system of the "training analyst," was a major source of institutional contradictions that affected the training of candidates, the scientific developments within psychoanalysis, and the nexus of psychoanalytic theory and practice with the surrounding scientific, social and cultural world.

The first part of this volume is focused primarily on the analysis of the nature of these problems and their effects on the personal analysis and supervision of candidates; on theoretical and clinical seminars; on selection, progression, and graduation; on educational principles and requirements, developments of theory and technique, and, particularly, limitation versus expansion of the realm of interests and applications of psychoanalysis. The second part of this volume deals with proposals of solutions to the problems encountered, and major suggestions for innovation in psychoanalytic education.

Chapter 1 is dedicated to the exploration of the nature of psychoanalytic identity and threats to this identity. It relates psychoanalytic identity with ideological temptations and problems related to psychoanalytic practice, and examines aspects of the nature of personal commitment to our field. Chapter 2 begins the exploration of the influence of group processes on the functioning of institutions and particularly, the organizational leadership of psychoanalytic institutes. I utilize psychoanalytic theories of group regression and leadership to examine the nature of tensions that evolve in the course of institutional psychoanalytic work. These considerations crystallize in Chapter 3, in which I reach a general conclusion regarding the contradiction between the ideology of psychoanalytic education that inspires the educators, on the one hand, and the reality that has evolved in psychoanalytic institutes as a consequence of its present structure, on the other. Chapter 4 proposes an important illustration of nonfunctional developments in institutes, namely, the development of authoritarianism, and explores the relationship between personality of leadership to the functions of leadership, and the nature of the external culture within which psychoanalytic institutions function.

Chapter 5 provides a potential respite from the seriousness of the earlier body of information, in an ironical set of proposals related to how institutional bureaucratization and routinization affects the creativity of psychoanalytic candidates. More seriously, in Chapter 6, I deal with the pressing need to increase research on psychoanalysis, and the exploration of some of the resistances against this development. Chapter 7 moves the focus of my critique to the nature of psychoanalytic supervision, considered to be the most essential aspect of the training program, and here the focus is on the responsibilities and problems facing the supervisor.

Chapter 8 brings together the description of the main symptoms of institutional regression and educational failure that affects psychoanalytic education, and an overview of early efforts to correct these failures and dysfunctional educational processes, and the beginning efforts to explore alternative methods of psychoanalytic education. Here the main critique is of the internationally dominant Eitingon system and the efforts to modify and innovate it. Chapters 9 and 10 jointly explore a major proposal for changes in psychoanalytic education derived from the analysis presented so far. They include concrete recommendations regarding the training analysis system, whether it should be maintained or not (Chapter 9), and refer to innovative efforts in all other aspects of psychoanalytic education, with particular emphasis on the development of new technical approaches to deal with the most severe characterological illnesses where psychoanalysis would not seem to be indicated, and often fails.

The recommendations of these two chapters are complemented by the analysis of the relation of psychoanalysis to university settings in Chapter 11. Here the question is to what extent the linkage with academia is essential for the future of the position of psychoanalysis in the world of science, and what strategies psychoanalysis may employ to reestablish its standing within university settings that have been lost in recent decades.

A new pause is offered to the reader with the ironic format of Chapter 13, in which proposals for change are presented in the form of a "suicide prevention guide" for psychoanalytic institutes and societies. This is followed, finally, by the last chapter of this book, Chapter 14, in which alternatives to the training analysis system are proposed in some detail, with the concrete example of the American Psychoanalytic Association as an illustration of the application of this analysis to the actual organizational structure of a major conglomerate of related psychoanalytic institutions.

I need to stress that, as this brief overview indicates, the most extended and in-depth experiences of my professional psychoanalytic life have been related to the development of psychoanalysis in the United States. Nevertheless, my active work, over many years, as member of the Executive Council of the International Psychoanalytic Association, Chairperson of an International Psychoanalytic Congress, and member of multiple committees and tasks forces of the International Psychoanalytic Association over the years—that culminated in my being elected President of the International Psychoanalytic Association for the period of 1997–2001—have powerfully influenced my perspective. They have given me the confidence that the studies presented in this volume correspond sufficiently to the psychoanalytic situation throughout the three continents with strongly developed psychoanalytic centers, to believe that the proposed solutions may, indeed, have value throughout the entire realm of professional and educational institutions of this international community.

---

# 1

# THE IDENTITY OF THE
# PSYCHOANALYST[1]

---

In what follows, I shall be speaking of identity in a broad sense that
includes the psychoanalyst's convictions as well as his vocation, his
personality as well as his technique skills.

Grinberg (1983), in exploring the analyst's professional identity,
stresses a particular kind of curiosity regarding the mind and psychic reality, a curiosity that extends to the analyst's own psychic
functioning; Grinberg also stresses the capacity for and interest in
introspection and self-analysis, a creative capacity, an ability to think
under adverse circumstances, ethical behavior that assures avoiding
acting out in the counter transference, tolerance for the frustration of
psychoanalytic work, particularly the ability to cope with uncertainties and with the temporary loss of the ability to understand. I would
add, as related qualities, the analyst's confidence in the possibility of
acquiring new understanding through introspection and insight and
of bringing about change through insight in oneself and others, at the
same time maintaining respect for the limitations of both understanding and the change derived from it. The analyst needs to have respect
for the powerful nature of human aggression as well as of libidinal
forces, a respect for the unavoidable ambivalence in all human relations, and the need to accept limitations in oneself, in others, and in
human enterprise in general.

I think additional characteristics of the psychoanalyst's identity
include what may be considered a parental attitude of holding or
containing the conflictual and chaotic nature of intrapsychic conflict.
Holding or containing has cognitive and affective components and

5

includes a basic attitude of concern for oneself and the patient and a psychological openness to the unknown in others as well as in oneself.

It hardly needs to be stressed that such ego aspects of psychoanalytic work, in order to be operative and realistic, must be embedded in a healthy ego identity. The intellectual brilliance, intuitive awareness of primitive conflicts, and emotional availability of candidates with borderline character pathology may initially appear to be professionally promising. Only after years may their chaotic intrapsychic organization become apparent to their colleagues and supervisors. They themselves may realize that they lack crucial discriminating functions in their assessment of patients, in handling the transference and countertransference. Unless their personal analysis radically modifies their character pathology, their lack of ego identity will eventually affect their analytic identity as well.

And the superego also makes a crucial contribution to the analyst's identity. Superimposed on a generally mature superego reflected in moral integrity and professional ethics are specific superego functions. These specific superego functions include a firmness of convictions moderated by a degree of flexibility regarding value systems. I think these attitudes regarding value systems are reflected in three characteristics: first, a degree of maturity in the level of personal identification with social, political, or religious ideologies; second, an ability to resist regression when subject to group processes; and third, an ability to adhere to a value system of one's own choosing as opposed to submitting to conventionality.

Regarding the first criterion, I agree with Green (1969), that the incapacity to commit oneself to any value system beyond one supplying self-serving needs usually indicates severe narcissistic pathology. The commitment to an ideology that includes sadistic demands for perfection and tolerates primitive aggression or one that assumes a conventional naiveté of all value judgments indicates an immature ego ideal. Commitment to ideologies that respect individual differences, autonomy, and privacy, that tolerate sexuality while rejecting the expression of primitive aggression would reflect characteristics of the mature ego ideal. I would therefore consider commitment to trivial social ideologies or to messianic systems that divide the world into good and evil (and thereby dehumanize half of humanity) a highly suspect development.

The second criterion, resistance to regression when subject to group processes, has relevance to the psychoanalyst not only as a member of society subject to social and political pressure, but also to his position vis-a-vis his psychoanalytic institute. Bion (1961), Turquet (1975) and Anzieu (1984) have described the regression that occurs when group processes take over. Impressive clinical evidence indicates that regardless of the individual's maturity and psychological integration, certain group conditions tend to bring on regression and activate primitive psychological levels. Groups that are small, closed, and unstructured, as well as groups that are large, minimally structured, and lacking clearly defined tasks to relate them to their environment, tend to bring about an immediate regression in the individual. This regression consists in the activation of defensive operations and interpersonal processes that reflect primitive object relations. The potential for this exists within all of us. When we lose our ordinary social structure, when our ordinary social roles are suspended, and when multiple objects are present simultaneously in an unstructured relationship, reproducing in the interpersonal field a multiplicity of primitive intrapsychic object relations, under such circumstances primitive levels of psychological functioning may be activated.

Combining the observations made of mobs, large groups, and small groups, I have proposed that group processes in general pose a basic threat to personal identity (Kernberg, 1980). This threat is linked to the proclivity in group situations for primitive psychological levels to be activated, including primitive object relations, primitive defensive operations, and primitive aggression with predominantly pregenital features.

The third criterion of specific superego functions mentioned, namely, firmness and differentiation of individual values as contrasted to conventionality, is tested in ordinary institutional functioning. Individual judgment and autonomy are threatened by the institutional pressures operating upon the psychoanalyst as part of his training experience and membership in psychoanalytic organizations. The derailing of institutional task systems, of committee structures, and of the collective evaluation of individuals under the effects of power struggles tangential to the actual tasks test the corruptibility of an individual's value systems as well. The ethically protected atmosphere of the psychoanalytic relationship contrasts with the potentially dishonest, opportunistic and sadistic atmosphere that may develop in psychoanalytic as well as in all other institutions. The contrast between the humanly ideal psychoanalytic relationship and the ordinary reality of institutional strife surrounding it may be sharp and disturbing to all involved. To stand up to this development in contrast to cynical opportunism, bitter withdrawal, or escape into messianic dream worlds express the psychoanalyst's superego maturity.

In short, I am suggesting that the superego aspects of a psychoanalytic identity are reflected not only in moral integrity (in a moral as opposed to a moralistic stance vis-a-vis the patient) but also in resilience to the corruptive or regressive pressures operating upon the superego within the social and cultural system.

I now turn to some factors that may strengthen or weaken the psychoanalyst's identity.

## Narcissistic deterioration

Major unresolved narcissism of the psychoanalytic candidate, reflected in a purely cognitive "learning" of the interpretation he/she has received during the training, and in, using them with his own patients without a process of internal reflection and working through is probably the single most important threat to the future psychoanalyst's identity. The narcissistic gratifications involved in psychoanalytic training, such as professional advancement, the unconscious misuse of the therapeutic relationship as an expression of power, basking in patients' idealizations, and the facilitation of vicarious living through patients may unfortunately remain unrecognized for many years. The eagerness with which the narcissistic candidate-analysand incorporates his own analyst's growth may be matched by a parallel eager absorption of intellectual knowledge in the institute courses and seminars and remain undetected.

A candidate's narcissistic identification with his own psychoanalyst and the pseudomaturity that accompanies the hidden grandiosity of the narcissistic personality may be mistaken for appropriate maturation. It is often only during supervision of control cases that a candidate's lack of curiosity about himself becomes apparent, or his inability to cope with uncertainty, or the fact that his interpretive endeavors are limited to those dynamics that have emerged in his own analysis and to those that correspond to the dominant concerns (or fashions) of his particular analytic group. The narcissistic candidate's intolerance to learning from his patients, from supervision, colleagues, and reading—in contrast to what is only "culturally" absorbed—may remain undetected.

Once graduated, the cumulative effects of these limitations may bring about a closure to new experiences that translates into an increasing sense of boredom with psychoanalytic work, frustration with its limitations, and a search for alternative professional activities to break this impasse. The counterpart of this development may be a defensive idealization of psychoanalysis (as practiced by himself), a rigid and doctrinaire attitude as a defense against the uncertainties about his own work and psychoanalytic discovery, plus an over dependency on institutional and social gratifications that may come from being a psychoanalyst in his particular culture.

The long-range effects of unresolved narcissistic pathology will thus threaten the analyst's identity. His skepticism may result in a rejection of psychoanalysis; a nihilistic relativism expressing the unconscious conviction that nothing is of real value, or a doctrinaire rigidity that protects him from the envy of whatever is new and unknown. The relentless, bitter attacks on psychoanalysis on the part of former graduates who have not come to terms with their own limitations to emotional introspection, their refusal to acknowledge the dynamic unconscious in themselves and others, are painful reminders of the limitations in our selection procedures and educational capabilities.

I think that possibly the single most important factor that strengthens the analyst's future identity is the discovery, by means of his psychoanalytic exploration, of unconscious meanings and intrapsychic change that, in contrast to intellectual speculations, comes as a surprise, unexpectedly, and brings home the reality of unconscious determinism. Authentic insight, a combination of cognitive and emotional awareness and concern for oneself and one's patients is the core of a psychoanalyst's professional identity. The experience of discoveries in the realm of the unconscious reconfirms the analyst's identity throughout his professional work, protects him against the envy of what is not his own knowledge or discovery, and facilitates the full deployment of the holding or containing attitude in the interpretive process.

## The narcissistic training analyst

Because narcissistic character pathology has only been assessed systematically in the last twenty years, our technique in dealing with narcissistic character defenses and transference resistances is still evolving. It should therefore not be surprising that unresolved pathological narcissism is an important contribution to limitations in psychoanalytic training. A training analyst with unresolved narcissistic pathology obviously poses a great danger to the resolution of narcissistic pathology in his candidates. What interests me here are the mechanisms by which narcissistic psychopathology is transmitted, figuratively speaking. These mechanisms include not only the narcissistic training analyst's obvious blind spots that prevent him from perceiving parallel psychopathology in his analysand, but also his lack of tolerance for the candidate's aggression, including the candidate's need to depreciate analytic work.

A major threat to the psychoanalyst's creativity in working with *his* patient is the patient's relentless, aggressive attack on the analyst's work with him. Attacks of this sort produce narcissistic lesions in the psychoanalyst. It is much easier for the analyst to tolerate aggression against any other aspects of his personality or behavior. The training analyst unable to tolerate the narcissistic candidate-analysand's aggression may foster an unconscious collusion with the analysand, so that the latter's aggression, particularly the destructive implications of unconscious envy, will not be explored. The analysand is thus condemned to insufficient resolution of his narcissistic pathology.

This unconscious collusion also fosters defensive narcissistic formations in the transference and counter transference, leading to the "great training analyst–great candidate" syndrome, a mutual idealization. This psychoanalytic "honeymoon" may sometimes persist undetected until the very end of the analysis. More frequently, it can lead to sudden disappointment, mutual rejection, and the end of the analysis. Abrupt terminations of training analyses may result from a final unconscious collusion in which the candidate denies to himself the limitations of his own training analysis, and the training analyst his own growing sense of alarm and dissatisfaction with this particular candidate.

Furthermore, collusion in denying aggression can result in the candidate-analysand's displacing his aggression onto other objects in the psychoanalytic institute (a socially predetermined channel of acting out in these circumstances). The training analyst's ability to tolerate the candidate's aggression in the transference may be a crucial determinant for the candidate's tolerance and acceptance of his own aggression and ambivalence. This tolerance reduces the pervasive needs for defensive idealizations and facilitates the analysis of

10

dissociative processes in superego functioning. The need to carefully analyze the dissociation between idealized and depreciated values is an important correlate of the analysis of conflicts around aggression. Failure to analyze defensive idealization processes may lead to persistence of superego pathology, which eventually threatens the analyst's identity along the channels mentioned earlier.

## The termination phase of psychoanalysis

Working-through of mourning, typical of the termination phase of psychoanalysis, brings forth the working through of the candidate-analysand's relation to his analyst, and, by extension, to psychoanalysis itself. In my experience, this can be an important opportunity for resolving conflicts about psychoanalysis as a science and as a profession, which may foster the psychoanalyst's professional identity later on or, in the absence of such working-through, potentially weaken that identity. I am referring specifically to the candidate's fears of having disappointed the training analyst, his fears that the training analyst will perceive still unresolved neurotic problems as permanent shortcomings, resulting in the candidate's becoming an inadequate psychoanalyst. Behind these fears are not only fantasies about the training analyst as being perfect but also a lack of confidence in one's ability to work further on one's own difficulties by means of self-analysis.

Equally important are the reactions of disappointment because of what the candidate feels he has not received from his training analyst, the disillusionment related to idealizations of the psychoanalytic process that were not fully analyzed, together with the resentment for having been "let down" by the training analyst. Here again, the training analyst's security in his work as well as his acceptance of its realistic limitations, his acceptance of his own shortcomings as well as his confidence in the candidate's capacity for further self-analysis, constitute a frame against which these depressive and paranoid anxieties, and the ambivalence toward the training analyst, may be worked through.

## Self-analysis

The capacity for self-analysis is a major indicator of the consolidation of the psychoanalyst's identity. Gertrude Ticho (1967) in a study of self-analysis concluded that it is a gradually developing, discontinuous function, which depends for its activation on multiple, individually determined circumstances, and basically is largely rooted in the past experiences during the training analysis. The extent to which self-analysis proceeds stems not only from identification with the training analyst's analytic function but from the internalization of the specific object relation with the training analyst, in which his analytic function and the candidate-analysand's capacity to establish a maturely dependent relationship with the training analyst are two equally important components.

I would add that the analysis of defensive dissociations between the idealizing functions of the ego ideal, on the one hand, and the sadistic devaluation derived from deep superego layers, on the other, is an important guarantee of the capacity for self-analysis. To accept the limitations of what one has learned and received in psychoanalytic work without devaluing it, and to accept one's own limitations without self-devaluation leads to the capacity to tolerate a continuing self-critical evaluation of oneself as a psychoanalyst.

As a result, self-analysis may provide help under extreme emotional crises and strengthen the psychoanalyst's identity or, if dissociative superego pressures have not been resolved, contribute to the deterioration of this identity. There is a double edge to such life experiences as severe illness, breakup of a marriage, death of a child, migration: they may lead to emotional growth sustained by self-analysis and related psychoanalytic learning, or deterioration of the confidence in psychoanalysis as self-analysis proves impotent. Typical symptoms of malfunctioning in the self-analytic role are the willingness to recommend psychoanalysis to patients but not consider it for oneself or one's own children; or the blind reliance on psychoanalysis that gives it a flavor of a religious conviction.

## The analyst's patients

Sometimes the candidate has patients with severe character pathology, borderline conditions, or narcissistic personality structure who have the capacity for an intense activation of primitive conflicts in the transference, which, even if the patient cannot benefit from them, reconfirm the truth of analytic understanding for the candidate. In contrast, patients who are emotionally dull and whose understanding does not extend beyond the obvious trivialities of daily life may have a deadening effect on their analysts-in-training.

An analytic education that focuses on the development of an analytic process rather than on the outcome of analysis is preferable. By the same token, it seems to me preferable that candidates start out with several patients in a short period of time, circumstances permitting, rather than in a slow progression from one to two to three patients.

To be effective, even in limited ways, reinforces the psychoanalyst's identity. Our patients contribute to keeping our science alive in our minds, and psychoanalytic skills may either develop or deteriorate depending on feedback from creative psychoanalytic work. The narcissistic analyst's restlessness with long-term treatments contributes to cutting him off from the creative potential of clinical work; a psychoanalyst's exclusive work with "healthier" patients may diminish his capacity for empathizing with the deepest sources of psychopathology. Work with children, with borderline or psychotic patients may provide an ongoing enrichment of contacts with the most turbulent aspects of the unconscious.

I am very doubtful about the assertion that the psychoanalyst can maintain his identity only if he confines himself to the clinical practice of psychoanalysis. Psychoanalytic psychotherapy with severely disturbed cases, the psychoanalytic study of marital conflicts, the psychoanalytic investigation of group processes and organizational functioning, any or all of these may enrich a psychoanalyst's identity by providing new evidence and data about unconscious functioning. The psychoanalyst's dedication to professional functions other than psychoanalysis, such as general psychiatry, research, or other academic pursuits, does not constitute, in my view, a threat to psychoanalytic identity *per se*. These activities may, however, lend themselves as anchoring points of dissatisfactions that stem from preexisting problems in professional identity.

## Supervisory experiences and consultation with colleagues

A psychoanalytic institute atmosphere that permits candidates to be candid about their mistakes and uncertainties, rather than excessively afraid of criticism, and discourages idealization of training analysts and suspicion of dissenting opinions will give the candidate an opportunity to use supervision not as a judgmental experience, but as a chance to learn from a senior colleague. In many psychoanalytic institutes, clinical seminars discuss only cases of the candidates but not of senior training analysts. And in all seminars it is frequently the youngest one who presents and the most experienced ones who consult. This arrangement militates against learning from more experienced colleagues, including from their mistakes and uncertainties.

My point is that the nature of the supervisory experience and of clinical seminars may either reinforce or decrease idealization processes affecting psychoanalytic identity. The splitting off of doubts, devaluation, and imaginary threats to the idealized version of psychoanalysis onto other groups reinforces parallel tendencies to splitting in the training analysis. Institutional dissociative processes contribute to obscuring superego pathology in the candidate by masking the splitting off of idealized segments of the ego ideal and persecutory segments of more primitive superego precursors. The eventual breakdown of the idealization of psychoanalysis may foster abandonment of the field, cynicism, or the search for compensating ideologies within the psychoanalytic field or elsewhere. Here arises the temptation of transforming psychoanalysis into a messianic ideology, or its blending with other messianic ideologies which provide, at one stroke, professional security, religious confirmation, and a transfer of an illusional power of the analyst *vis-à-vis* the patient to the analyst *vis-à-vis* society.

## Psychoanalytic ideology

Chasseguet-Smirgel and Grunberger (1986) have described how psychoanalytic thinking and understanding can be transformed into an ideology or political program containing messianic and/or paranoid characteristics that are in dramatic contrast to the very nature of psychoanalytic insight.

Habermas (1971–1973) described ideology as motivated false consciousness of social classes. He outlined the potential resolution of this false consciousness by means of a "critical theory" that would provide self-reflective enlightenment together with social emancipation. Ideology, within this conception, and also related ones of Marxist writers, implies, according to Althusser (1976), an unconsciously determined system of illusory representations of reality. This system, said Althusser, derived from the internalization of the dominant illusion a social class harbored about the conditions of its own existence, is achieved by means of the internalization of the "Paternal law" as part of the internalization of the oedipal superego. Habermas drew a parallel between the philosophical analysis of ideologies by means of critical theory, on the one hand, and the psychoanalytic situation, on the other. In psychoanalytic treatment, the patient also starts out with a "false consciousness," and is helped by the analyst to gain enlightenment by means of self-reflection, an enlightenment geared to emancipation of the patient.

If psychoanalysis frees the individual from an ideology as a false consciousness, one effect of psychoanalysis would be to eliminate the proneness to embrace ideologies. But Marxist thinkers, as Kolakowski (1978) points out, are caught in the dilemma that Marxism itself represents an ideology (notwithstanding the traditional Marxist efforts to solve the paradox by declaring Marxism to be a science rather than an ideology).

I believe that psychoanalysis, in its understanding of the psychological determinants of idealization processes as part of superego development throws light on the fundamental nature of ideologies, but I do not think that such a light necessarily implies that we should dismiss ideologies as comprehensive value systems that orient the individual toward his society. Rather, I think that what is relevant is the nature of the identification made with the ideology. At one extreme is a facile acceptance of trivial and/or conventional ideologies. At the other end is a fervent embracing of an ideology and even expansion of it (in narcissistically grandiose individuals) together with paranoid ideas regarding ideologies that conflict with the one embraced. In between is a flexible, open-ended attitude with varying degrees of criticizing in regard to the ideology in question. Psychoanalysis may help to analyze the failure or the deterioration of an individual's integration of his value systems into the conventionally trivial, the narcissistically messianic, or the paranoid-persecutory, thus protecting the individual from regressive psychological processes that would otherwise make him a victim of what might be called the regressively extreme polarities of ideologies.

Now, psychoanalysis itself may become a *Weltanschauung*, an ideology in its own right. In my view, the transformation of psychoanalysis into an all-embracing value system obscures superego pathology in the candidate, fosters the defensive idealization of psychoanalysis as a protection against deeper unconscious conflicts, and sharply limits psychoanalytic curiosity, openness, and awareness of the limits of psychoanalysis itself.

Elsewhere, (1986, Chapter 3) I have examined organizational conflicts that foster such a transformation of psychoanalysis into a religion and, I would now add, interfere with full exploration of superego pathology and the related dangers to the establishment and preservation of the professional identity of the psychoanalyst.

In my view, the psychoanalyst who condenses psychoanalysis with a political ideology as a comprehensive philosophical system on the one hand, and the psychoanalyst who turns his back on politics, philosophy, and religion in total dedication to "pure" psychoanalysis (or totally incorporates these fields into "applied" psychoanalysis) represent two sides of the same coin. Both extremes militate against a stable professional identity by fostering unrealistic idealization processes, and their corresponding dissociated devaluation and paranoid fears of alternative views. The analyst's capacity to invest in value systems other than psychoanalysis proper may be crucial in permitting him to maintain an active and rich contact with life.

In conclusion, I believe that psychoanalytic identity is based upon ego and superego structures. The ego is responsible for curiosity, flexibility, respect for the unconscious, and creativity. The superego is responsible for firmness and flexibility of convictions, and a stable and autonomous system of values. Subtle but significant superego pathology may easily go undetected throughout psychoanalytic training and only emerge later in trivialization, cynical relativism, messianic deterioration, and rigidly dogmatic and paranoid stances regarding psychoanalysis.

## Note

1 Originally published in: Psychoanalytic Identity and the Intrapsychic Organization of the Analyst. In: *Maintenance of the Psychoanalytic Identity and Functioning in a World of Flux*, No. 6, International Psychoanalytical Association Monograph Series, J. Chasseguet-Smirgel (ed.), pp. 63–76, 1987.

## References

Althusser, L. (1976). *Positions*. Paris: Editions Sociales.

Anzieu, D. (1984). *The Group and the Unconscious*. London: Routledge & Kegan Paul.

Bion, W.R. (1961). *Experiences in Groups*. New York: Basic Books.

Chasseguet-Smirge, I.J. & Grunberger, P. (1986). *Freud or Reich? Psychoanalysis and Illusion*. New Haven, CT: Yale University Press.

Green, A. (1969). *Sexualité et ideologie chez Marx et Freud*. Paris: Etudes Freudiens, 1–2, pp. 187–217.

Grinberg, L. (1983). Discussion of Joseph and Widlocher. In *The Identity of the Psychoanalyst*, (eds.) E.D. Joseph & D. Widlocher. New York: Int. University Press, pp. 51–66.

Habermas, J. (1971). *Knowledge and Human Interests*. Boston, MA: Beacon Press.

_____. (1973). *Theory and Practice*. Boston, MA: Beacon Press.

Kernberg, O. (1980). *Internal World and External Reality: Object Relations Theory Applied*. New York: Aronson.

_____. (1986). Institutional Problems of Psychoanalytic Education. *J. Amer. Psychoanal. Assn.*, 34: 799–834.

Kolakowski, L. (1978). *Main Currents of Marxism*, vol. 3: The Breakdown. New York: Oxford University Press.

Ticho, G.R. (1967). On Self-Analysis. *Tnt. J. Psychoanal.*, 48: 308–318.

Turquet, P. (1975). Threats to Identity in the Large Group. *The Large Group: Dynamics and Therapy*, (ed.) L. Kreeger. London: Constable, pp. 87–144.

# 2

# THE COUCH AT SEA

## Psychoanalytic studies of group and organizational leadership[1]

Psychoanalytic contributions to the theory of group and organizational psychology have a puzzling quality. A few key theoretical contributions in this area occupy a territory somewhat peripheral to the mainstream of psychoanalysis, and most psychoanalysts tend to shy away from them. These contributions have nevertheless had a significant impact on the intellectual, scientific, and even political scenes. Their impact, however, has been limited in the field of organizational intervention, and there are good reasons for that: More about this later.

In what follows I present a brief overview of this field, with an emphasis on an area that seems to have received less attention than it merits—that of leaders of groups and organizations. The title of my article is intended to convey the sense of uncertainty and even danger that I have come to associate with attempts to apply psychoanalytically gained knowledge to large groups and organizations.

### Freud and leadership

Freud (1921) initiated the psychoanalytic study of group processes, explaining them in terms of his then newly developed ego psychology. Freud understood the immediate sense of intimacy that individuals established with each other in mobs as derived from the projection of their ego ideal onto the leader, and their identification with him as well as with each other. The projection of the ego ideal onto the idealized leader eliminates moral constraints and the higher functions of self-criticism and responsibility that are so importantly mediated by the superego. The sense of unity and belonging protects the members of the mob from losing their sense of identity, but it is accompanied by a severe reduction in ego functioning. As a result of all these developments, primitive, ordinarily unconscious needs take over and the mob functions under the sway of drives and affects, excitement and rage, stimulated and directed by the leader.

Freud linked these concepts with his hypotheses regarding the historical origin of the primal horde (1913). The leader who is idealized is both the oedipal hero who killed his father and who symbolically represents the alliance of all the sons, and also the father and his law, obeyed as the result of unconscious guilt for the parricide.

These formulations have been very influential in the history of contemporary thought, not only in the fields of psychology and sociology but even in political theory. As Lasch (1981) pointed out, these formulations have provided a theoretical underpinning for generations of Marxists and other socialist philosophers from Wilhelm Reich (1935) to Louis Althusser (1976). The patriarchal bourgeois family was seen as the place where the repressive ideology of capitalism was introjected and linked with the sexual prohibitions of the oedipal father.

Whereas Freud thought that the repression of sexuality was the price paid for cultural evolution, Reich thought that the repression of sexuality represented the effects of a pathological superego determined by the social structure of capitalism. Soviet Russia's sexual repressiveness, Reich explained, reflected the development of a Soviet authoritarian power structure.

In illustrating his theories of group psychology, Freud used the organization of the church and the army as examples of the relation of the group or, rather, the total organization, to its leader. But, Francois Roustang reminds us in his book *Dire Mastery* (1982) that Freud was never actually in the army, nor was he a member of any church. His personal experience of leadership came from the psychoanalytic movement. Roustang points to the paradox that Freud, who critically described the irrational relations between leaders and followers in organized institutions, should have been the author of "On the History of the Psychoanalytic Movement," written in 1914. Freud's paper clearly indicates, according to Roustang, his conviction that a truly scientific commitment to psychoanalysis coincided with loyalty to his (Freud's) ideas, whereas any questioning of key

19

psychoanalytic concepts represented unconsciously determined resistances to truth. The ad hominem nature of the arguments Freud advanced against Jung and Adler is painful reading for any admirer of Freud's genius. One could dismiss Freud's relations to his immediate followers as an irrelevant historical curiosity, were it not so intimately linked with subsequent psychoanalytic history. Roustang, in his study of the relation between master and disciple, calls attention to a contradiction inherent to psychoanalytic movements: The goal of psychoanalysis is to resolve the transference. But psychoanalytic education attempts to maintain the transference that psychoanalysis tries to resolve. If fidelity to Freud, the charismatic founder of psychoanalysis, were required, the members of the societies could not be scientifically independent. The tradition has persisted, as Roustang makes clear in his discussion of Lacan.

Was Freud describing his psychoanalytic movement or unconsciously using it as a model while writing "Group Psychology and the Analysis of the Ego"? And how can one explain his lack of interest in examining the personality of the organizational leader itself? Freud seems to consider the nature of the leader mostly in terms of the leader's symbolic function as the youngest son of the symbolically murdered father. Freud simply attributes to the leader characteristics of self-assuredness and narcissistic self-investment, in contrast to the libido the group invests in him.

## Bion and leadership

Bion's contributions to small group processes, summarized in his book *Experiences in Groups* (1961), are sufficiently well known not to warrant their summary here. I consider his psychoanalytic explanation of the regressive processes that occur in small groups in terms of the three basic emotional assumptions of dependency, fight/flight, and pairing, and their activation when the task structure of the group (Bion's "work group") breaks down the most important single contribution psychoanalysis has made to small group psychology. I hasten to add, however, that, whereas Bion's method of exploring primitive defenses, object relations, and anxieties in small unstructured groups may be of great value in learning about small group psychology and group processes, even in large organizations and large unstructured groups, I find the therapeutic value of his technique questionable.

In fact, inherent in Bion's method is the refusal of the leader to participate in the group. The leader observes and interprets all transactions, even those directed toward himself, in terms of group processes as if the leader were a cipher. This strategy reduces the ordinary social role relation between the members and the leader. The attempt to eliminate the leader as a distinct personality not only prevents the ordinary structuring of the group situation by means of socially accepted and reassuring roles and interactions, it creates— when applied to group psychotherapy—an artificiality in the posture of the leader. It results in making a mockery of the psychoanalyst seated unobserved behind the couch.

Confusing the psychoanalyst's technical neutrality with "disgruntled indifference," to which Freud himself (1927) objected, is still prevalent today. Some analysts think that to be technically neutral requires not only not sharing their inner life with the patient (which is entirely appropriate), but the creation of the illusion that the analyst has no personality at all, which is hardly being realistic. I doubt whether it could have been said of Freud that he appeared to his patients as a "man without qualities."

This issue is related to the current analytic controversy regarding the extent to which the transference is based in the reality of what the patient observes in the analyst or belongs to the patient's past. This discussion neglects the fact that the transference usually crystallizes around realistic aspects of the analyst's personality, exaggerated and distorted as a consequence of the patient's unconscious transfer from experiences in the past. To differentiate the reality of the stimulus for the transference from the transference per se as a distortion or an exaggeration of that stimulus has always been a primary technical task. My point is that the fantasy or wish to erase any reality stimulus derived from the analyst only serves the patient's unconscious need for idealization.

There are advantages and dangers in Bion's technique. Among the advantages are the sharp highlighting of primitive modes of mental operations and the possibility of examining unconscious processes that influence group behavior. On the negative side, questions have been raised (Scheidlinger, 1960; Malan, Balfour, Hood & Shooter, 1976) to what extent the artificial distancing of the group leader, the elimination of ordinary supportive features of group interactions, and the failure to provide cognitive instruments for self-understanding to individual patients regarding their particular psychopathology may be too strenuously demanding on the individual patient and thus be therapeutically counterproductive. I think Bion's technique may also artificially foster the idealization of the therapist.

Bion stresses the basic assumption that group leaders are sucked into their leadership role by the very nature of the regression in the group. Hence, Bion's leader is really a prisoner of the group atmosphere; or rather the group utilizes his personality characteristics for its own purposes. In contrast, the leader of the work group has a rational approach to reality and an awareness of the boundaries of the group. This rational leader has the capacity for reality testing, an awareness of time, and the capacity to stand up to the hatred of rationality activated under basic assumptions conditions. The distinctions Bion draws between the two types of leaders offer seminal concepts for the understanding of the ascendancy of narcissistic and paranoid personalities under basic assumptions group conditions; but they also convey a strange failure to consider the reality of the person who is the work group leader. Did Bion assume that his own extremely powerful personality (obvious to everybody who met him) was submerged by his refusal to fulfill the ordinary role expectations in the group?

Again, this might appear to be a trivial issue, if it were not that, after many years of silence regarding group issues, the theme of the group and its leadership reemerges in Bion's book *Attention and Interpretation* (1970). Here Bion refers to the "exceptional individual" who may be a genius, a messiah, a mystic, or a scientist. Bion offers Isaac Newton as an outstanding example, pointing to Newton's mystical and religious preoccupations as the matrix from which his mathematical formulations evolved. It is hard to avoid the impression that Bion is referring here not only to the work group leader and his creativity but also to a very special type of leader whose convictions have a religious core, and whose behavior, as indicated by the collective term "mystic" with which Bion frames this category, implies the secrecy of one initiated, an obscure or occult character, someone mysterious or enigmatic.

Bion, I think, is here referring to himself, and the question of whether he was aware of it resonates with the question of whether Freud was aware of the nature of the model of the unmentioned leaders of the army or the church. Be that as it may, there is a sense Bion conveys of the impotence of rationality, fragility in the creative mystic, which is endangered by the envious, paranoid, pedestrian, conventional, and limited nature of what Bion calls the establishment. Bion describes three types of interaction between mystic and establishment; a mutually enriching or "symbiotic" one, a mutually destructive or "parasitic" one, and a mutual ignoring or "commensal" one. His emphasis is on the risk of the destruction of the mystic who cannot be "contained" by the establishment, or vice versa, on the risk that the disruptive creativity of the mystic will destroy the establishment.

## Kenneth Rice's school

Kenneth Rice's systems theory of organizations treats the individual, the group, and the social organization as a continuum of open systems. Rice (1965) integrates Bion's theories of small group functioning with his own and with Turquet's (1975) understanding of large group functioning and an open systems theory of social organizations.

Within this model, psychopathology may be conceptualized as a breakdown of the control function, a failure to carry out the primary task, and a threat to the survival of the system. In the individual we see breakdown of the ego and emotional regression; in the group, breakdown of leadership and paralysis in basic assumptions; and in the institution, breakdown of the administration, failure to carry out the institutional tasks, and loss of morale. Breakdown of boundary control is the principal manifestation of breakdown in the control function.

Rice's theories form the background to the Tavistock Clinic group relations conferences in Leicester and the A. K. Rice group relations conferences in this country. These are time-limited conferences for learning about group, organizational, administrative, and leadership functions. The conferences include small group meetings conducted according to a strictly Bionian technique, large group meetings applying this same technique as described by Rice and Turquet, inter-group exercises, theoretical conferences, and "application groups" to discuss problems of home organizations.

Rice and Turquet studied the behavior of large unstructured groups—of 40 to 120 persons—in ways similar to Bion's study of small group processes. Turquet stressed the individual member's sense of total loss of identity in large group situations, and the simultaneous dramatic diminution in the ability to evaluate realistically the effects of one's own acts or the acts of others within such a group setting. The individual is thrown into a void, even projective mechanisms fail, because it is impossible to evaluate realistically the behavior of anyone else; projections therefore become multiple and unstable, and the individual desperately tries to find some means of differentiating himself from the others.

Turquet also described how the individuals in the large group feared aggression, loss of control, and the emergence of violent behavior. The fear is the counterpart to provocative behaviors among the individuals, behaviors expressed in part randomly but mostly directed at the leader. It gradually becomes evident that it is those individuals who try to stand up to this atmosphere and maintain some semblance of individuality who are most subject to attack. At the same time, efforts at homogenization are prevalent, and any simplistic generalization or ideology that permeates the group may be easily picked up and transformed into an experience of absolute truth. In contrast to the simple rationalization of the violence that permeates the mob, in the large group a vulgar or "common-sense" philosophy functions as a calming, reassuring doctrine which reduces all thinking to obvious clichés. One cannot escape the impression that in the large group aggression largely takes the form of envy of thinking, of individuality, and of rationality.

In my experience with both large and small groups, including group relations conferences, several phenomena emerge with impressive regularity and intensity: First, the activation of intense anxieties and primitive fantasies in the small study groups, and, second, the activation of a primitive quality to both group functioning and potential individual aggression in the large group. The rapid development of ad hoc myths about the leadership or about the conference, and the search for a comprehensive and simplistic ideology in contrast to discriminating reasoning, illustrates in one stroke what happens during the breakdown of organizational functioning. The crucial function of boundary control in task performance and of the role of task oriented leadership emerges in contrast to the dramatic temptations, at points of regressions, to select the most dysfunctional members of subgroups to basic assumptions group leadership and to blur all boundaries in the emotional turmoil that pervades the group.

One important drawback to group relations conferences is the relative failure to consider the effects of their temporary nature. Katz and Kahn (1966) pointed out that the learning of new attitudes on the part of staffs of social and industrial organizations, in the context of exploring the irrational aspects of group processes in an experiential setting, frequently fails. This failure results from their neglecting to analyze the stable features of the organizational structure and the relation between that structure and the real (in contrast to fantasized or irrational) conflicts of interests which such organizational structures mediate.

I think that short-term learning experiences in groups do not allow time for studying the impact of personality structures on members of organizations, particularly the personality of key leaders.

Here we are touching again, now at the level of the relation between large groups and organizational structure, the same, almost unnoticeable, neglect of the impact of the personality of the leader on organizational conflicts. Rice has the great merit of having fully developed a theory of organizational functioning that permits the diagnosis of both organizational regression—"loss of morale"—and of administrative distortions which facilitate such regressive group processes, a theoretically elegant and eminently practical approach to organizational dynamics. But, once again, the effects of the distorted personality on stable social organizations are missing here. It is almost as if the optimal, rational leader were a "man without qualities," or perhaps *should be* a man without qualities?

I think that the more severe the leader's personality pathology and the tighter the organizational structure, the greater are the destructive effects of the leader on the organization. It might be that, under extreme circumstances, the paranoid regression of an entire society maintains the sanity of the tyrant, and, when his control over that society breaks down he becomes psychotic: The final months of Hitler point to this possibility.

Under less extreme circumstances, the effort to "correct" organizational distortions by changing the behavior of the leader may have disastrous consequences for him as well as for those in the next hierarchy. If the organization has to live with a characterologically dysfunctional leader, it may be preferable to adapt the administrative structure to an optimal balance between task requirements and the leader's needs, a solution remarkably opposite to Rice's model.

But how is one to know where to draw the line between restructuring the organization to protect it from the leader's pathology and acknowledging that the organization requires a different leader?

The application of a combined psychoanalytic and open systems theory model of institutional functioning to therapeutic community models (see Main, 1946) illustrates the limits of the therapeutic use of large group analysis. (For a critique of therapeutic community models see Kernberg, 1982.)

I would like to stress that there is an enormous danger within a therapeutic community setting. The danger is that the open exploration of the total social field, wherein patients and staff interact by analyzing the content of the communications which emerge in the community meeting, may be transformed into a messianic denial of reality should the group come under the sway of a leadership characterized by narcissistic and paranoid features. To view the content of large group meetings as a reflection of the unconscious of the organization, and to trace the origin of distortions in the social system to its administrative structure or to the psychopathology of individual patients, or to conflicts at the boundary between patients and staff or of a particular service with the total hospital is exciting and potentially helpful. By the same token, the transformation of trust and openness into the messianic spirit of the dependent or pairing group or, rather, the large group that has found a narcissistic leader and a soothing simplistic ideology is a great and constant temptation for the group and the leader alike. The threat to rational evaluation of task boundaries and constraints, to the ordinary political negotiation around boundaries, is enormous. The proverbial disillusionment and burning out of staff involved in this process who overextend themselves in a messianic over evaluation of what can and should be accomplished needs no illustrations.

Here, we find a paradoxical effect of psychoanalytic illumination of the unconscious in institutions: The deepest, hidden agendas of the institution appear at the surface in verbal communication at large group meetings. But this is an illusion: The immediate availability of understanding basic issues is no guarantee that they will be resolved. Unlike individual psychoanalysis, there is no direct link between emotional reality in groups and their resolution by actual institutional mechanisms of change. The neglect of the personality issues of leadership in the psychoanalytic contributions to group and organizational functioning mentioned before is compounded by the underestimation of the risk for disruption of all rationality by the snowballing effects of expanding small group and large group regressions in the process of self-exploration. The diagnostic instrument self-destructs, the collective patient becomes psychotic.

## Didier Anzieu and Janine Chasseguet-Smirgel

We come now to one more field of application of psychoanalytic theory to group and organizational processes, namely, the study of group processes as the breeding ground for social ideologies, perhaps the most exciting, but also the most controversial and most explosive application of psychoanalytic thinking to social phenomena. I am referring here to the work of French analysts, particularly Didier Anzieu (1971, 1981), Rene Kaes (1980), Janine Chasseguet-Smirgel (1975), and Denise Braunschweig and Michel Fain (1971).

Anzieu (1971) proposed that, under conditions of regression in the unstructured group, the relationship of individuals to the group as an entity acquires characteristics of fusion of their individual instinctual needs with a fantastic conception of the group as a primitive ego ideal equated to an all-gratifying primary object, the mother of the earliest stages of development. The psychology of the group, at that point, reflects the shared illusions (1) that the group is constituted by individuals who are all equal (thus denying sexual differences and castration anxiety); (2) that the group is self-engendered, that is, a powerful mother in itself; and (3) that the group itself might solve all narcissistic lesions (the group becomes an idealized "breast-mother").

Chasseguet-Smirgel (1975), expanding on Anzieu's observations, suggests that under such conditions groups (both small and large) tend to select leadership that represents not the paternal aspects of the prohibitive superego, but a pseudopaternal "merchant of illusions" who provides the group with an ideology (defined as a system of ideas shared by a group and serving to unify the group), which confirms the narcissistic aspirations of fusion of the individual with the group as a primitive ego ideal: the all-powerful and all-gratifying preoedipal mother. Basically, the identification with each other of the members of the small or large group permits them to experience a primitive narcissistic gratification of greatness and power. The violence of groups operating under the influence of ideologies adopted under such psychological conditions reflects the need to destroy any external reality that interferes with this group illusion. The loss of personal identity, of cognitive discrimination, of any individuality within such a group is compensated for by the shared sense of omnipotence of all its members. The regressed ego, the id, and the primitive (preoedipal) ego ideal of each individual are fused in this group illusion.

27

Writing earlier under the pseudonym "Andre Stephane," Chasseguet-Smirgel and Grunberger (1969) analyzed the social psychology of both French fascism and the new left in light of the student rebellion of 1968, describing infantile characteristics common to both movements. Given the heated political atmosphere in France in 1968, Chasseguet-Smirgel and Bela Grunberger decided to publish their probing and disturbing analysis under a pseudonym. Here, we might say, rationality went into hiding; the observers of the social scene start from an acknowledgment of the (at least temporary) impotence of reason.

## Rational leadership

Combining the psychoanalytic observations made of mobs, large groups, and small groups, I earlier proposed (1980) that group processes pose a basic threat to personal identity, linked to a proclivity in group situations for the activation of primitive object relations, primitive defensive operations, and primitive aggression with predominantly pregenital features. I proposed that Turquet's description of what happens in large groups constitutes the basic situation against which (1) the idealization of the leader in the horde, described by Freud; (2) the idealization of the group ideology and of leadership which promotes narcissistic self-aggrandizement of the group, described by Anzieu and Chasseguet-Smirgel; and (3) the small group processes described by Bion are all defending. Obviously, large group processes can be obscured or controlled by rigid social structuring. Bureaucratization, ritualization, and well-organized task performance are different methods with similar immediate effects.

Large group processes also highlight the intimate connection between threats to retaining one's identity and fear that primitive aggression and aggressively infiltrated sexuality will emerge. The point is that an important part of nonintegrated and unsublimated aggression is expressed in vicarious ways throughout group and organizational processes. The exercise of power in organizational and institutional life constitutes an important channel for the expression of aggression in group processes that would ordinarily be under control in dyadic or triadic relations.

I would now modify these earlier formulations. I still believe that large group processes threaten individual identity and therefore activate defenses against identity diffusion and a defensive idealization of the leader. But this formulation underestimates the primary gratification to be found in dissolving in fantasy the boundaries between the self and the primitive forerunners of the ego ideal, in what Freud (1921) (referring to falling in love) called the fusion of ego and ego ideal in mania, in hypnosis, and in the excitement of identifying with others in the group. Anzieu and Chasseguet-Smirgel clarified this illusion of merger more fully when they pointed to its preoedipal nature, in contradistinction to the illusion of merger with a cruel but morally sophisticated superego that characterizes Freud's group member. To put it differently, the messianic characteristic of small and large group regression, with its pregenital features and its denial of intra-group aggression, has to be differentiated from the spirit of the mob, which satisfies every member's need to eliminate a sense of separateness in a common, powerfully self-righteous, emotionally laden movement forward, the destructive expansion of a rioting mob (Canetti, 1978).

But these two levels of regressive temptation (of the small and large group as opposed to that of the crowd) also call for two layers of regressive leadership. At one extreme we find the self-indulgent narcissist who can lead the small dependent assumption group or pacify the large group with a simplistic ideology that soothes while preventing envy of the leader, or, in a more "sophisticated" combination, the sexually "liberated" narcissist who preaches sexual liberation in the group's (symbolic or actual) bathtub and condenses polymorphous preoedipal sexuality with messianic merger. At the other extreme, and more disturbingly, we find the sadistic psychopath, with a well-rationalized cruelty, who energizes the mob into destructive action against a common enemy and frees it from responsibility for murder.

In an earlier work (1980, Chapter 13), I attempted to describe the effects on organizational regression of personality characteristics of the leader, with particular reference to schizoid, obsessive, paranoid, and narcissistic personalities, and I shall not repeat these characteristics here. In my earlier description, however, I limited my observations to small organizations, such as psychiatric hospitals and university departments, where there are usually no more than three levels of hierarchies and where, therefore, there is still some semblance or possibility of leader and followers knowing each other.

The question is to what extent such small, self-contained types of social organization surround the leader with a structure of rationality that would avoid the takeover by a sadistic or narcissistic leader or neutralize his regressive effects over an extended period of time. The possibility that the leader will be personally acquainted with those at the grass roots level of the organization protects the reality aspects of the total institution. But larger organizations, such as national bureaucracies or international corporations, where four to seven hierarchic levels of leadership are the rule, may no longer offer such a possibility of ordinary social control. In such large organizations, any direct contact between all levels of staff becomes impossible or unreal, and the replacement of reality by projective mechanisms increases.

Elliot Jaques (1976) has made a systematic analysis of bureaucracy. He finds that well-functioning bureaucracies have merit. They provide the social system with rationally determined hierarchies, public delineation of responsibility and accountability, stable delegation of authority, and an overall accountability of the organization to its social environment by both legal and political means and a parallel organization of employees and/or labor unions. Bureaucracies may thus provide an optimal balance between the potentially regressive consequences of hierarchically determined relations between individuals, on the one hand, and the possibility of redress of grievances and protection from arbitrariness, on the other.

Jaques's assumption is that the leaders of large social institutions are accountable to, or controlled by, the state or by law. The implicit counterpart to this assumption is that when such social controls are unavailable, the distortions at the top will go unchecked and will be communicated throughout the entire organization. A well-functioning bureaucracy in a democratic system may be one ideal model of organizational structure. In contrast, a tightly organized bureaucracy, controlled by a totalitarian state with a paranoid psychotic or a sadistic psychopath at the head of it, would necessarily represent a social nightmare into which the regression of all included groups would very easily fit, without any possibility of rational correction from anywhere. The totalitarian bureaucracies of Nazi Germany and the Soviet Union were able to murder millions of people without any internal convulsions. These examples suggest that the authoritarian power generated within organizations, stemming from both individual psychopathology and from organizational regression, not to mention the ordinary discharge into the organization of unacknowledged narcissistic and aggressive needs by all individuals, may rapidly escalate, given certain social and political conditions, into socially sanctioned cruelty and dehumanization. The distinction between an ordinary dictatorship in which the right to privacy is preserved as long as no direct actions are taken against the regime and a totalitarian system in which all social interactions are regulated by an imposed ideology may be one of the painful discoveries of our time.

Elias Canetti, in his book *Crowds and Power* (1978), describes the universal temptation to become part of a crowd and of assuring personal survival and immortality by killing others as a basic unconscious motive for wanting the leadership of the crowd.

The psychoanalytic study of a particular subgroup of narcissistic patients with aggressive infiltration of their pathological grandiose self elaborated by Herbert Rosenfeld (1971) provides a counterpart to Canetti's description.

Psychoanalytically oriented consultants for institutional problems, whether they follow the model of Rice, Jaques, Harry Levinson (1972), or Abraham Zaleznik (1979), assume that regressive manifestations in group processes indicate institutional malfunctioning and that these group processes potentially point to the nature of the conflicts affecting the system. The usual procedure is to study the primary tasks of the organization, its administrative structure, how authority is distributed and delegated, whether the system has checks and balances, and whether it provides for a redress of grievances. With the possible exception of Levinson's, all these approaches focus on the leadership only after other factors have been studied, by the process, as it were, of elimination. Personality problems always appear at first in the foreground, but can only be diagnosed as causal features once all the other institutional issues have been analyzed and discarded.

Jaques's (1976, 1982) findings regarding an individual's capacity for work as measured by his capacity to estimate the time it will take to accomplish certain tasks and his effective capacity to organize and carry out such tasks (the maximum time span of discretion in his work) are a truly important contribution to organizational psychology and to selection criteria for leadership. Yet the psychoanalytically oriented consultant may be averse or reluctant to take this factor into consideration, and would more likely think in terms of psychopathology than in terms of the inequalities of a leader's capacity for performing his various tasks. In fact, it may be more difficult to assess this quality than to assess or even to sift out the aspects of personality that produce optimal leadership functioning. The leader of an organization as well as the consultant must be constantly alert to the danger of giving rein to their own narcissism and aggression and therefore may have difficulty in acknowledging that managerial leaders do differ in their administrative capabilities. The leader (and the consultant) must also resist any tendency to allow themselves to be influenced by fears of arousing unconscious envy by exposing the differences between people. The leader's task is to judge. Perhaps the best he can do is to maintain alertness to the implications of standing in judgment of others.

On the basis of my experience as psychoanalyst, leader of groups (including therapeutic communities), medical director of psychiatric hospitals, and consultant to mental health institutions, I can attempt to describe the desirable personality characteristics for rational task leadership. First is high intelligence, which is necessary for strategic conceptual thinking; second is personal honesty and non-corruptibility by the political process; third is the capacity for establishing and maintaining object relations in depth, which is essential for evaluating others realistically; fourth is what might be called healthy narcissism in the sense of being self-assertive rather than self-effacing; and fifth is a sense of caution and alertness to the world rather than a naive credulousness, what someone I once knew called justifiable anticipatory paranoia.

The need for high intelligence, expressed in the capacity for strategic conceptual thinking, and probably also in creative imagination, may seem self-evident. The need for honesty and non-corruptibility may also seem self-evident, but requires testing under conditions of stress and political constraints. In practice, to be fair and just to those the leader knows personally is still possible; but to be fair and just to those who depend on him without his knowing them personally is the test of an integrity that transcends personal commitments to others. The fairness to many will necessarily appear as rigidity to the few; the leader's incorruptibility faced with the temptations of leadership will be experienced as sadistic rejection by the tempters, as may the leader's maintenance of fair rules applying to all. Here the narcissistic investment in moral righteousness may protect rational leadership, together with the paranoid distrust of temptations from the surrounding group. These functions require a well-integrated and mature superego, which assumes the sublimatory nature of ideals and value systems and signifies the preconditions for normal (in contrast to pathological) narcissism.

Under optimal conditions, the leader's narcissistic and paranoid features may neutralize each other's potentially negative effects on the organization and on the leader himself. The paranoid implications of suspiciousness toward subordinate efforts of kowtowing may prevent the disastrous consequences of a narcissistic leader's needs to be obeyed *and* loved at the same time. The narcissistic enjoyment of success in leadership may prevent the erosion of self-confidence that derives from paranoid fears about potential attacks or criticism from others. In stark contrast to such optimal combinations, severe character pathology in the leader in the form of pathological narcissism complicated by paranoid features may prove disastrous (see Kernberg, 1980, Chapter 13).

What is the "right" dosage of normal narcissism and paranoia required for rational leadership? Is it firmness without sadism, incorruptibility without rigidity, warmth without manipulativeness, or emotional depth without the loss of distance required to focus on the total gestalt of the group and on the task as contrasted with its human constraints? The optimal leader of an organization might have to blind himself to the awareness of the impact of his own personality on the organization sufficiently so as to be able to resonate with the needs of the group, but not so much as to lose his capacity for using his personality in the leadership role.

A small dose of narcissism and paranoid traits may reinforce the power of rationality and honesty, and a small dose of sadism in the leader may protect the task systems from regression. Yet, an excess of these ingredients may suddenly trigger regression in leaders: A sense of justice and fairness may become self-righteousness and sadistic control. Regression in the leader may trigger regression in the organization.

In the psychoanalytic situation, the psychoanalyst has sufficient boundary control to help a patient discover his unconscious and, by the same token, to permit the development and potential resolution of the patient's unconscious conflicts around sex and aggression in the transference. In transferring the psychoanalytic investigation to group processes an easy activation of primitive processes may occur, which would immediately exceed the boundary control of the exploring psychoanalyst. By the same token, the psychoanalytic consultant exploring organizational issues that deal with the personality of the leader may trigger off a storm that would destroy not only the consultative process but the very capacity of the organization to tolerate it. The complexities of the technique of communication of organizational dynamics may be one factor

limiting the consultant's task. But, it is not, in my view, the dominant one. The discrepancy between the analytic instrument-group
shared unconscious fantasies, basic assumptions groups and system
theory of organizations and the capacity for containment on the
part of the institution may provide a more important and perhaps
intimidating barrier to advances in this field.

I hope I have made clear why I think a nebulous ambiguity surrounds the subject of leadership in Freud, Bion, and others. I also
hope my metaphoric title, The Couch at Sea, has communicated
some of the excitement I find in exploring the social unconscious,
even if the uncertainties still facing us mean having to navigate in
troubled waters—and on the couch rather than behind it.

## Note

1 Reprinted from *International Journal of Group Psychotherapy* Volume 34,
Number 1, International Universities Press, Inc., New York.

## References

Althusser, L. (1976). *Positions*. Paris: Editions Sociales.
Anzieu, D. (1971). L'illusion groupal. *Nouvelle Revue de Psychanalyse*, 4:7
    3–93.
—— ( 1981). *Le groupe et linconscient: Limaginaire groupal*. Paris: Dunod.
Bion, W. R. (1961). *Experiences in Groups*. New York: Basic Books.
—— (1970). *Attention and Interpretation*. London: Heinemann.
Braunschweig, D. & Fain, M. (1971). *Eros et Anteros*. Paris: Petite Bib-
    liotheque Payot.
Canetti, E. (1978). *Crowds and Power*. New York: Seabury Press.
Chasseguet-Smirgel, J. (1975). *L'Ideal du Moi*. Paris: Claude Tchou.
Freud, S. (1913). Totem and Taboo. *Standard Edition*, 13. London: Hogarth
    Press, 1955.
—— (1921). Group Psychology and the Analysis of the Ego. *Standard
    Edition*, 18. London: Hogarth Press, 1955.
—— (1914). On the History of the Psychoanalytic Movement. *Standard
    Edition*, 14. London: Hogarth Press, 1957.
—— (1927). Letter to Oskar Pfister of 10/22/1927. *Sigmund Freud Oskar
    Pfister Briefe 1909–1939*. Frankfurt am Main: Fischer Verlag. (English
    Translation: *Psychoanalysis and Faith: The Letters of Sigmund Freud and Oskar
    Pfister*, eds. H. Meng & E. L. Freud.) New York: Basic Books, 1963.
Jaques, E. (1976). *A General Theory of Bureaucracy*. New York: Halsted.

—— (1982). *The Form of Time*. New York: Crane, Russak.

Kaes, R. (1980). *L'idiologie: Etudes psychanalytiques*. Paris: Dunod.

Katz, D. & Kahn, R. L. (1966). *The Social Psychology of Organizations*. New York: Wiley.

Kernberg, O. (1980). *Internal World and External Reality: Object Relations Theory Applied*. New York: Jason Aronson.

—— (1982). Advantages and Liabilities of Therapeutic Community Models. In *The Individual and the Group*, Vol. 1, eds. M. Pine & L. Rafaelsen. London: Plenum Publishing Corp.

Lasch, C. (1981). The Freudian Left and Cultural Revolution. *New Left Review*, 129: 23–34.

Levinson, H. (1972). *Organizational Diagnosis*. Cambridge, MA: Harvard University Press.

Main, T. F. (1946). The Hospital as a Therapeutic Institution. *Bull. Menninger Clin.*, 10: 66–70.

Malan, D. H., Balfour, F. H. G., Hood, V. G. & Shooter, A. M. N. (1976). Group psychotherapy: A Long-Term Follow-Up Study. *Arch. Gen. Psychiat.*, 33: 1303–1315.

Reich, W. (1935). *The Sexual Revolution: Toward a Self-Governing Character Structure*. New York: The Noonday Press, 1962.

Rice, A. K. (1965). *Learning for Leadership*. London: Tavistock Publications.

Rosenfeld, H. (1971). A Clinical Approach to the Psychoanalytic Theory of the Life and Death Instincts: An Investigation into the Aggressive Aspects of Narcissism. *Internat. J. Psycho-Anal.*, 52: 169–178.

Roustang, F. (1982). *Dire Mastery: Discipleship from Freud to Lacan*. Baltimore, MD: The Johns Hopkins University Press.

Scheidlinger, S. (1960). Group Process in Group Psychotherapy. *Amer. J. Psychother.*, 14: 104–120; 346–363.

Stephane, A. (1969). *L'Univers contestationnaire*. Paris: Petite Bibliothèque Payot.

Turquet, P. (1975). Threats to Identity in the Large Group. In *The Large Group: Dynamics and Therapy*, ed. L. Kreeger. London: Constable.

Zaleznik, A. (1979). Psychoanalytic Knowledge of Group Processes: Panel Report. *J. Amer. Psychoanal. Assoc.*, 27: 146–147; 149–150.

# INSTITUTIONAL PROBLEMS OF PSYCHOANALYTIC EDUCATION[1]

## The symptoms

Psychoanalytic education today is all too often conducted in an atmosphere of indoctrination rather than of open scientific exploration. Candidates as well as graduates and even faculty are prone to study and quote their teachers, often ignoring alternative psychoanalytic approaches. The disproportionate amount of time and energy given to Freud, in contrast to the brief and superficial review of other theorists, including contemporary psychoanalytic contributions (other than those of dominant local authorities), and the rigid presentation and uncritical discussion of Freud's work and theories in the light of contemporary knowledge give the educational process a sense of flatness.

Candidates are systematically prevented from knowing the details of their faculty's analytic work. They are usually even sheltered from sharp disagreements within their own institute, so that, at best, they may learn about these at society meetings rather than within their formal educational program. In the case of seminars and personal supervision, candidates learn only about cases treated by themselves and other candidates, presumably treated with less than an optimal psychoanalytic technique. The more senior the analyst, the less he shares his analytic experience with students. To illustrate the teaching of technique with selected vignettes is very different from presenting ongoing clinical material fully to students. The only experience candidates have regarding how psychoanalysis is optimally carried out derives from their own psychoanalysis and from their readings. If it is true that their own analyses are highly contaminated by their transferences, and that the literature case material is highly distorted by a variety of factors and thus of questionable value as a model of psychoanalytic technique, this failure to provide experience with optimal technique is a most astonishing and rarely discussed aspect of psychoanalytic education.

A candidate authentically dependent on his training analyst may identify with his analyst's analyzing attitude. But even under optimal conditions, the candidate will not learn general technique. That the candidate may learn and identify himself with his analyst's "style" is a far cry from his learning about his analyst's theory of technique. And, unless this learning of "style" is enriched and deepened by learning optimal psychoanalytic technique, it may end up as a ritualized and cliché-ridden mode of approaching patients. Candidates with narcissistic pathology, who are exquisitely attuned to all of their training analyst's interventions and to his thought processes as these reveal themselves in his eventually predictable behavior, miss, by the same token, the opportunities of learning about psychoanalysis from their own unconscious.

It hardly needs to be stressed that all published clinical data reflect a carefully selected segment of any psychoanalysis, typically of those aspects in which the psychoanalyst was either successful or, if unsuccessful, still managed to learn from and overcome that momentary failure. This selectiveness results in conveying an idealized and unrealistic conception of the true nature of psychoanalytic work.

The reluctance of senior analysts to share their clinical experience and technique (as reflected in extended, detailed case presentations) with their junior colleagues is carried to extremes with candidates. There may be good reasons why a candidate's own training analyst should not share other clinical experiences with him, but I can see no good educational reasons for the general practice of training analysts not sharing any of their ongoing clinical experience with candidates as a group or with individual candidates in the supervisory relationship.

Preventing candidates from learning about the difficulties and uncertainties of psychoanalytic practice and technique leads, under the best of circumstances, to a subsidiary symptom: the candidate's unrealistic idealization of psychoanalytic technique and of the senior members of the faculty. It can happen that senior members of the faculty who never discuss a case, present a paper, or share their work in any public way are even more highly idealized.

The ultimate authority of most institutes is invested in the training analyst; the authority of the faculty suffers by comparison. This apportioning of authority results in a fragmentation of the supervisory and monitoring process throughout a candidate's training. Particularly in large institutes, it is as if each seminar leader and each supervisor were operating in a vacuum. Opportunities for communication among faculty regarding the candidate's functioning are minimal. Individual faculty members feel they have very little influence on the overall evaluation and progress of the candidate. One might argue that such fragmentation of the faculty may protect some candidates against arbitrary persecution from single senior faculty members with inordinate influence. In practice, however, a public faculty discussion of discrepant views about a particular candidate offers greater protection against arbitrary evaluations. In large institutes, the information from seminar leaders and supervisors tends to be transmitted to a committee rather than to the entire faculty, further fragmenting and depersonalizing the supervisory monitoring functions of the candidate's educational progress. In small institutes, where the same people train, teach, and supervise, a cautious attitude tends to prevail, focusing on who is the training analyst of any particular candidate, as if any criticism of the candidate might reflect on the training analyst, or any negative evaluation of the candidate be considered an attack on his training analyst.

In fact, the assumption that the candidate reflects the power or influence of his training analyst is so pervasive that Greenacre (1959) described what she called a "convoy" system by which training analysts safely monitor the voyage of their analysands through the perilous seas of the training years. Training analysts so engaged reflect the loss of the analytic attitude and the institutional corruption of the analytic process.

Linked with this phenomenon is the implicit assumption that the "real" psychoanalytic education is the training analysis, that supervision is secondary, and courses only tertiary aspects of that training. The often implicit additional assumption, that monitoring a candidate's learning and capability in the light of anything but his own training analysis is of doubtful value, contributes to the self-demeaning consequences of the supervisory and instructional faculty's lack of sufficiently shared knowledge and authority. Insofar as seminar leaders who are not training analysts also contribute to underestimate their own didactic functions, the junior faculty implicitly contributes to this self-devaluation.

The traditional assumption that training analysts should report on the candidate's progress, a highly questionable custom derived from naive earlier times of psychoanalytic education, has fortunately now been recognized as a major cause of distortion of the psychoanalytic process in the training analysis itself, and as the origin of the still existing practice of the candidates' having a "first analysis" for the institute, and a "second analysis," after graduation, "for themselves." Lifschutz (1976) has reviewed the literature and has convincingly argued for the non-reporting training analyst position.

Behind the tradition of reporting training analysts is the assumption that supervision, seminars, group discussion, and faculty evaluation are of far less importance than the knowledge the training analyst presumably has about the value and capacities of his analysands. The faculty's self-protective withdrawal from candidates who are perceived as particularly privileged or untouchable, and "compassionate graduation" of inadequately performing candidates who have remained in training for many years are other typical symptoms of the failure to invest adequate authority in the faculty body.

A lack of accountability of faculty for their evaluation of candidates is the counterpart of their lack of sufficient and functional authority. Although, under the influence of changes in the surrounding educational system in universities and medical schools candidates as a group tend to have more authority and spelled-out channels for redress of grievances, psychoanalytic institutes—as convinangly reported again by the national organization of candidates (Franzen, 1982)—are characteristically vague and imprecise in describing all the requirements for candidate acceptance, progression, graduation, and their channels of communication and for redress of grievances.

This situation is complicated by a specific characteristic of psychoanalytic education that is astonishingly ignored. I am referring to the paranoid atmosphere that often pervades psychoanalytic institutes and its devastating effect on the "quality of life" in psychoanalytic education. Members of some South American psychoanalytic institutes speak of the phenomenon of the "unhooked telephone": the fact that candidates' open criticism of faculty, largely constituted of training analysts, is inhibited because the candidates are in personal analysis with those same training analysts. Thus candidates as well as graduates and faculty have to be extremely careful about what they say about training analysts in the presence of students and colleagues who may still (or again) be in analysis with that person. Training analysts, of course, are in the unhappy position of having to hear through their candidates (particularly at times of strongly negative or split-off negative transference) what their colleagues and students are saying about them. The assumption that the training analyst's narcissism is healthy enough for him not to take offense is, as we well know, an illusion.

Several phenomena potentiate each other and strengthen the paranoid atmosphere that pervades many psychoanalytic institutes. Candidates' displacement, splitting, and acting out of the negative transference may be expressed in underground criticism of the senior faculty, particularly when the institute does not provide ordinary channels for students' and faculty's joint evaluation of the educational process. The narcissistic lesions absorbed by senior training analysts through the phenomenon of "unhooked telephones" may increase their countertransference reactions to their own candidates and the displacement of these reactions onto other training analysts and candidates, thereby increasing their paranoid reactions toward the institution.

The training analysts' acting out of countertransference reactions frequently takes the form of confidential communications about candidates to other training analysts, often only expressed by subtle gestures or pregnant silences. Dulchin and Segal (1982a, 1982b) have pointed to the breakdown of confidentiality about candidates' analyses in one psychoanalytic institute, and it is reasonable to assume that this is a widespread phenomenon, particularly, although not exclusively, in institutes that have reporting policies. While "reporting" is officially disappearing from psychoanalytic institutes at this time, it tends to linger on in this informal way.

A consequence of these developments is an atmosphere among senior faculty of sharing secrets, of being an in-group of "being in the know," in contrast to the out-group of junior faculty who are not training analysts and the candidates. As Roger Dorey (personal communication) has pointed out, this actualizes the fantasy of the secretive oedipal couple and the excluded children so prevalent in psychoanalytic institutes. The "paranoiagenic" (Jaques, 1976) atmosphere of psychoanalytic institutes, the threat of persecution that permeates them, is the counterpart to the institutionally sanctioned and fostered idealization (particularly of senior training analysts) that also pervades them.

The apparent or real arbitrariness in the appointment of junior faculty and training analysts is another easily recognized major problem in psychoanalytic education. It is an open secret that the appointment of training analysts is politically motivated, that the actual qualifications of the training analyst may be less important than his or her reliability with regard to local politics. This corruptive aspect of psychoanalytic education is often apologetically rationalized as the unavoidable repetition of "family life" (with intergenerational conflicts, sibling rivalry, "primal scene" material, etc.) in psychoanalytic institutes. But the failure to make a distinction between an educational institution and a family reflects a failure to develop and preserve an organizational structure that is oriented to the tasks to be performed. Such a failure directly causes paranoiagenic deterioration of the institution's social life and functions. This point, arbitrariness in the appointment of faculty, could be misunderstood as a rejection of the necessarily subjective criteria, the personal judgments that must enter the decision of whom to appoint training analyst.

What I question is the lack of explicit, public policies and criteria for the selection of training analysts and the lack of explicit, public information regarding the locus of and the accountability for the decision-making. The formal locus and the real locus of decision-making are often very different. The policy of "gently tapping" selected graduates, rather than explicit encouragement for manifestation of interest on the part of candidates for training analyst appointments, illustrates the social hypocrisy surrounding such appointments, which poisons the atmosphere of psychoanalytic institutes.

The lack of explicit criteria for the appointment of faculty in general, and the lack of explicit policies and criteria for the quality control of faculty functioning, particularly of training analysts' functioning, reflects the political nature of these appointments. The avoidance of explicit criteria for the retirement of faculty, particularly training analysts, and the proverbial conspiracy in institutes that protect incompetent training analysts to the point of their becoming a public nuisance are well known. Here the lack of discussion of the actual clinical work of senior training analysts has one more negative consequence.

A final symptom of the sick psychoanalytic institutes is the diminished creative thinking and scientific productivity on the part of faculty, students, and graduates. A narrow intellectual frame determined by the locally prevalent views within the broad theoretical spectrum of psychoanalysis, intellectual toadyism or kowtowing to venerable fathers of the local group, petty "cross-sterilization," and discouragement of original thinking are painful indicators that not all is well with psychoanalytic education.

Cross-sterilization is manifest in the suspicious and envious way in which new ideas are received, faculty fearfulness of expressing new ideas that might challenge local dogma, and the general collusion in public applause of rehashed formulations, while privately many depreciate the monotonous repetition of concepts that, by the same token; also reassure the faculty that nothing new is threatening their present convictions. The net effect is a deterioration of scientific work and original thinking. The question could be raised whether the general scientific domain of psychoanalysis actually has nothing new to say. But the exciting developments at the boundaries of psychoanalytic theories and technique belie such a narrow and pessimistic view.

## Immediate causes: primary task and organizational structure

So much for the symptoms. Now to trace back to their causes. I have chosen to approach the problem by first examining the organizational structure of psychoanalytic institutes and then examining the primary tasks (or aims) of the institutes, for if there is a discrepancy between the primary tasks of an organization and its structure, problems ensue. The structure of an organization corresponds, in practice, to the administrative structure of the institute. In what follows, I explore the relation between primary tasks and the administrative structure of psychoanalytic institutes.

What are the primary tasks of a psychoanalytic institute? And how would different concepts of such primary tasks relate to a correspondingly functional administrative structure? I propose four models of education, each of which corresponds to explicit aims that have been formulated as desirable primary tasks for psychoanalytic institutes. Each of these models warrants a specific organizational structure corresponding to its respective aims. These models are (1) an art academy, (2) a technical trade school, (3) a monastery or religious retreat, and (4) a university college. I shall spell out the theoretical implications of these models, the corresponding organizational structures functionally linked to them, and examine the actual structure of psychoanalytic education in light of these models.

In the first model, the art academy, the primary task of psychoanalytic education is to train expert craftsmen and, it is hoped, artists, so that their talents can be brought to fruition. To employ this model would be to assume that psychoanalysis is more than a technique; it is an art, and highly specialized training in craftsmanship will facilitate the expression of creativity of the apprentices. This model fits with the highly individualized nature of psychoanalytic training, with the tutorship and mentorship aspects of psychoanalytic education and criteria for progression, and with the assumption (characteristic of many institutes) that there exists one ideal technique that needs to be mastered as a basis for subsequent creativity within that art. The discussion of theories would be circumscribed by the need to establish their relation to the ideal technique perfected in that institute. Some psychoanalytic institutes, in fact, operate as if such an ideal technique, elevated to perfection by the local masters, existed and learning it from these masters is the best way for candidates to absorb and master it.

There is, however, a striking contradiction between the art academy model and the way institutes actually function. Unlike the art teacher in the art academy, the senior training analyst functions in privacy and his techniques remain shrouded in secrecy. To conform to the aim of the art academy, psychoanalytic training would allow candidates to observe and critically judge the process of a psychoanalytic treatment carried out by their local masters. In addition, the focus would have to be on the nature of the product of the actual psychoanalytic work rather than on the nature of the personality structure facilitating this work. It would therefore also imply taking the supervisory and seminar structures much more seriously in their evaluation of the candidate's work.

The second model, that of a technical or trade school, would conceive the primary task of psychoanalytic education to be the learning of a clearly defined skill or trade, with no emphasis on artistic creativity. Teachers would be able to document their mastery of psychoanalytic skills without assuming or pretending that unique personal inspiration or creativity is required in carrying them out. Psychoanalytic institutes, according to this model, would be highly specialized trade schools with a program of efficient training, monitoring of the students' progress, and, once the optimal level of skill has been reached, graduation. An essentially bureaucratic structure of institutional organization might be similar to that of other specialized technical schools, such as industrial and technical skills in applied arts.

Most psychoanalysts would probably strongly reject this model and consider it a degradation of the analyst's personality attributes and personal creativity and the artistic aspects of psychoanalytic work. It needs to be pointed out, however, that insofar as great emphasis is currently put on the careful monitoring of the progress of the candidate's skills, without any emphasis on the public display of corresponding skills on the part of the faculty, the institute does resemble a trade school. A student can learn, for example, accounting techniques, budgeting, and financial analysis without observing his teachers carrying out such functions in detail in their personal work.

Less obviously, but more importantly, in my view, the trade school model highlights the advantages of a bureaucratic organization that has explicit criteria and standards of professional functioning for both teachers and students. Such a model provides a system for objective monitoring and qualification which reduces arbitrary, private subjective judgments carried out in secret; it provides for an easy system of checks and balances between students and faculty, for redress of grievances of both students and faculty with regard to the administration. The responsibility of the trade school administration to graduate students with socially acknowledged and sanctioned technical expertise also provides a clear accountability of the institution which protects all its members from arbitrary redefinitions of the nature of the work, the qualifications for admission, progression, and graduation.

This model illustrates Jaques's (1976) thesis that bureaucratic systems of organization, at their best, permit a reduction of paranoiagenic features in the organization. Such a reduction may have very salutary effects on psychoanalytic institutes, which, as mentioned earlier, are particularly paranoiagenic. However, insofar as psychoanalysts tend to conceptualize psychoanalysis as an art and a science, they would probably reject a trade school model.

A third model would consider psychoanalytic institutes as monasteries or religious retreats and psychoanalysis as a system of religious beliefs. Whereas psychoanalysts would probably vehemently reject such a model, insisting on the scientific in contrast to the religious and ethical nature of psychoanalytic theory, there are important features of psychoanalytic education, as it is actually carried out, that would justify such a designation.

First of all, the religious assertion of faith in the existence of the deity and the essentially irrational nature of such a faith are not unlike the sense of conviction about the truth of psychoanalytic theory, particularly about the unconscious. This sense of conviction is usually traced to an emotional experience connected with the discovery of the unconscious in oneself and the experience of psychological change following this discovery. In both instances a highly subjective personal experience, an emotional encounter with the unknown, rather than rational analysis constitutes the anchoring pillar of the educational program.

In addition, this deeply transforming emotional experience is carried out in the context of an intense relation to another person, idealized and experienced as a spiritual guide. That spiritual guide as mentor is complemented by other mentors, who focus on the limitations, shortcomings, mistakes, and inadequacies of the student's performance, while sustaining the assumption that they are working at a higher level, which the student must reach through ongoing self-exploration as well as learning about the formulations of the masters, in the end, the original master of the school, Freud.

The idealization of Freud in psychoanalytic education is illustrated in the detailed, frequently obsessive and relatively non-critical study of his work, the invocation to Freud's ideas when new developments in the field appear to threaten one of his formulations, the genealogical retracing of psychoanalytic training from a candidate's own training analyst to his training analyst, to one of the original disciples, and finally to Freud. All of these features reflect an extraordinary emotional investment in the original founder and his beliefs, quite similar to religious practice.

Above all, the quality of faith required to undergo a process explicitly designed to face an individual with the unknown, and the shrouding in secrecy of the work and the personality of those who help the student, reproduce the emotional atmosphere of monasteries and religious retreats. The exposure of the personalities of the trainees to a total scrutiny, while the personalities of the teachers are maintained in as much secrecy as possible, is a requisite characteristic of religious education.

However, although the organizational structure of psychoanalytic institutes may be impressively similar to one used for theological training, I agree that psychoanalysis should stand or fall as a science and not as a system of emotional belief.

This leads us to my fourth model, that of the psychoanalytic institute as a university college, as an institution for the transmission, exploration, and generation of knowledge, including the transmission of methodological tools for the generation of new knowledge. That this knowledge should have a practical application, namely, helping human beings in distress and particularly helping psychologically ill people with psychological treatment, places psychoanalytic education close to the model of medical schools and other helping professions and fits with a definition that Freud (1922) gave of psychoanalysis as a theory of the mind, a method of investigation of unconscious processes, and a method of treatment. Such a model would include the following as major organizational requirements.

First of all, the candidate, in addition to personality characteristics commensurate with the capacity to explore his own unconscious and to learn how to explore the unconscious of patients without undue risks to himself or to others, would have to be exposed to and educated with a critical sense regarding all theories and techniques, be expected to learn the latest developments in the theory of technique—not a closed system of beliefs—and would have to accept the uncertainty resulting from a critical examination of all knowledge, theories, and procedures in the light of all available evidence. He would have to absorb not only Freud's writings, but also those of psychoanalysts who reached theoretical and/or technical conclusions that differ from Freud's.

The faculty would have to be able and willing to tolerate scientific debate, to expose their theories and actual clinical work to the critical analysis of the students. Faculty selection, while necessarily containing a subjective, personal element, would have to be carried out by publicly known criteria and with publicly known and sanctioned procedures open to review by a legally designated authority, and the institute would be accountable for the selection, monitoring, and ongoing reconfirmation of faculty.

Both faculty and student bodies would have independent organizations that could challenge the actual carrying out of policies by the school's administration in the light of such publicly sanctioned policies. The hierarchical relation between the director and his administrative subordinates in the institute would be balanced by the sanctioned authority of the faculty. This model may be the most congenial to the aspirations of most psychoanalysts, but, in my view, it fits very poorly with the actual structure of psychoanalytic institutes.

My conclusion is that a serious discrepancy exists between the prevalent, explicitly formulated or implicitly acknowledged aims of psychoanalytic education and the dominant organizational structures that characterize psychoanalytic institutes. In my view, while psychoanalytic educators think they are transmitting what is both an art and a science, they have structured their institutes so that they correspond most closely to a combination of the technical school and the theological seminary. If instead, psychoanalytic educators adopted a model combining the features of the art school and the university college, they would be closer to achieving their aims and would eliminate the symptoms listed above.

## Underlying causes: psychoanalytic treatment in an institutional setting

Having examined the relation between primary tasks and organizational structure of psychoanalytic education let me now turn to a motivational analysis of the distortions in these relations. By analogy, one might say that we shall now turn to the unconscious motivations determining the psychopathology of psychoanalytic institutes. The simplest explanation one might be tempted to propose in analyzing the discrepancy between primary task and organizational structure in psychoanalytic institutes would be of a self-perpetuating power elite of training analysts that utilizes the exacerbation of idealization processes inherent in psychoanalytic training to consolidate its power and the related narcissistic gratification by exercising control over a small social organization.

Insofar as a power motive is a universal quality of human beings, the power exerted by education committees, particularly if they coincide with the executive committees of psychoanalytic institutes, may play into an important human motive. One might speculate that, insofar as a senior faculty status in psychoanalytic education also coincides with late middle age and old age, the correspondingly waning gratification in creativity, productivity, and sexuality may also reinforce the power motive. The financial security of older training analysts in power and the distraction from the ordinary uncertainties of aging may play an important role here.

These, however, are universal conflicts and motives, which cannot be attributed exclusively to psychoanalysts. The collusion with and confirmation of functionally excessive or authoritarian power that a senior group of training analysts obtain from their institution at large must reflect further issues. One frequently observes that when senior analysts step down from positions of power and authority they are immediately able to point to the distorting nature of such positions (for example, Keiser's [1969] and Arlow's [1973, unpublished] analyses of problems in psychoanalytic education point in many ways to the symptoms I mentioned earlier). In addition, political minorities within an institute, who protest against the institute's authoritarian structure, may easily become as authoritarian as those they have replaced.

I think that, in addition to the vicissitudes of individual power motivations, the widespread ignorance of the importance of organizational structure, and the regressive consequences of group processes activated under conditions of nonfunctional administrative structures (Kernberg, 1980, and Chapter 2 of this volume), there are underlying sources of insecurity pervading psychoanalytic institutes and psychoanalysis as a profession. I suggest that these insecurities derive from the nature of the product handled in psychoanalytic institutes, namely, the uncovering of the unconscious, in the context of the institutional boundaries of the psychoanalytic institute, and the particular effects of this operation on candidates and training analysts alike. Using a fashionable contemporary analogy, one might say that the therapeutic process of psychoanalysis liberates radioactive products and the dispersal of this radioactive fallout, which ordinarily occurs in psychoanalytic treatment carried out in an open social setting, is interfered with by the constraining and amplifying effects of the closed environment of the psychoanalytic institutions.

In ordinary psychoanalytic treatment, much of the transference and countertransference activated is dispersed in the form of displacement, working through, and the ordinary dilution of the emotional impact of the psychoanalytic session, as patient and analyst move in totally separate social environments between the sessions. The advantages of this arrangement in protecting the technical neutrality of the treatment situation and in reducing the potential for transference acting out and countertransference acting out are evident. In contrast, the training analysts' treatment of candidates occurs within the confines of a shared social setting and organizational structure. This creates ample opportunities and temptations for transference and countertransference acting out and for amplification of these powerful emotional forces within the institution.

Both the training analyst and the candidate analysand are more exposed to each other than is the case in ordinary psychoanalytic treatment; they are more vulnerable to their directly exerted and indirectly expressed mutual influence, and yet, are perceived as inordinately powerful by the other person of their patient–analyst dyad. The training analyst is exposed in terms of the easy availability of direct observations of him and information about him on the part of the analysand, and the analysand is more directly exposed in terms of direct observation and indirect information about him available to the training analyst.

Displacements of the transference, splitting and displacing the transference onto other members of the faculty, acting out the negative and positive transference at seminars and in supervision, all contribute to making the training analyst more vulnerable to his candidates' acting out. The training analyst actually exerts power in the "reporting" institutes, but the experience of him as extremely powerful is present in non-reporting institutes as well, for he is part of the administrative structure of the institute, a senior and influential member of the faculty.

In my view, this "radioactive fallout" is a basic cause of disturbances in the psychoanalytic institute and of the activation of primitive defensive operations in the institution to deal with them. Why primitive defensive operations? Because when people function in groups, and especially when these groups exist in an organization structurally out of tune with its aims, regressive group processes tend to become operative (see Kernberg, 1980, pp. 209–273, and Chapter 2 of this volume). The exploration of the dynamic unconscious carried out in multiple therapeutic psychoanalyses within a social organization increases the regressive potential of group processes to an intensity probably matched only by institutions that are tightly controlled by authoritarian leadership.

Idealization processes and an ambience of persecution are practically universal in psychoanalytic institutes. Jointly, these mechanisms also point to the prevalence of splitting operations, the division of the institutional world into idealized and persecutory objects. While these regressive features might be reduced, if not eliminated, by an organizational structure optimally adapted to the organizational tasks, in fact, the opposite developments take place. Because psychoanalytic institutes have not attempted to develop such functional administrative structures, the prevalent defenses of idealization and feelings of persecution have contributed to pushing the organizational structure into further reinforcing these defensive operations.

49

At the very center of the activation of these prevalent defensive operations is the idealization of the training analysis and the training analyst. In a somewhat oversimplified generalization, one might say that the technical school model, in combination with the monastery or religious retreat model is unconsciously geared to prevent the open examination of the training analysts' work or the open exploration of their theoretical systems and technique. Idealization of the training analysis reflects the unconscious need for personal and institutional security, control, and certainty, which would shield all concerned from the radioactive fallout of the psychoanalytic process.

Before proceeding further, I should say that I recognize that there are also external sources of insecurity that have an important impact on psychoanalytic education. But because I am attempting to focus in detail on the internal sources of insecurity of psychoanalytic institutes, I cannot do justice to those external sources here. In what follows, I examine the mutual effects of the psychoanalytic institution and the training analysis in more detail.

The need for the training analyst to maintain a position of technical neutrality in regard to his candidate-analysand has powerful and unforeseen consequences on the nature of psychoanalytic education. Some of what follows has already been referred to in the psychoanalytic literature on the problems of the combined therapeutic and educational objectives of the training analysis. What I wish to stress, in particular, are the consequences of this dual nature of the training analysis for psychoanalytic institutes and psychoanalytic education.

The training analyst's efforts to avoid that any of his personality characteristics, viewpoints, idiosyncrasies, and institutional conflicts become evident to his candidate-analysand fosters a process of secrecy in his institutional functioning. There is a prevalent confusion between, on the one hand, the training analyst's need to maintain privacy in connection with his personal life, his emotional reactions, and his countertransference and, on the other hand, the appropriateness of his making public his stance regarding organizational, educational, clinical, and professional issues. This confusion tends to foster the ideal of the "anonymous" analyst, a person with assumed perfect morality, nothing distinctive in his personality, vast human understanding, equally vast psychoanalytic knowledge, and no convictions or opinions regarding anything else.

In the case of the "reporting" training analyst, that secrecy veers into hypocrisy and dishonest manipulation, even if the training analyst is otherwise essentially honest; the dramatic contradiction between hiding one's personality in order not to influence the candidate's analysis while actually influencing the candidate's progression behind his back has been, in my view, one of the most problematic aspects of psychoanalytic training. Fortunately, the practice is now disappearing in even the most traditional institutes. But the training analyst's efforts to conceal his professional functions from the analysand-candidate still exist. This unrealistic attempt to be a non-person seems to be unwarranted.

The training analyst's "going into hiding" on the professional level is, I think, a well-rationalized manifestation of insecurity regarding his method. It operates in unconscious collusion with the candidate's assumption that it is the training analyst "who knows" about the candidate's unconscious, rather than the candidate who is himself finding out about his unconscious with the help of the training analyst. Roustang (1982) rightly points out that the analysand's fantasy that his own analyst "is the one who knows" should be analyzed until the analysand realizes that all interpretations are only hypotheses. The analysand has to learn that new knowledge will emerge in unexpected ways from his own unconscious by means of free association and the exploration of the transference, that this process may have been facilitated by his analyst's interpretations, but is *au fond* a surprising, and often moving and startling, discovery of the unknown in himself.

In addition, the idealization of the training analyst as the one who knows is realistically reinforced by the fact that the training analyst is also an essential part of the educational institution, so that unanalyzed idealizations of the training analyst, reflected in the identification with him and the related wish to become an analyst and a training analyst as well, are never resolved. Arlow's (1970, unpublished) discussion of this problem in psychoanalytic training is relevant here, as is his comment (1973, unpublished) that, in the British Psychoanalytic Institute, where candidates have the opportunity of entering either Kleinian or Anna Freudian seminars, the seminars they select are almost invariably determined by the orientation of their training analysts.

As both Arlow and Roustang point out, the unanalyzed ambivalence against which the idealization is a defense is expressed in splitting off the negative transference onto other training analysts and, eventually, onto other psychoanalytic schools and orientations, with the consequent maintenance of the idealization of one's own training analyst and institute, and, ultimately of Freud, all of which then perpetuates blind spots regarding such idealizations and perpetuates, too, the "family romance" of generations of candidates (Arlow, 1973, unpublished). My main point here is that the training analyst may unconsciously use "technical neutrality" as a disguise, as a rationalization for his unconscious wish to maintain the candidate's idealization of him.

It used to be thought that the analyst's office should contain nothing that might reveal something personal about him, that the office look something like a monk's cell so as to reinforce the idea of technical neutrality. These excesses, fortunately, are now a thing of the past. However, the behavior of many training psychoanalysts still seems to reflect the fantasy that technical neutrality is equivalent to having no personality. Does there exist behind the training analyst as a "man without qualities" the fantasy of the training analyst as the man who pretends not to be God?

This whole issue is related to the current controversy over the extent to which the transference is based both in the patient's past and in the reality of what the patient observes in the analyst, or exclusively in the patient's past, a controversy that neglects the fact that the transference usually crystallizes around real aspects of the analyst's personality, exaggerated and distorted as a consequence of the patient's unconscious transfer from experiences in the past. To differentiate the reality of the stimulus for the transference from the transference *per se* as a distortion or an exaggeration of that stimulus has always been a primary technical task.

That an analyst may defensively deny the reality of the stimulus he provides for the patient's transference is a product of countertransference. To describe a proneness to countertransference reactions as a complementary issue to the development of the transference is something very different from calling the transference itself a compromise formation between contributions of patient and analyst. My point is that the training analyst's wish to eliminate himself as a faculty member in the psychoanalytic institute only serves to perpetuate the analysand's unresolved idealization of him, the institute, and of psychoanalysis itself.

Another major issue derived from the candidate-analysand *vis-à-vis* his training analyst is the assignment of roles automatically carried out during psychoanalytic exploration. Insofar as the candidate is exploring his unconscious motivations, his repressed or dissociated libidinal and aggressive impulses, the training analyst carries out the dominant function of a reasonable and mature ego, while the id or the unconscious aspects of the superego are activated in the candidate.

This development, true for all psychoanalytic treatments, becomes a danger for the candidate-analysand because it again fosters his idealization of his analyst-teacher as unusually mature, and a danger for the training analyst because it fosters in him an internal sense of pressure to live up to such expectations in his other educational functions as well. Idealization corrupts the idealizable. Collectively, the faculty is under pressure to reinforce the image of the rational and reasonable supermen the candidates' collective fantasies expect them—and unconsciously induce them—to be.

In addition, the training analyst's control over the candidate's treatment gradually tempts him to extend that control to the educational process in the institute. We underestimate the training analyst's temptation to extend the control over his candidates as a consequence of the fact that they are both submerged in the same social institution. The early history of psychoanalysis is the product of more than the paternalistic tendencies of the forefathers.

Conflicts that arise in connection with the classroom frequently are interpreted as acting out of transferences, and the first solution to be heard is, "back to the couch!" This attitude reinforces the idealization of the training analysis; it also obscures possible shortcomings in the institute's educational program. Faculty and students come to share an unconscious image of the entire institute as a huge couch behind which sits the collective body of training analysts and on which lies the collective body of students.

The training analysts' fantasy of omnipotence expressed in "back to the couch" can also be perceived in the faculty's amusing tendency to blame the training analyst for his candidate's shortcomings. Education committees, admission committees, or progression committees have a habit of throwing questioning glances at the training analyst whose candidate is misbehaving; the training analyst maintains the obligatory silence and struggles with or against resulting guilt feelings. Rarely, a highly narcissistic training analyst may be tempted to terminate prematurely the analysis of a particularly notorious candidate. Other narcissistic training analysts may not let their candidate-analysand go, to avoid launching a less than perfect product of their work. Many institutes now try to avoid discussing the candidate's progression in the training analyst's presence. The information nonetheless usually reaches the training analyst, particularly if resentment against the candidate exists elsewhere or the institute is small.

As a member of an educational institution, the training analyst carries out implicit and explicit administrative functions. When he supervises or conducts a seminar or participates in committee work or represents the institute at the local society or at the national level, he carries out a boundary function, that is, a function of communication between two connecting systems, at the boundary of which he stands. For example, as a teacher, the training analyst is at the boundary between the group of students he is teaching and the institute itself; he should, therefore, clarify the needs, expectations, and distortions each has about the other. This managerial or leadership function is essential to all social organizations. It would be trivial even to mention it, were it not that it happens to be in precise conflict with the requirements of carrying out a training analysis.

The training analyst has to maintain strict silence regarding what he learns from his patient-candidate about what goes on in the institute, in order to minimize the danger of the "unhooked telephone" syndrome I mentioned earlier. At the same time, the training analyst is in a position to hear about his candidate-analysand from many sources within the institute, particularly if the candidate's behavior is unconsciously provocative. The training analyst now also has to be able to absorb, contain, and tolerate internally such information about his candidate without acting on it. He must keep himself open to explore his internal reactions to such information in the light of his candidate-patient's material and transference developments. In other words, the training analyst must maintain a *barrier* between his candidate-patient and the institute in connection with these double vectors of acting out, even as he must act as liaison between other students and the institute.

It is not surprising but very unfortunate indeed that the training analyst tends to extend this "barrier" function to his other educational activities in the institute, thus causing a breakdown of boundaries between groups, task systems, and faculty and students, while letting his functions as a member of the faculty contaminate the boundaries between himself and the candidate. The result is the proverbial indiscretions he commits in regard to his candidate, and his emotional reactions to third parties about whom his candidate has spoken.

The analyst in private practice does not have to experience the normal limitations of personal authority regarding other people, required in ordinary social organizations. Furthermore, he is protected from the regressive pull that even reasonably well-functioning organizations exert from time to time over their members. These circumstances may foster a false sense of personal maturity and autonomy in the analyst. An "ivory tower" atmosphere is characteristic of the training analyst in full-time private practice, especially one whose patients are for the most part not severely ill and include a number of "normal" candidates. The reanalysis of colleagues, often rightly considered "difficult" is still very different from the ordinary spectrum of patients of non-training analysts. In fact, the temptation for prestigious psychoanalysts to gradually select an ever healthier spectrum of patients may increase this ivory-tower atmosphere, which enters into a sharp and even violent contrast to what is required of him when he is working within a psychoanalytic institute.

The sense of power and security the analyst enjoys in his office is legitimate in that his technically appropriate control of the psychoanalytic situation is also socially sanctioned. And it is only natural for the analyst to seek the same gratifications of power and security from his institute. But when the wish or need to control is transplanted to a psychoanalytic institute, it immediately fosters an authoritarian, hierarchical system of social control and management, which is rationalized by training analysts as a group on the basis of the need to preserve their "anonymity."

Another and related issue is the temptation for the training analyst to displace repressed or dissociated sadistic and narcissistic needs onto the psychoanalytic institute. To represent reason and rationality behind the couch is one thing; to avoid the expression of frustrated, dissociated, repressed, or projected narcissistic and aggressive impulses in the course of organizational interactions is another. We assume that psychoanalysts' sexual needs are sufficiently fulfilled outside their professional situation so that, under ordinary circumstances, these would not create problems within the institute. The sexual barrier between analysts and patients naturally extends to that of training analysts and candidates in psychoanalytic institutes. The same is not true, however, for the expression of narcissistic needs, of the frustrated exhibitionism of the "silent" analyst behind the couch, and of sadistic needs stemming from many sources. Dissociated sadistic needs, usually well controlled in dyadic and triadic relationships, are often acted out in social organizations, and psychoanalytic institutes provide special channels for narcissistic gratification and injury.

The uncertainties attending the selection of candidates, their progression and graduation, and the selection of training analysts are real enough. These uncertainties are compounded by vague and diffuse, institutionalized ideals of perfection and their counterpart, suspiciousness and rigidity at all points of transition. Arlow (1973, unpublished) has called attention to the oedipal roots of the initiation rites in psychoanalytic institutes. I would expand on his formulation by including the collective institutional temptation to project dissociated sadism onto the "guardians of the gate," those who are delegated to carry out selection procedures and supervise other initiation rites. One former chairman of a committee that qualified candidates for membership in the American Psychoanalytic Association told me how, in contrast to his usual behavior, his chairmanship role had made him rigid and suspicious, and how, retrospectively, he perceived himself as the policeman of the organization, although he had never been given any explicit "orders" from anybody to behave this way!

Arlow (1970, 1973, unpublished) has suggested that the counterpart of the unresolved idealization of the training analyst is the newly appointed training analyst's unconscious fantasy produced by his new status. He has successfully rebelled against the father, which leads to a guilt–determined identification with the father as the aggressor, and the consequent temptation to dominate and suppress the next generation of candidates, graduates, and non-training analysts alike as potentially dangerous usurpers.

This unconscious identification with an aggressor may be reinforced, in my view, by unconscious envy of the candidate as the immature, regressed, and therefore "guilt-free" representative of gratification of instinctual needs forbidden to the supposedly mature and rational training analyst. The exaggerated conventionality and even provincial puritanism that sometimes permeates older and larger institutes, the inordinate outrage (and explicit sexual excitement) that follows any breach of sexual boundaries within the psychoanalytic organization, illustrate this development.

The conscious fear and (presumably mostly unconscious) enjoyment of crisis and chaos at times of organizational conflicts in institutes may also be related to the projection onto the institute of intolerable instinctual impulses. The suspicion of "dissenters," the relief when a split in the institute finally creates "external" enemies, and the transformation of psychoanalytic theory into a self-sustaining belief system that becomes the ideology of an "in-group" (the guilt-determined alliance of the brothers) contain both oedipal elements and the preoedipal defenses and group valences characteristic of regression in the "basic-assumptions groups" described by Bion (1961).

It has probably become obvious by now that, as a consequence of the problems derived from the nature of the "product" handled in psychoanalytic institutes, namely, the activation of the dynamic unconscious in training analysis, additional complications develop: unconscious fears that the institution will be invaded by uncontrollable instinctual forces, which strengthens the senior faculty's experienced need for an authoritarian, hierarchical organization as a security system. We can thus see the temptations for establishing a monastery or religious retreat model of organization. The hierarchical organization and religious ideology also protect the institutionalized fantasy of omniscience of the senior group of training analysts.

In spite of the explicit and genuine conception of psychoanalysis as a science and an art that predominates among psychoanalysts and would optimally be expressed in corresponding institutional models of organization, powerful forces tend to transform the ideology of psychoanalytic institutes into a religious organization or rather, into an organizational structure that would be most commensurate with a theological seminary.

Psychoanalysis, in this transformation, is no longer a scientific theory to be continually reexamined, but a firmly established doctrine that also has an implied value as a *Weltanschauung,* a view of the world that readily explains the unconscious motives and resistances of those who do not agree with it. Psychoanalysis thus becomes a powerful ideological instrument in combating the unfaithful, in using unconscious motivation of others as a social weapon. Personal imperfections in the behavior of individuals in the psychoanalytic institution are understood to be signs of regression, to be cured by a return to the couch. The institutionally activated aggression of the members of this psychoanalytic community is gratified by the attack on "outgroups"; their dependency needs are gratified by the unremitting idealization of their training analysts—teachers of the past generations, culminating with Freud; and their sexual, particularly oedipal, needs are symbolically gratified in the "family romance" fantasies Arlow (1972) described.

57

It could be argued at this point, not without reason, that all these characteristics of psychoanalytic' institutions are at least in part an extension of the historical circumstances of the origins of the "psychoanalytic movement," of Freud's struggle for assuring his revolutionary discoveries against the hostility of organized academic "science" of his time. Roustang (1982) mentions Freud's paternalistic personality, the cult of his personality engaged in by his immediate followers and reflected in the efforts to maintain an inordinate secrecy regarding all aspects of Freud's personal life, and the historical enactment of a sequence of oedipal dramas involving Freud's disciples and relatives. Roustang points to the intimate connection between these historical aspects of psychoanalytic institutes and current pathology of their unresolved idealizations in the transference. Mahony (1979) has called attention to the intimate connections between these same historical circumstances and aspects of Freud's writings. I find these historical analyses of interest, but propose that the organizational distortions in psychoanalytic institutes are self-perpetuating, owing to active institutional processes that go beyond such a purely historical explanation. I have attempted to specify some of these processes here.

We may assume, if the organizational distortions of psychoanalytic education were resolved, if the administrative structure of psychoanalytic institutes were altered so as to correspond to an explicit concept of the aims of psychoanalytic education, that new challenges and difficulties would emerge in response to new developments at the boundaries of psychoanalysis as a science and a profession. The revolutionary developments in, for example, neurophysiology, infant development, and small group psychology, and in philosophical inquiries pose potential challenges to psychoanalytic theory, that may facilitate new research and discoveries within psychoanalysis itself. When psychoanalytic education remains excessively concerned with protecting idealization processes within the institution, however, persecutory fears may easily be projected onto the external environment, and new scientific developments in other fields may be perceived as threats to psychoanalysis.

The predominant educational culture, the more regulated or freer educational system in different countries, for example, may also stimulate corresponding educational structures within the psychoanalytic institutes, often without conscious effort or even awareness of this relation (E. D. Joseph, personal communication). It is striking that, in spite of these potential environmental influences, psychoanalytic institutes in many countries and in very different social, cultural, and educational environments suffer from very similar problems related to the internal structural and conflictual issues explored so far in this paper. The resolution of these internal constraints may also contribute to a more creative interchange of educational philosophy across the institutional boundaries of psychoanalytic institutes.

## Some general principles of treatment

What follows are some general guidelines that derive from the ideas I have just presented. I am suggesting strategies for institutional reorganization, strategies for dealing with the immediate and underlying causes of what I have described as the stagnation of psychoanalytic education. These guidelines do not imply that I think there is a single solution for all institutes; what I am offering is a common theoretical frame from which to explore alternative solutions and their respective advantages and disadvantages. If it is true that the underlying causes of the problems in psychoanalytic education have to do with intrinsic qualities of the psychoanalytic situation, we have to be prepared to live with conflict, and with the limited effectiveness of all corrective measures. It would seem reasonable to propose, however, that significant improvement of the educational functions of psychoanalytic institutes is possible.

First, it is essential that the administrative models selected correspond to explicit goals of psychoanalytic education. In my view, the combined model of a university college and an art academy is the most promising for psychoanalytic education. There are undoubtedly technical aspects of training, of the need for developing professionalism, to indicate that aspects of a technical school model should be integrated. If psychoanalysis has, among other functions, that of a helping profession, standards of technical sophistication for that profession are an important aspect of psychoanalytic education.

By the same token, aspects of the monastery or religious retreat model, with its central focus on faith, are probably unavoidable because, particularly in the early stages of learning about psychoanalysis, much work on oneself and with patients has to be carried out without any immediate evidence of the specific effectiveness of that work. To open oneself to exploring one's unconscious requires

59

an act of trust that has a religious aspect to it (or, if one prefers, a religious attitude is one expression of basic trust).

With these reservations, however, a model based predominantly on the university college and art school would seem to me optimal. It should be kept in mind that I am referring to *models*, and not to how universities or art schools actually do function. Conflicts will always be found in all human institutions. My point is that if the primary task and the organizational structure are in harmony, the self-regulatory functions of university colleges and art schools can be relied upon to limit the disturbances in their operations derived from unavoidable human factors. A university college model of organizational structure would imply full academic freedom for the faculty, rewards for scientific productivity (as opposed to rewarding submission and subservience to local ideologists and kowtowing to the masters), and would generate both faculty and students' interest in scholarly and scientific work. This could electrify psychoanalytic seminars and transform them into focal points for the generation of new knowledge in psychoanalysis.

To place functional authority in the hands of the faculty, of supervisors, seminar leaders, and lecturers would go a long way toward reducing the pathological idealization of training analysts. The students would know that their progress depends on performance in classes and under supervision, on an open interchange with their teachers.

This model would offer clear, precise criteria for admissions, progression, and graduation, decisions about students made by committees publicly known with publicly known channels of redress of grievances. The faculty would have the obligation to share their evaluations with the students; and a clear system of student evaluation would go far in diminishing the paranoid atmosphere within institutes.

The selection of faculty would also have to correspond to clear and publicly expressed criteria and would be carried out by committees accountable for their decisions. The selection of training analysts, particularly, would have to be based on explicit criteria, and a selection process that permits all eligible psychoanalysts to apply for faculty positions and to be assured of a fair and open process. That subjective judgments operate in the selection of faculty, particularly training analysts, does not mean that the criteria according to which these judgments are made are not public and that those who carry out such judgments should not be held accountable for them. Within a university model, it should not be difficult to devise systems that provide the guarantee for a fair selection and monitoring of faculty, which, by itself, would help reduce the paranoiagenic atmosphere of psychoanalytic societies and institutes. It may be helpful to stress that I am not proposing to make public the reasons for which, for example, a particular analyst was not appointed training analyst—but the method, the procedure, the locus of this discussion and decision must be public, so that the person affected by the decision has the means of informing himself who made that decision and for what reasons. The corresponding committee's discussion is not public, but its chairman or a representative should be authorized to discuss the issue with the affected individual.

The task is to destroy the myth and the reality or perception that there exists a privileged group of training analysts whose selection is dependent as much on personal and political factors as on their professional capacities. One problem centers on the number of training analysts to be appointed by a given institute. Various countries have experimented with selecting training analysts on the basis of explicit standards and requirements, complementing the appointment of a large number of training analysts by allowing the candidates to freely select their training analyst from a list provided by the institute.

In other countries some institutes have opted for "democratic" methods of selecting training analysts. For example, appointing as training analysts all "full members" of the society, the "full members" having been elected by vote of the constituent membership, thus replacing strictly academic criteria by a purely political mechanism. The trouble with this method is that it is based on a fallacy. The expectation that "democratic" solutions will solve the problems of arbitrariness reflects a confusion between organizational requirements of an educational system and the political governance of a community.

Democratic decision-making may protect individuals in institutions from arbitrariness, but it does not resolve the issue of insuring that the aims—or primary tasks—correspond with the organization's structure. The quality of the product—in this instance, the competence of the training analyst—may suffer equally whether the institution is authoritarian or democratic. The appointment of a large number of training analysts, selected on the basis of criteria that have to do with assuring their quality is probably the best way to demystify the function of training analysts and to produce a healthy competition for academic excellence among them.

By the same token, limiting the number of candidates that any one training analyst may treat analytically at any time should help to eliminate the "convoy" phenomenon of a training analyst with a large cohort of candidates-analysands, and result in training analysts' treating a broader spectrum of patients. Generally speaking, a large number of faculty members, offering seminars and supervision, may also diminish the control of certain key courses by a small self-perpetuating group. Again, the selection of seminars and seminar leaders should be based on educational criteria, with built-in quality controls and not on political, "democratic" ones.

Clear lines of organizational structure are the essence of the university model: clear administrative boundaries, but no boundaries or restrictions for the transmission, exploration, and generation of new ideas.

From all that I have said, it should be clear that I do not favor reporting analysts. At most, I think the training analysts might report the day the training analysis started, the number of sessions per month or year, and the date the analysis is either interrupted by one or both participants or is completed. This arrangement would offer a reasonable compromise between the need to know whether a candidate has been or is in training analysis as part of his training requirements, and an otherwise complete separation of the training analysis from all other educational functions of the institute.

At the risk of beating what some colleagues might consider a dead horse, but which I do not think quite moribund, I would like to add a few words on this subject. "How To Catch a Psychopath" could be the heading beneath which lie all the reasons given in support of the reporting training analyst. But a true psychopath may conceal psychopathic behavior from his own training analyst. Against the argument that only the training analyst will be aware of a candidate's serious psychopathology is the fact that much concealment goes on in reporting institutes, typically expressed in the practice of a candidate's having a first analysis "for the institute" and a second analysis "for himself." Those in favor of the reporting system justify it on the grounds of its being able to detect unsuitable candidates. But I see no reason why a training analyst cannot interrupt an analysis with a candidate he thinks is unsuitable, without prejudice to the candidate's request for another training analyst from the institute. I firmly believe that the damage done by the reporting system is far worse than the safeguards it provides, and I strongly endorse Lifschutz's (1976) analysis of this issue.

To keep training analysts truly separate from the educational and supervisory system of their own candidates would put greater pressure on supervisors and seminar leaders for evaluating the candidate's progress, and this seems to me a very salutary pressure. Supervisors and seminar leaders would then have an increased sense of authority and responsibility. This alone could influence positively the educational atmosphere of an institute. By the same token, once training analysts are really reassured that their responsibility is exclusively to their candidates–analysands, they in turn may experience a greater degree of freedom in their handling of transference and countertransference.

A university model implies open scientific discussions, the sharing by training analysts of their own cases in scientific meetings, which include both graduates and candidates. It would seem reasonable that a training analyst not present his own cases to a seminar in which his own candidate participates, but this should not be a problem in any but the smallest of psychoanalytic institutes. The training analyst should, however, not have to refrain from teaching seminars in which his own candidates participate. The supervisory situation may be a particularly favorable opportunity for senior analysts to share their own experiences with their supervisees. At the same time, the supervisors would have the responsibility for communicating honestly their evaluation to their candidates–supervisees, an essential aspect of a functional educational system.

The model of an art academy for psychoanalysis would be expressed in the opportunities for candidates to learn from the analytic work of faculty and training analysts, in addition to learning psychoanalytic technique with their own cases and those of other candidates presented in supervision and seminars. The custom by which, in gatherings of junior and senior faculty, it is usually the junior people who present case material would gradually disappear. The subservience of junior faculty to senior faculty would also diminish, both because the appointments of training analysts would be institutionalized, formalized, and subjected to the checks and balances of an academic institution, and because sharing the universal difficulties in analytic work, even in the best hands, would contribute to reducing the irrational idealization of senior colleagues.

The introduction of some bureaucratic organizations with formal policies and procedures, publicly known mechanisms of redress of grievances, and socially sanctioned authority and accountability at all levels are challenging but not impossible tasks. These policies and procedures might combine the best aspects of a university model with that of a technical school.

In conclusion, the changes in the structure of psychoanalytic education proposed, tending to strengthen the university college and art academy models at the expense of reducing the technical school and, particularly, the monastery or religious retreat models should go a long way in reducing the pervasive idealization and persecution processes that plague psychoanalytic institutes. The firm protection of the boundaries of the personal analysis of candidates, matched by the open participation of training analysts in all other aspects of the educational process, and a fair, rational, and open system of selection, monitoring, and progression of both candidates and faculty may not eliminate the conflicts created by psychoanalysis carried out in an institutional setting, but such measures would facilitate the creative utilization of the awareness of these conflicts for deepening psychoanalytic understanding and knowledge, and developing psychoanalytic technique. I believe that adopting the measures suggested herein would significantly contribute to reactivating the excitement of psychoanalytic education and contribute to generating new knowledge in our field.

## Note

1 Reprinted from *Journal of the American Psychoanalytic Association*, Volume 34, Number 4, International Universities Press, Inc., Madison, CT.

## References

Arlow, J. A. (1972). Some Dilemmas in Psychoanalytic Education. *J. Amer. Psychoanal. Assn.*, 20: 556–566.

Bion, W. R. (1961). *Experiences in Groups*. New York: Basic Books.

Dulchin, J. & Segal, A. J. (1982a). The Ambiguity of Confidentiality in a Psychoanalytic Institute. *Psychiat.*, 45: 13–25.

_____. (1982b). Third Party Confidences: The Uses of Information in a Psychoanalytic Institute. *Psychiat.*, 45: 27–37.

Franzen, S. (1982). Editorial. *Council Advancement Psychoanal. Ed.*, 2(2): 2.

Freud, S. (1922). Two Encyclopedia Articles. S. E. 18.

Greenacre, P. (1959). Problems of the Training Analysis. In *Minutes of Training Analysts' Seminar*. Chicago Institute for Psychoanalysis, November 21.

Jaques, E. (1976). A *General Theory of Bureaucracy*. New York: Halsted.

Keiser, S. (1969). *Report of the Outgoing Chairman of the Committee on Institutes to the Board on Professional Standards*. Bull. Amer. Psychoanal. Assn., 25(2): 1168–1169; In *J. Amer. Psychoanal. Assn.*, 17.

Kernberg, O. F. (1980). *Internal World and External Reality: Object Relations Theory Applied*. New York: Aronson.

Lifschutz, J. E. (1976). A Critique of Reporting and Assessment in the Training Analysis. *J. Amer. Psychoanal. Assn.*, 24: 4–59.

Mahony, P. (1979). The Budding International Association of Psychoanalysis and Its Discontents. *Psychoanal. Contemp. Thought*, 2: 551–593.

Roustang, F. (1982). *Dire Mastery: Discipleship from Freud to Lacan*. Baltimore, MD: Johns Hopkins University Press.

---
4
---

# AUTHORITARIANISM, CULTURE, AND PERSONALITY IN PSYCHOANALYTIC EDUCATION[1]

---

In the previous chapter, I recommended developing strategies for institutional reorganization that would reduce the pathological symptoms within psychoanalytic education. In essence, my recommendations centered upon a combined art academy and university college model, and a corresponding functional administrative structure.

Here I wish to elaborate on the factors that contribute to the combination of idealization processes and paranoiagenic developments in psychoanalytic institutes, and their negative consequences on the educational process and for psychoanalytic creativity.

I have been able to observe at least three psychoanalytic institutions in depth over a period of time: the Chilean Pyschoanalytic Institute, the Topeka Psychoanalytic Institute, and the Columbia University Psychoanalytic Center for Training and Research. In addition, I have had briefer experiences as guest student and faculty member of other institutes. The experiences gathered in all these activities have strongly influenced the following observations. My basic thesis is that the principal cause of authoritarianism in psychoanalytic institutes is the *motivated* discrepancy between explicit educational goals and actual administrative structure. However, unacknowledged influences from the surrounding culture, from prevalent political crosscurrents—particularly totalitarian ideologies—from the educational system generally, and the personality of the psychoanalytic leader, all have the potential to contribute to authoritarianism in subtle or not so subtle ways. Sometimes even ordinary social conventionality may be transformed into a focused oppression.

## Power, authority, authoritarianism

The most immediate effect of a nonfunctional administrative structure is the growth of authoritarian tendencies in the organization. The development of chaos is another consequence, but insofar as organizations continue their operations, chaos is usually complemented or followed by authoritarianism. The immediate symptoms of authoritarianism include fearfulness, submissiveness, rebelliousness, and passivity throughout the organization. In psychoanalytic institutes, for the reasons mentioned, idealization and paranoiagenesis become dominant under such circumstances.

Authoritarianism depends on the extent to which the power invested in, and the authority exercised by faculty, particularly training analysts as a group, are appropriate to their functions; that is, "functional." Faculty may be either "powerless," that is, without the power commensurate with the authority required to carry out its tasks, or with power totally exceeding that which would be functionally required by the task. This latter defines "authoritarianism." I am saying that power must be adequate for legitimate authority, in turn defined by that needed to carry out the required tasks (Kernberg, 1979).

One example of authoritarianism, in one institute controlled by an extremely powerful training analyst who was, at the same time, the head of the psychiatric institution within which that institute functioned, is the following: A senior candidate was assigned a patient who had murdered her infant son. The candidate considered the case unanalyzable, while his supervisor (our powerful leader) insisted that it was an acceptable analytic case. All senior psychoanalytic consultants involved had agreed that psychoanalysis was contraindicated, and the candidate refused to continue the analysis, referring the patient instead for psychotherapeutic treatment. His supervisor later objected to the candidate's graduation for an extended period of time, although, in the opinion of the other members of the senior faculty, the candidate had fulfilled all the requirements for graduation. Many extra-official meetings took place among the senior members of the faculty to see if it was possible to help the candidate to graduate by by-passing the leader's veto. The postponement of this candidate's graduation eventually became an open secret throughout the Institute, increasing an existing atmosphere of fearfulness and cynicism about psychoanalytic training.

## The surrounding culture and institutional blind spots

On shifting from one culture to another, the differing nature of the concepts of technical neutrality and of acting out may become apparent, thus influencing the definition of acting out behavior. In Santiago, Chile, in the 1950s, it was culturally acceptable to go to extended lengths to avoid paying taxes; a rather liberal, European-style attitude regarding sexual morality also existed, and a prevalent "double morality" that combined the influence of a paternalistic tradition with that of the Catholic Church. Divorce was frowned upon, while extramarital affairs, particularly on the part of men, were tolerated rather freely. These attitudes were reflected, I realized later, in our attitude toward patients' and candidates' sexual behavior as well.

I moved from Santiago to Topeka, Kansas, which is in the heart of the American Bible Belt. This completely different cultural surrounding was characterized by a very strict adherence to the responsibility for paying taxes, in fact, a strong moral attitude invested in that social responsibility (which, of course, is part of the American culture and has also permeated Chilean culture in recent years). Regarding issues of sexual morality, the Topeka Institute accepted divorce, and very often considered it a reasonably mature solution to marital conflicts, but extramarital affairs were severely frowned upon. This corresponded to the prevailing culture. The reflection of these cultural differences in analysts' attitude toward their patients' clinical material was startling to say the least. In fact, a joke circulating among psychoanalytic candidates in Topeka who had immigrated from various Latin American countries had it that, in the United States a man had all the women of his life in sequence, while, in Latin America, they were available simultaneously. A training analyst in Topeka, wanting to be helpful, once warned me that she had observed me the day before in a movie theater kissing my wife. She was concerned that such public display might endanger my future appointment as a training analyst.

## Political ideology

In Chile, during the presidency of Salvador Allende, a sharp split took place between the leftist supporters of the Allende government and the center and rightist opposition to it (including center-left Social Christians). This division extended to Marxist-oriented training analysts identified with the Allende regime and non–Marxist training analysts identified with the opposition. A Social Christian candidate happened to be in analysis with a Marxist training analyst. The Marxist training analyst interpreted the candidate's participation in a physicians' strike against the Allende government as a submission to the capitalist ideology representing his oedipal father. The candidate protested, stating that he did not want to discuss politics with his training analyst. The training analyst then suggested immediate termination of the analysis. He was willing to retract his idea only after a lengthy and painful discussion with the Institute's education committee a few days later. Upon discovering from his analyst that he would be resuming his analysis with the same analyst, the candidate, panic stricken, left the country to continue his psychoanalytic training elsewhere.

We tend to forget that technical neutrality is based upon the implicit assumption that analyst and patient share a common cultural and ideological ground. The reproduction, in the analytic situation, of ideological conflicts in the political culture that destroy this underlying consensus may lead to a breakdown of functional preconditions for analytic work, and consequent authoritarianism. The transformation of psychoanalysis itself into a *Weltanschauung* may become a risk for the position of technical neutrality.

## Educational systems

The association in the United States of psychoanalytic institutes within a university setting, particularly a department of psychiatry, may significantly influence the educational procedures. Where the psychoanalytic faculty conducts a large private practice and a true isolation of the psychoanalytic institute develops, the risk of a narrow, insulated educational program increases. In some places, biologically oriented departments of psychiatry have almost no representation of faculty with psychoanalytic orientation while the local psychoanalytic institute lacks the challenge from the development in biological sciences at their boundaries with psychoanalysis. This separation tends to restrict scientific inquiry and debate and flatten psychoanalytic education. At the other extreme, psychoanalytic institutes within departments of psychiatry may be at risk of undue influences from the changing attitudes of departmental chairmen toward psychoanalysis. However, when a chairman of a department appreciates the contributions of psychoanalysis, psychoanalytic institutes exposed to the challenge and stimulation of an academic ambience may develop exciting enrichments of their curriculum, stimulate a scholarly atmosphere, and develop innovations in the educational program.

One of the reasons for the increasing attraction of the Columbia University Psychoanalytic Center in recent years has been its encouragement of scientific dialogue within its department of psychiatry, with Columbia University, and its development of interdisciplinary symposia and conferences.

## The personality of the leader

Roustang (1982) points to the paradox that Freud, who critically described the irrational relations between leaders and followers in organized institutions, should have been the author of "On the History of the Psychoanalytic Movement," written in 1914. Freud's paper clearly indicates, says Roustang, his conviction that a truly scientific commitment to psychoanalysis coincided with loyalty to his (Freud's) ideas, whereas any questioning of key psychoanalytic concepts represented unconsciously determined resistances to truth. We might dismiss Freud's relations to his immediate followers as an irrelevant historical curiosity, were they not so intimately linked with subsequent psychoanalytic history. Roustang, in his study of the relation between master and disciple, calls attention to a contradiction inherent to psychoanalytic movements: the goal of psychoanalysis is to resolve the transference. But psychoanalytic education attempts to maintain the transference that psychoanalysis tries to resolve. If fidelity to Freud, the charismatic founder of psychoanalysis, were a requirement, the members of the societies could not be scientifically independent. The tradition has persisted, as Roustang makes clear in his discussion of Lacan.

It could easily be argued that the tradition of the structural characteristics of the psychoanalytic movement initiated by Freud and

70

consolidated in the prevalent arrangements of psychoanalytic institutes are primarily responsible for the authoritarian developments
that I summarized in the earlier part of this chapter. While respecting
the historical origins of authoritarian features of psychoanalytic education, I have argued that it is the nature of the very task which, by
activating organizational defenses particularly along the lines of training analysts' and candidates' group regression, tends to perpetuate
the distortion between task and structure. But the personality of the
leaders within each psychoanalytic institution does have a significant
influence, for better or worse, on institutional functioning.

The Chairman of the Department of Psychiatry of the University
of Chile, in Santiago, Chile, from the late '40s to the early '60s was
also the founder of the Chilean Psychoanalytic Association and its
Institute. A strong leader, he was mostly concerned with the development of new ideas, and remarkably free of the need to impose these
ideas (and his will) on those working with him. In fact, the dynamics
of the institute centered around the faculty's effort to systematize and
normalize psychoanalytic education, while the leader's chief emphasis
was on the revolutionary content of psychoanalytic thinking and the
need for ongoing exploration of new territories. As a result, a strong
personal leadership coincided with a remarkably informal structure
of psychoanalytic education. While it is true that the enthusiasm and
commitment of an early generation of psychoanalysts in that country
contributed to the high morale of the institute, the informality of
the leader's relation to both faculty and candidates counteracted the
natural division of training analysts and candidates. During his tenure,
idealization and paranoiagenesis were remarkably low.

The Topeka Institute of Psychoanalysis in the early '50s and '60s
was under the influence of the leadership of a senior training analyst
who at the same time was Chief of Staff of the Menninger Foundation
within which the Topeka Institute of Psychoanalysis functioned: He
was everybody's ultimate boss. He was also a powerful personality
both admired and feared; and his strong personal leadership of the
Menninger Foundation included the psychoanalytic institute. The
atmosphere in seminars and in supervision of candidates was remarkably tense in comparison to my experiences in Santiago, Chile. In
fact, I was struck by the cautious, at times frankly fearful attitudes
of candidates as individuals and groups. The leader was less concerned about the particular orientation of psychoanalytic education:
Topeka was more closely identified with American ego-psychology,

than with loyalty to himself and to the Menninger Foundation. The emphasis was on the hierarchical structure of the psychoanalytic institute, and resulted in the usual hierarchical organization of teaching and latent division between faculty and candidates, and between training and nontraining analysts.

The founder and leader of the Columbia University Center for Psychoanalytic Training and Research left the New York Psychoanalytic Institute to set up a new psychoanalytic institute within a department of psychiatry at a prestigious medical school. He had expressed a strong commitment to psychoanalysis as a science, and believed in a strong, centralized leadership. The degree of authoritarian pressure he had generated was very concretely revealed to me when I moved from Topeka to New York, years after this leader's retirement.

By then, a new generation of Columbia-trained analysts were dedicated to transforming an authoritarian into a functional administrative structure. They explained to me at a private dinner that they welcomed my joining them but wanted to be sure that I understood and would subscribe to their commitment to a non-authoritarian administrative structure, and an open scientific attitude to theory and practice.

More recently, under the leadership of a woman director, the Columbia Institute has developed an administrative structure that corresponds remarkably well to the requirements of a combined university college and art academy model that I outlined at the beginning of this paper. In my view, this leader's commitment to a model of psychoanalytic education that fosters a spirit of inquiry, an open discussion of the broadest range of psychoanalytic thinking, encourages research, and, above all, carefully limits the authority vested in training analysts and faculty to what is functionally required has placed the Columbia Institute at the center of the intellectual life of the American Psychoanalytic Community.

The level of idealization and paranoiagenesis at the Columbia Institute has been remarkably low in recent years, as it was during the 1950s and early '60s in Santiago, and in contrast to what I had observed in the early '60s at Topeka. I should stress, however, that similar variations in the amount of idealization and paranoiagenesis and of authoritarian structure may be observed in institutes where strong personalized leadership is not present or defended against by bureaucratic or political arrangements.

In the '60s and '70s a struggle was in progress at the New York Psychoanalytic Institute between an in group of senior psychoanalysts who maintained a firm control of the institution and an out group including both a minority of training analysts and a large number of nontraining analyst faculty who were challenging what they saw as the rigid control of their Institute, particularly the process of appointing training analysts, a process that had become highly politicized. When I first arrived in New York I simultaneously joined the faculties of Columbia and New York, and during the three years of my participation in the New York Psychoanalytic Institute I was able to compare the two. The level of idealization and paranoiagenesis at the New York Psychoanalytic Institute was very high, and the contrast between the relaxed, open, inquisitive spirit at seminars, panels and conferences at Columbia and the high tension and anxiety on the part of candidates as well as nontraining analyst faculty at the New York Institute was impressive. Yet both institutions were directed by groups of faculty rather than any particular leader. In fact, some of the most prestigious training analysts at the New York Institute at that time were part of the outgroup.

An authoritarian structure may evolve in a system characterized by a collective leadership, and a functional institution may evolve in a system with strongly individualized leadership. In this connection, it needs to be stressed that the effort to correct for authoritarian institutional structure by the development of *democratic* processes may backfire, because, as I have pointed out elsewhere (1989), when political decision-making replaces task-oriented decision-making, functional authority also may suffer. For example, the appointment of the members of the faculty by secret vote on the part of all of the members of a psychoanalytic society may be a democratic process, but may not be the optimal way for selecting faculty: to the contrary, it may foster a politization of the membership around an ideology tangential to the functional needs of psychoanalytic education.

In my previous discussion of this subject (Chapter 3), I focused on some major corrective measures available to reduce the negative effects of the development of paranoiagenesis and idealization in psychoanalytic education. These include the elimination of all reporting functions of the training analyst; a public, functional method of training, selection, and monitoring of faculty; an insistence on the training analysts' communicating their own clinical work; the organization of faculty and of candidates to facilitate open communication, redress of grievances, and correction of distortions in the educational process; the demystification of all aspects of selection, progression, and graduation of candidates; and the participation of candidates individually and in groups in generating new developments in psychoanalytic knowledge.

Perhaps the most pernicious effect of authoritarianism on psychoanalytic education and psychoanalysis generally is the restriction and flatness of the teaching and learning about psychoanalysis. The willing confrontation of alternative theories and practice is essential for scientific development and education.

## Note

1 Published in *Journal of the International Association for the History of Psychoanalysis*, 5: 341–354, 1992.

## References

Arlow, J. A. (1972). Some Dilemmas in Psychoanalytic Education. *Journal of the American Psychoanalytic Association*, 20: 556–566.

Jaques, E. (1976). *A General Theory of Bureaucracy*. Portsmouth, NH: Heinemann Gower.

Kernberg, O. (1989). Paranoiagenesis in Organizations. In *Comprehensive Textbook of Group Psychotherapy*, 3rd Edition. H. Kaplan and B. J. Sadock (eds.). Baltimore, MD: Williams and Wilkins Press, 47–57, 1993.

_____. (1979). Regression in Organizational Leadership. *Psychiatry*, 42: 24–39.

Miller, E. J. & Rice, A. K. (1967). *Systems of Organization*. London: Tavistock Publications.

Roustang, F. (1982). *Dire Mastery: Discipleship from Freud to Lacan*. Baltimore, MD: Johns Hopkins University Press.

# 5

# THIRTY METHODS TO DESTROY
# THE CREATIVITY OF
# PSYCHOANALYTIC CANDIDATES[1]

Some years ago, in the context of a discussion with a colleague about ways to increase the creativity of candidates in psychoanalytic training, that colleague told me, with a smile: "Our problem is not so much to foster creativity but to try not to inhibit the creativity naturally stimulated by the nature of our work" (Lore Schacht, personal communication). Her comment triggered memories and observations in the course of my studying, teaching and participating in psychoanalytic education in different psychoanalytic societies and institutes. I decided to gather these observations, discuss them with colleagues, and finally, put together in a negative format, what, at the bottom, is a plea for the fostering of psychoanalytic creativity. For a positive format of this study, I refer the reader to Chapter 3, in which I present a systematic analysis of the relationship between organizational structure and functioning of psychoanalytic institutes, on the one hand, and their effects on psychoanalytic education on the other. As an excellent overview of present day problems in psychoanalytic education, Wallerstein's (1993) summary of the 5th IPA Conference of training analysts in Buenos Aires may serve as an important background to what follows.

The following list of ways to *inhibit* the creativity of psychoanalytic candidates is not expected to be exhaustive, although, I hope, it covers dominant problems. Here, then, is my advice on how to effectively inhibit creativity in the learning process in our institutes:

1. Slow down the processing of applications; delay accepting candidates; slow down the provision of information to candidates: this will help to slow them down in turn. If candidates' progression is systematically slow and cumbersome, if their written case material is subjected to numerous revisions, and, particularly, if long periods of waiting in uncertainty become a regular part of their progression experience, they will tend, in turn, to become slow to respond and to take initiatives. The slower the process of acceptance and progression, the more candidates themselves will avoid the final steps to graduation, autonomy, and joining the membership of the society; and, of course, the longer it will take them to produce scientific contributions, if indeed they ever do.

2. Freud's writings can be put to good use in damping candidates' interest in thinking for themselves. Instructors should insist that candidates read Freud carefully, in historical order, completely and exhaustively, making sure that the candidates learn exactly what his theory was at any point. Teachers should convey the clear message that any critical analysis of Freud's conclusions has to be postponed until students have read Freud completely (and until they have much more experience and knowledge in the psychoanalytic field). To begin with, they need to know what Freud thought, and as much of it as possible: it is helpful, therefore, to disconnect the teaching of Freud's writings from any outside or contemporary critique of his work, or from contemporary controversial issues, or from clinical problems of burning actuality. The protection of Freud's work from contamination with other theories or critique will do wonders to gradually decrease candidates' interest in further developments of psychoanalytic thinking.

It is important for the instructor to keep in mind that it is the *conclusions* that Freud arrived at that have to be taught and memorized, not the *process of Freud's thinking*: in fact, if the students acquire a grasp of the methodology of Freud's thinking, which was unavoidably revolutionary, this may lead them to dangerous identifications with his originality and thus defeat the purpose of the isolated and exhaustive focus on his conclusions (Green, 1991).

3. A helpful reinforcement of the deterioration of any possible excitement with Freud's writing may be achieved by assigning some of Freud's most creative and important papers, at the beginning of each new seminar, going in great detail over everything Freud said in these

by now familiar articles, and stressing his conclusions. This reassuring repetition of permanent aspects of Freud's works, combined with giving them a very special emphasis in the curriculum, desensitize the students to his contribution, a lulling process much enhanced by asking the students to write extensive summaries of Freud's work, or to summarize to the rest of the class what everybody has already read. One may further the process by setting up specific examinations on the content of the entire work of Freud as a precondition for progressing to other seminars.

4. Be very attentive to candidates who tend to question the views of any major theoretician or contributor who is a favored author of your particular psychoanalytic institution. Convey clearly the message that critical thinking is welcome as long as it leads to a confirmation of your dominant leader's views. Make sure to reward those students who are excited and fully convinced by what you assign to them (except, of course, the contributions of "deviant schools": these should be expected to arouse appropriate incredulity and indignation among the students). If, tactfully but consistently, you show your appreciation of those students who agree with the official view of your institution, the temptations to develop new, different, questioning, or divergent views may gradually disappear (Giovannetti, 1991; Infante, 1991; Lussier, 1991).

5. Try to protect your candidates from participating too early in scientific meetings of your psychoanalytic society, or from being invited to gatherings where respected colleagues may sharply disagree with each other. This may be justified by pointing to the advisability that the personal training analysis be undisturbed by premature external influences, particularly those that might disturb the anonymity of the training analyst. Within a small psychoanalytic society, it is always possible to justify forbidding candidates to attend psychoanalytic society meetings because such a small group might not be able to avoid contacts between candidates and their analysts outside the sessions, and this justifies perfectly the isolation of the institute teaching from the active scientific world of psychoanalytic thinking.

6. Carefully control elective courses: These are often used by junior members of the faculty to present new and challenging ideas. Watch carefully over elective seminars in general and remain alert to the possibility that they may disturb the harmonious, integrated

approach to psychoanalysis that corresponds to your society's or Institute's dominant views.

7. Maintain a strict separation between undergraduate and postgraduate seminars. Fortunately, most psychoanalytic institutions have an intuitive understanding of the importance of avoiding a premature mixing of candidates and graduate analysts in the same seminars: the candidates are too likely to discover uncertainties and questioning attitudes in the graduates that candidates are learning to suppress. This may disturb a healthy idealization of the effectiveness of psychoanalytic training, and the illusion of enormous differences between candidates and graduates.

8. The preservation in the students of a healthy respect for their elders may be achieved by assembling teams of senior training analysts and junior analysts interested in becoming training analysts to teach certain courses or seminars. Keep a clear hierarchy of older and younger members of the faculty. If the junior analyst respectfully bows to the senior analyst's views, and conveys by his total behavior his unquestioning acceptance of senior authority; if, in fact, he shows uncertainty as to the extent to which he may take initiatives in teaching any particular seminar, the message of the need to accept and not to question established authority will be strengthened. You may accentuate hierarchy by simple means: for example, reserving the front seats of professional meetings for senior faculty.

9. Strengthen the graduation rituals by whatever intelligent means you find: this is a field with great potentialities. For example, you may ask the candidates to write up a case for graduation, and then subject their manuscripts to numerous revisions and corrections. Through this experience the candidates acquire a healthy respect for the enormous difficulties in writing an acceptable paper for publication. Or else, require the candidate to present a paper before the psychoanalytic society. The discussants should be the most senior members of that society (who may not have written a paper themselves for a long time). Their demanding expectations of what a scientific paper should include may be communicated by the exhaustive criticism of the candidate's presentation. Or else, a committee constituted by such senior psychoanalysts may convey the same message. In some countries, the same effect has been obtained by a secret vote on the part of all the society members of whether a candidate's paper

is acceptable to fulfill criteria for admission to the psychoanalytic society itself. When significant political divisions within the society make young graduates automatically drift to the power group of their own training analysts, the qualifying scientific paper may become an excellent source of anxiety about the dangers connected with scientific work (Bruzzone *et al.*, 1985.

10. Stress the message that it takes many years of clinical experience before one's understanding of psychoanalytic theory and technique, not to speak of applications of psychoanalysis to other fields, are profound and solid enough to justify one's attempt to contribute to the science of psychoanalysis. Raise delicately but early the question, to what extent candidates' attempts not only to present papers but to have them published (!) may reflect unresolved oedipal competitiveness or narcissistic conflicts. If junior psychoanalysts publish sparsely, and make sure to have senior members of their society approve their manuscripts before they submit them for publication, this custom should become common knowledge among the candidates, and may reinforce their fear of publishing. Naturally, avoid stimulating candidates to put any new, original idea of their own into writing: Writing should be a chore, an obligation, never a pleasure, an early source of pride in contributing to the science of psychoanalysis while still being a student (Britton, 1994).

11. It may be very helpful to point out that psychoanalysis is understood and carried out properly only in places far away from your own institution, and preferably in a language not known by many of your students. If the demands of the training are such that the students would not be able to spend an extended part of the time in that distant ideal land, they may become convinced that it is useless to attempt to develop psychoanalytic science in a place so far from where the true and only theory and technique are taught. And that conviction will last.

12. Candidates should be discouraged from premature visits to other societies or other institutes, from participating in congresses and meetings or in analytic work in other institutions. This holds true, particularly, for those gatherings in your own city, region, or country, and complements the idealization of places so far away or of a different language that they are inaccessible to your candidates. Fortunately, some psychoanalytic societies and institutes have erected

powerful walls against intrusion by foreign visitors, except the very occasional ones to be shot down in a well-prepared meeting; and in many parts of the world it would be very difficult for a candidate to transfer from one institute to another, from one country to another, and even from one city to another without having to overcome multiple obstacles. This helps to avoid potentially damaging comparisons, the awareness of psychoanalytic institutes' and societies' experimentation with new educational methodologies, and the contamination by a questionable spirit of change and innovation.

13. Assign always double the number of publications that one could reasonably expect students to absorb from one seminar to the next. Ask them to present summaries to their colleagues, test the extent to which they have read these papers in detail, and as mentioned before, don't forget to throw in those papers of Freud's that they have already read in many seminars. An additional, helpful message may be to not assign any paper that has been published less than twenty years ago: this conveys the message that the really important contributions have already been made, and that little is to be expected from recent or new developments in theory or technique, including, of course, any ideas that might be germinating in the minds of the students.

14. In contrast to some institutes that leave the decisions of whether candidates should attend seminars given by their own training analysts open to the joint exploration of that issue by that analyst and his analysand, make it a strict principle that candidates should never participate in a seminar given by their own training analyst. In fact, make sure that candidates do not show up at meetings, panels, or any other professional gatherings where the transference might be disturbed by objective information about their analyst's professional work, lest the anonymity desirable for analytic training may be disturbed. Anonymity fosters unanalyzable idealization and healthy insecurity (see Chapter 3).

15. It may be very helpful to give prominence, in the reading lists, to the works of the leading members of your own institution, ideally to be taught not by themselves but by their own, present or former students. Make sure to assign concordant papers that reinforce the views of the local leaders, and only include one or two dissident views, in order to expose their weaknesses. This focus on the reference lists may be complemented by the assignment of a scientific paper or

a case study as part of the progression requirements, with a careful emphasis on the need to quote the locally preferred theoreticians in support of the observations of the student's paper.

16. Ideally, exposure of the students to alternative psychoanalytic schools should be avoided as long as possible. In seminars for advanced students particular papers representing dissident or deviant approaches should be reviewed briefly, in the context of balancing opposite views, and appropriately criticized. It is very helpful to invite leaders of different viewpoints for brief seminars which may, as an exception, include students, graduates and course instructors. The latter may participate to make sure that the students can witness the merciless dismantling of the representative of the alien view. One–day seminars with a leading dissident whose views are attacked in a respectful but unwavering way may contribute to the reassurance that the local school knows best, that the student's mind can rest at peace, and that new ideas, though dangerous, can be robbed of their subversive potential.

17. Always have the least experienced candidates present cases in the presence of more experienced ones and of the faculty. It should never be the most experienced analysts who present a case to a candidate's group: the uncertainties of the work, the inevitable mistakes of senior analysts may erase the sense of self–criticism, the fear over reprimands, and the natural modesty of candidates who are starting their professional work. The conviction that graduates do much better work than candidates, that training analysts do much better work than graduates, and that the older training analysts do much better work than the younger ones, assures the self–doubts of the candidates.

18. Make sure that some unusually critical or rebellious candidates who threaten the atmosphere of harmony at seminars, challenge their senior instructors, or dare talking publicly against training analysts in the presence of their analysands (likely, of course, to report such conversations in their sessions) are gently kept back or stimulated to resign. It is not too difficult to do this, for example, by long delays in approving their supervised analytic cases. One may also arrange meetings of their seminar leaders in which the problematic candidates are critically discussed. The information about these discussions gets back to the candidates in question only indirectly through personal advisors or ombudsmen, who, in friendly ways, convey the

negative attitude that exists in the institute toward them. If a candidate receives sufficient information through third and fourth parties of what is said about him, it will eventually either change his attitude about the institute in the desired direction or else it will stimulate him to resign. Once a candidate has resigned or been asked to resign, don't mention his name again, and maintain a discreet silence about the whole affair: the message that something frightening and dangerous has occurred about which, mercifully, nobody wants to talk, will have a powerful impact on the student body.

19. In recent years, a wonderful new method for dampening the excitement with psychoanalytic training has been devised in the form of an introductory informal, preparatory year of classes: here the entire psychoanalytic theory and technique may be briefly summarized at a simple, introductory college level, already referring to the highlights of Freud's thinking that will be discussed in detail later on, as well as providing the students with a brief introductory history of psychoanalysis from its beginning to the present, while stressing that all of these are areas in which their knowledge will be deepened later on. As many candidates will have studied psychoanalytic theory already at various levels, the process of dulling by repetition will begin already at this introductory level. The effect of a sense of not really knowing fully what will be taught and impatient wishes for deeper exploration may be induced in this way, together with a routinized simplification of basic concepts that will rob them of the excitement when, much later, they are explored in detail. And, naturally, you may use this method for inducing the loss of interest by any course taught at an "introductory" level, insinuating that the "real stuff" will be presented elsewhere.

20. Don't teach an up-to-date course on psychoanalytic technique. Concentrate the teaching of psychoanalytic technique on Freud's introductory papers on the psychoanalytic method, and on his case studies: The Ratman, The Wolfman, Dora, Little Hans will, of course, already have been covered in the comprehensive study of Freud's work; but now, these papers may be read again with the purpose of teaching general principles of psychoanalytic technique. If the candidates acquire knowledge from elsewhere (as, unfortunately, is almost unavoidable at this time) about new developments and alternative approaches to the psychoanalytic process, their anxiety over their own lack of familiarity with the different approaches

of say, Ego Psychology, the French schools, the British schools, etc., will motivate an increased insecurity about their work. This will dampen their confidence in contributing to the challenges that our present day patient population presents to us. If, at the same time, the subtle message is conveyed that psychoanalytic work is really an art that will be mastered intuitively, and that growth and intuition will depend on the progress in their personal analysis and in supervision, that anxiety may maintain its helpful inhibitory effects for a long period of time (Arlow, 1991).

21. Supervisors may carry out a crucial function in inhibiting can--didates' trust in their own work and in the possibility of learning by means of their own experience. It is important that supervisors talk as little as possible. In fact, it may help that the candidate experience a natural continuity between his being a patient in analysis and the relationship with his supervisor. The supervisor's listening carefully and silently to the candidate's presentation of work with his patients, with an occasional comment illustrating what the candidate has done wrong, may keep the candidate in a healthy uncertainty and humility regarding his work. His effort to construct, for himself, the mental frame that determines his supervisor's views will occupy his mind to the extent of influencing significantly his work with his patient. The candidate should feel that following his supervisor's advice without questioning, and demonstrating to the supervisor that he has done the kind of interpretation that he understood the supervisor would have made will absolve him from severe mistakes in his work. This development will prevent the dangerous process by which the candidate might otherwise integrate for himself a theory and a personal frame of technique that evolves and changes creatively as he tests his views in the treatment situation while respecting the patient's autonomous development. If supervisors never come together to discuss their educational approaches to supervision, and if a complete split is maintained between the faculty who teach psychoanalytic technique and the supervisors of control cases, a productive chaos and confusion may bring about the candidates' awareness that it will take many years before they will master the analytic skills sufficiently to dare to contribute creatively to them.

22. A certain degree of paranoid fear, the counterpart of the idealization processes fostered by the training analysis, permeates most psychoanalytic institutions, but, it is important to remember, in fact,

that all social organizations struggle with such developments. Such paranoid fear may contribute to discouraging candidates from independent work, from courageous initiatives, from challenging inquiries. Fortunately, it is not difficult to increase paranoid fears by multiple measures: the most effective has been the reporting by training analysts on the development of the candidates in analysis with them.

The tradition of reporting training analysts, that is, of training analysts informing the education committee about the readiness of their analysands to start classes, or to take a first control case, etc. has been the most paranoiagenic instrument invented as part of psychoanalytic education. It is regrettable that this instrument has now been eliminated and even declared unethical by most psychoanalytic institutes. Fortunately, the irrepressible tendency of some training analysts to indicate with slight gestures and without a word what their true feelings are about various candidates is still being kept alive: this attitude may be fostered by the use of the system of "unhooked telephones," that is, the utilization of what candidates tell their training analysts about what other candidates have been saying about them, as an inspiration for retaliatory moves on the part of these training analysts. At least, the fear about such consequences of a careless comment is a healthy support for paranoid developments (Dulchin & Segal, 1982a, 1982b; Lifschutz, 1976).

23. Another perfectly legitimate method for increasing paranoid fearfulness in candidates is simply not conveying full and adequate information about requirements, expectations, rules and regulations, and channels for redress of grievances. To begin, don't inform candidates regularly about how they are progressing, how they are viewed by teachers and faculty at large, and only let them know about their shortcomings or failures in the indirect ways already described. That supervisors should not be outspoken and explicit with their supervisees, so that these only learn indirectly from the candidate advisor, the director of the institute, or through the rumor mill how they are being evaluated may contribute powerfully to reinforcing paranoid attitudes. It is perfectly legitimate to refer all candidates' questions to the official brochure, and to avoid periodic information gathering and information sharing meetings. In some institutes, the director meets with the entire candidates' body, which tends to produce an atmosphere of relaxation, autonomy, and potential challenges of authority, all of which is dangerous!

24. The messages conveyed by senior leaders of the local psycho-analytic community are extremely important. Manifest, outspoken indications of great insecurity and fearfulness over writing on the part of the most senior and powerful training analysts may foster a healthy identification with them. An even more effective example may be represented by the old fashioned but, fortunately, still exist-ing "convoy" system: a small number of very senior training analysts are the most desirable analysts in their local group, and have such a large number of candidates in personal analysis that they do not have any energy left to go to scientific meetings, let alone participate actively in the scientific work of the society. In order to protect the purity of the transference, they never open their mouths in public, and the mutual friendships, alliances as well as rivalries among those candidates fortunate to be in analysis with one of the great masters feeds into a stabilizing idealization and passivity. This model is highly effective in inhibiting candidates' independent and critical thinking.

25. Try to maintain a relatively uniform student body in terms of the professional aspirations of your students. The true analyst should only wish to do psychoanalysis, to experience the freedom of working in his office with analytic patients, and should be very averse to diluting true analytic work by applying it to other aspects of his professional background such as carrying out psychothera-peutic work with severely regressed patients, or with children, or with psychotics, or participating in academic pursuits outside the psychoanalytic setting, carrying out research, assuming institutional leadership, or participating in the arts.

Major challenges to psychoanalytic theory and technique occur at the boundary of our professional field, and the avoidance of investment in such boundary pursuits protects not only the purity of psychoanalytic work, but also the raising of challenging and potentially subversive questions regarding the limits as well as the applications of psychoanalysis. Avoid accepting and training the mav-erick who wishes to learn psychoanalysis to apply it to another realm of professional endeavor, the philosopher interested in the bounda-ries between philosophical and psychoanalytic understanding, the empirical researcher wishing to complement his neuropsychological background.

If such a protective selection of candidates has been carried out effectively, then you may tolerate a few "special students" interested in the intellectual aspects of psychoanalysis. But you must clearly keep them separate from the true student body, limit their attendance at clinical seminars, and in short, convey the message that a gulf exists between true analytic training and "secondary" enterprises. Don't give "partial clinical training" to academicians from other fields, who always should feel your wrath about unauthorized clinical work, and the impossibility of ever understanding psychoanalysis fully if they are not in a full fledged clinical training program.

26. By the same token, all interdisciplinary scientific inquiry should be relegated to very advanced stages of the training, tucked into elective seminars in the last year of courses, once the basic identity of the candidate is assured enough to be able to withstand the diluting and potentially corroding effects of the psychoanalytic approach to art, societal problems, philosophy, and research in the neurosciences. The opposite to such an approach would be to bring in studies of peripheral sciences at a point when psychoanalytic theory is just beginning to be explored, for example, when psychoanalytic drive theory needs to be assimilated without contamination or questioning from alternative models or schools of human motivation: or else, relating psychoanalytic technique to alternative psychotherapeutic methods. Or, for example, when teaching the psychoanalytic theory of depression, premature introduction of the relationship between psychodynamics and biological determinants of depression might threaten an authentic psychoanalytic conviction.

27. Refer all problems involving teachers and students, seminars and supervision, all conflicts between candidates and the faculty "back to the couch": keep in mind that transference acting–out is a major complication of psychoanalytic training, and that there are always transference elements in all students' dissatisfactions. A candidate's inordinate pressure towards challenging questions, imaginative thinking, or developing alternative formulations usually has profound transference roots and should be resolved in the personal analytic situation. This means also that the faculty has to remain united, that teachers faced with challenges from individual students, or from the student body at large, have to stick together. A united faculty provides a firm and stable structure against which the transference regression of the student body can be diagnosed and referred back to their individual psychoanalytic experience.

28. All the principles and recommendations outlined would not suffice if the teaching faculty were imbued with a spirit of creativity of their own. It is a difficult but not impossible task to inhibit the creativity of the faculty: faculty whose creativity is inhibited will be the best guarantee to reproduce such a process unconsciously in the relationship with the students. This is your major challenge: what can you do in the psychoanalytic society to inhibit the creativity of its members? Fortunately, long experience has taught us that the hierarchical extension of the educational process into the social structure of the psychoanalytic society is easily achieved and can be most effective. Here, what is particularly helpful is the development of powerful barriers at each step of the candidate's progression from institute graduate to associate member of the society, to full member, to training analyst, to becoming a member of the education committee, and/or in charge of a major ongoing seminar. Make sure that it is clear that the allegiance to powerful political groups is more important in fostering such a development than actual professional or scientific achievements. Make sure that the ways to proceed from one step to the next are uncertain and indefinite enough to maintain a constant air of insecurity and paranoia in the society. Have frequent secret votes determining progression at all levels, with a clear message to everybody that such votes are influenced by the political processes in your group.

29. Above all, maintain discretion, secrecy, and uncertainty about what is required to become a training analyst, how these decisions are made, where and by whom, and what kind of feedback or mechanism for redress of grievances anybody can expect who is fearful of the traumatic implications of being considered and rejected as a training analyst. The more the body of training analysts maintains itself apart and cohesive as the holders of authority and prestige, the more the inhibitory effects of the selection process will influence the entire educational enterprise. This is your most reliable and effective tool for keeping not only candidates but the entire faculty and the entire society in line.

30. Keep in mind, when uncertain about dangerous developments that may challenge proven methods of inhibiting the creativity of candidates, that the main objective of psychoanalytic education is not to help students to acquire what is known in order to develop new knowledge, but to acquire well proven knowledge regarding psychoanalysis to avoid its dilution, distortion, deterioration, and misuse.

Always keep in mind: where there is a spark there may develop a fire, particularly when this spark appears in the middle of deadwood: extinguish it before it is too late!

## Note

1 Published in *International Journal of Psychoanalysis*, 77:(5) 1031–1040, 1996.

## References

Arlow, J. A. (1991). Address to the Graduating Class of the San Francisco Psychoanalytic Institute, June 16, 1990. *American Psychoanalyst*, 25(1): 15–16, 21.

Britton, R. (1994). Publication Anxiety: Conflict between Communication and Affiliation. *Int. J. Psycho-Anal.*, 75: 1213–1224.

Bruzzone, M. *et al.* (1985). Regression and Persecution in Analytic Training: Reflections on Experience. *Int. Rev. Psychoanal.*, 12: 411–415.

Dulchin, J. & Segal, A. J. (1982a). The Ambiguity of Confidentiality in a Psychoanalytic Institute. *Psychiat.*, 45: 13–25.

_____ (1982b). Third Party Confidences: The Uses of Information in a Psychoanalytic Institute. *Psychiat.*, 45: 27–37.

Giovannetti, M. de Freitas (1991). The Couch and the Medusa: Brief Considerations on the Nature of the Boundaries in the Psychoanalytic Institution. Unpubl. ms. 5th IPA Conference of Training Analysts, Buenos Aires.

Green A. (1991). Preliminaries to a Discussion of the Function of Theory in Psychoanalytic Training. Unpubl. ms. 5th IPA Conference of Training Analysts, Buenos Aires.

Infante, J. A. (1991). The Teaching of Psychoanalysis: Common Ground. Unpubl. ms. 5th IPA Conference of Training Analysts, Buenos Aires.

Lifschutz, J. E. (1976). A Critique of Reporting and Assessment in the Training Analysis. *J. Amer. Psychoanal. Assn.*, 24: 43–59.

Lussier, A. (1991). Our Training Ideology. Unpubl. ms. 5th IPA Conference of Training Analysts, Buenos Aires.

Wallerstein, R. S. (1993). Between Chaos and Petrification: A Summary of the Fifth IPA Conference of Training Analysts. *Int. J. Psycho-Anal.*, 74: 165–178.

# 6

# THE PRESSING NEED TO
# INCREASE RESEARCH IN AND
# ON PSYCHOANALYSIS[1]

## An overview

I believe that the psychoanalytic community is faced with a pressing need to significantly increase research on all aspects of psychoanalytic theory, technique, and applications. For the purpose of this presentation, I am referring to research as systematic observations, under controlled conditions, leading to new knowledge. This, admittedly broad, definition includes historical research, clinical investigation, and naturalistic as well as empirical research.

Empirical research that does not consider fully the complex conceptual issues involving key psychoanalytic concepts runs the risk, in its operational definition of variables, of equivocating the nature of that which is being measured, while failing to do justice to the scope and depth of the relevant psychoanalytic concepts under investigation. Conceptual research, focusing on the historical development, conflictual definitions, and predominant present social usage of a certain concepts, runs the risk of sterility unless such study is linked to empirical investigation that may clarify controversies in the conceptual field and the related theories reflected in this concept.

Why this appeal regarding the urgent need for major increase in psychoanalytic research? In short, the urgency of this task involves, first of all, the scientific need to reassess and advance our knowledge; second, our social responsibility to reassure the public regarding the effectiveness of psychoanalysis and the psychoanalytically based psychotherapies we are developing, and to demonstrate our ongoing efforts to increase the range and efficacy of these treatments. All of this should also justify and assure the reimbursement systems for psychoanalysis. Third, we must increase our professional and scientific relationships with boundary sciences and disciplines, and strengthen our relationships with the clinical and the academic world.

Without an ongoing exploration of the efficacy of psychoanalysis and derivative treatments, we run the risk of being discarded by the mental health delivery systems. The financial pressures that militate against support of long-term psychotherapy at this time, the stress on evidence-based treatments in the medical field, the competing claims of non–psychoanalytic psychotherapies and psychopharmacology require a creative development of comparative research, which demonstrates our contribution to the social and medical environment, and may affect the cultural attitude toward psychoanalysis as well.

## Current empirical research and its critique

Within the neurobiological field, the study of the relationship between affect activation and cognitive control systems, has revealed the structures related to storage of affective memory and its activation in the context of new affective stimulation (Panksepp, 1998). We know, for example, that the excessive activation of negative affect related to hyper-reactivity of the amygadala and to abnormality of certain neurotransmitters, if and when complicated by a lack of adequate activation of controlling and contextualizing prefrontal and preorbital cortical structures may determine an excessively aggressive temperament and lack of impulse control. These findings need to be related to theoretical and clinical questions regarding the concepts of affects, drives, and ego functions. The neurobiology of consciousness, dissociated mental states, and alterations of consciousness under acute traumatic conditions need to be related to the psychoanalytic study of primitive defensive operations centered on splitting, and the psychology of dissociative functioning. The study of normal and pathological attachment provides information on the relationship between early object relations and disturbances in the capacity for later object relations, which, when combined with the study of temperamental predisposition provides an important potential bridge between psychoanalytic and neurobiological research.

90

Undoubtedly, there is a serious risk here of an over-simplifying reductionism, that has motivated a justifiable critique from psycho-analysts who question the clinical and theoretical relevance of infant observation (Green, 2000; Stern, 2000). This critique seems valid if directed against theoretical conclusions based on behavioral observations that, frequently, do not consider their intrapsychic correlates, and ignore the importance of profound unconscious developments of sexual and aggressive fantasy. Yet, by providing behavioral landmarks of early development that are relevant for the tracing of cognitive and affective processes, our knowledge of the development of intra-psychic life can be enriched. This happened with the abandonment of the Mahlerian concept of primary autism under the impact of the observation of the highly differentiated relationships between infant and mother from birth on.

The critique that empirical research cannot capture the wealth of unconscious processes evolving in patient and analyst, and that, characteristically, empirical research misses the deeper aspects of oedipal and pre-oedipal, sexual and aggressive fantasy life and con-flicts, seems correct. As André Green (Green, 2000) has pointed out, the description of the infant misses the infantile aspects of the adult. The gradual deepening of our knowledge of the neurobiological basis of cognitive and affective functioning, however, facilitates the understanding of the characteristics and preconditions for symbolic psychic functioning. The relationship, for example, between over-whelming trauma and psychological development may be better understood by relating real life experiences to specific sequelae of psychopathology.

The issue of relating observed behavior to psychoanalytic investigation is particularly relevant for the empirical study of the psy-chotherapies. Psychoanalytic institutions have traditionally neglected the application of psychoanalytic knowledge to techniques of deriva-tive psychotherapeutic procedures that may be of enormous social importance, facilitating the treatment of patients whose severity of illness precludes their being treated by standard psychoanalysis. Psychoanalysis, almost without being fully aware of it, has helped to develop effective and focused psychotherapeutic treatments for spe-cific psychopathologies that correspond to pressing social needs, such as the psychoanalytic psychotherapy of borderline patients (Clarkin, Yeomans & Kernberg, 1989; Bateman & Fonagy, 2004). The relative lack of concerted efforts by the psychoanalytic community to develop systematic studies of objective evidence of the efficacy of psycho-analytic psychotherapies has left the field to the cognitive behavior therapists, who have been enthusiastically willing and prepared to carry out empirical research on their modalities of treatment, and are increasingly challenging psychoanalytically inspired psychothera-pies everywhere. It is true that this latter development corresponds in part to financial pressures from Managed Care which privileges short term treatments, and to cultural dispositions toward empirical research that dominate in the Northern Hemisphere, particularly the Anglo–Saxon and Nordic countries, in contrast to an openness to a more philosophically inspired, subjectivistically focused attitude in Latin countries. The problem, however, is universal and increasing.

Despite the controversies about the possibility and plausibility of conducting research, major studies have been carried out regard-ing the effectiveness of psychoanalysis. In Germany, a pathbreaking study, sponsored by the German Psychoanalytic Association, was carried out under the leadership of Marianne Leuzinger-Bohleber (Leuzinger-Bohleber & Stern, 1997); a study in Sweden under the direction of Sandell (Sandell *et al.*, 1997) demonstrated the long-range effects of psychoanalysis in comparison to psychoanalytic psycho-therapy. In the United States, studies of the relationship between transference exploration and psychotherapy outcome were carried out by Lester Luborsky with the CCRT method (Luborsky & Crits-Christoff, 1990); Samson and Weiss (Weiss & Samson, 1986) studied superego functions in psychoanalysis; the long–term follow–up stud-ies of psychoanalytic treatment have been carried out at the Columbia University Center for Psychoanalytic Research and Education, the New York Psychoanalytic Institute, and the Boston Psychoanalytic Institute (Weber, Bachrach & Solomon, 1985a, 1985b; Erle & Goldberg, 1984; Kantrovitz *et al.*, 1987). The still earlier Menninger study directed by Robert Wallerstein (1986), and in its final stage under my direction (Kernberg *et al.*, 1972), was the first to system-atically compare psychoanalysis and psychoanalytic psychotherapies. The analysis of clinical change by means of the study of significant content change in the analytic hours throughout time has been attempted by using computerized methods, such as Mergenthaler (1996) in Horst Kaechele's group in Ulm, Germany, and by Wilma Bucci (1997) in New York.

These studies represent major efforts to deal with the relation-ship of psychoanalysis to the psychotherapies, and, indirectly, with its place in the field of psychological science and the delivery of psychic healthcare methods. Within the psychoanalytic community, however, these studies have been criticized for being intended to demonstrate, to a skeptical world, the effectiveness of psychoanalytic psychotherapy and psychoanalysis, without achieving a major impact or modification of biases against psychoanalysis, on the one hand, and without contributing to psychoanalysis as a science, on the other. The findings of these projects were often deemed superficial or trivial, and the operational definition of major psychoanalytic concepts questionable. A major critique within the psychoanalytic community of all those research efforts was also the neglect, on the part of such quantitative studies, of the nature of the psychoanalytic process, and their lack of focus on the specific effects of psychoanalysis in bringing about structural intrapsychic change as opposed to behavioral change.

I believe that much of this critique is relevant, and reflects the enormous methodological difficulties in carrying out research on the psychoanalytic and psychotherapeutic process; nonetheless, the level of research already achieved represents a significant advance over earlier pioneering efforts in that area. At this point, projects with newer methodologies and conceptual specifications are in various stages of development. They include, for example, the ongoing Borderline Psychotherapy Research Project carried out at the Department of Psychiatry of the Cornell University Medical College and the Westchester Division of the New York Hospital (Clarkin, Yeomans & Kernberg 1999). Our most recent project was a randomized controlled study of ninety patients diagnosed with Borderline Personality Disorder, assigned to one of three cells: (1) a manualized cognitive behavior therapy, namely Dialectic Behavior Therapy (DBT), (2) a manualized supportive psychotherapy based on psychoanalytic principles (SP), or (3) Transference Focused Psychotherapy (TFP), a specific psychoanalytic psychotherapy for patients with severe personality disorders.

An important finding so far, that I wish to stress here because of its key theoretical and clinical relevance to this discussion, is that there was a significant improvement in reflective function in the TFP group, compared with little or no improvement of reflective function in the other two treatment groups. Reflective function corresponds to the capacity to assess appropriately mental states in self and others, and, therefore the nature of self-representations and object representations that determine identity integration or identity diffusion (Fonagy & Target, 2003). Structural change, in this project's theoretical formulation, is reflected in changes in the internalized world of object relations, that is, in self and object relations, leading to identity integration. This study provides empirical evidence in support of a specific mechanism of change for psychoanalytic psychotherapy, namely, the effects of interpretation.

The main critique of empirical research within the psychoanalytic community is, that, so far it has not helped psychoanalytic practice, and that the significant developments in psychoanalytic theory and technique have come, not from empirical research, but from the inspired work of theoreticians and clinicians: Melanie Klein, Edith Jacobson, Winnicott, Bion, André Green, and others have been much more important and relevant in their contributions than any empirical research in psychoanalysis. There is no doubt in my mind about the fact that the subtlety, complexity, and richness of the psychoanalytic process cannot be captured in the necessarily restricted quality of particular research projects. But the cumulative effect of well-directed research programs moves in that direction. The relationship between our creative psychoanalytic theoreticians and clinicians, on the one hand, and the psychoanalytic researchers on the other, may be compared to the race between the hare (clinicians and theoreticians) and the tortoise (empirical research). Clinical and theoretical developments in psychoanalysis have evolved much faster than systematic research, given all its difficulties, apart from the distrust toward empirical research in our institutional life related to the sense that it does not do justice to the complexity of clinical phenomena.

I believe, however, that in the long run, the integration of empirical and conceptual research will contribute significantly to develop psychoanalysis proper, broaden its applications, and provide mutually beneficial links with the neurosciences that, in turn, will enrich and help psychoanalysis to develop, while psychoanalysis, based on a century of analytic inquiry, has much to contribute to these other sciences. I believe that this interchange will assure the position of psychoanalysis, not only within the sciences, but also within the field of mental health delivery services, and assure its future beyond its major contributions to the culture of the twentieth century.

In the corresponding relationship of psychoanalysis to the social sciences, empirical research has been much more difficult to develop, although conceptual research by creative psychoanalytic theoreticians and clinicians has both made important contributions to the field of social science. (Freud, 1921; Erickson, 1950; Mitscherlich, 1963; Moscovici, 1981; Kernberg, 1998; Volkan, 2004). Paradoxically, however, despite these contributions, the psychoanalytic community itself has maintained a "safe" distance from these findings, and it is only a very small contingent of psychoanalysts who have worked in this area.

## Resistances to research in psychoanalysis

The classical definition of psychoanalysis describes it as a theory of mental functioning, a means of investigating the human mind, and a method of treatment. Significant questions have been raised that signify an urgent need for more intense, consistent, and comprehensive research in all three of these domains.

In the area of theory, the classical psychoanalytic metapsychology has been challenged by the explosion of knowledge in the biological sciences. The theory of drives as fundamental motivators of human behavior and psychoanalytic theories of the origins and structure of psychic functioning, psychopathology, and psychic change need to be integrated with the implications of current research in neuroscience as well as in psychiatry, psychology, and sociology. New findings about the relationship between exploration of the dynamic unconscious, the lifting of repressions as contrasted to the effects of suggestion, and the effects of the interactive therapeutic process on exploration of the unconscious have raised important scientific challenges to psychoanalysis as an instrument of investigating human functioning. The efficacy of treatment by psychotherapeutic methods derived from psychoanalysis as well as such nonanalytic treatments as cognitive, behavioral, and non-verbal therapies has yet to be systematically compared with that of psychoanalysis. Recognition of the non-specific effects of various psychological treatments and of the complex relation between treatment process and treatment outcome poses challenging research questions regarding psychoanalysis as an agent of structural psychic change and the indications and limitations of psychoanalysis as a treatment method.

Given these challenges, the advances in scientific knowledge in boundary fields, and new developments in the practice of psychoanalytic treatment itself, it is puzzling that significant resistance to psychoanalytic research persists within the psychoanalytic community itself. What follows is an attempt to examine and understand common reservations about psychoanalytic research in the international psychoanalytic community.

Perhaps the main reservation stems from appreciation of the complexity of the psychoanalytic theory of mental functioning, the theory of psychoanalytic technique, and the rationale of actual clinical interventions. In fact, it has been questioned whether psychoanalytic procedures may accurately be subsumed under theories of "technique" rather than considered to be aspects of a method that cannot be described with any precision, given the complexity of the interactional field involving patient and analyst. This leads, in turn, to consideration of the complexity of the interactional psychoanalytic process, of "intersubjectivity" as a challenge to "objectification," and of the actual or potential disruption of the psychoanalytic situation created by the use of external observational instruments. At a simple, guts level, psychoanalysts are concerned that anything beyond the retrospective description of a clinical situation by the analyst—that is, any recording or direct observation—would disrupt the psychoanalytic process to the point of falsification.

A leading psychoanalytic clinician, after listening to audiotaped psychoanalytic sessions, exclaimed: "One thing I can tell you for sure; whatever this is, it is not analysis." At a seminar on psychoanalytic research in a major psychoanalytic institution overseas, 50 percent of a full-day workshop had to be dedicated to discussing the anxieties expressed regarding the recording of psychoanalytic sessions. There is abundant evidence that psychoanalysts are more concerned than their patients are about audiotaping psychoanalytic sessions and that their apprehensions about the reaction of colleagues and their insecurity about their interpretive interventions are important aspects of this reluctance.

Another major source of resistance to psychoanalytic research derives from the widespread perception within the psychoanalytic community that empirical methods of evaluating the psychoanalytic situation are relatively simplistic and thus do not do justice to the complexity and subtlety of the encounter. Such sophisticated research approaches as Luborsky's "Core Conflictual Relationship Theme" methodology for studying the transference (Luborsky & Crits Christoph, 1998), Gill and Hoffman's research on transference resistance (Gill & Hoffman, 1982), Kächele's computer based analysis of themes shifting over time within the psychoanalytic process (Kächele, Luborsky & Thomä, 1988), and Sampson and Weiss's analysis of the relationship between superego functions, repression, and anxiety (Sampson & Weiss, 1986) have all been attacked as partial and oversimplified, not directly relevant or helpful in answering the concrete challenges in the clinical situation. These approaches, further, have been said to restrict and potentially distort core psychoanalytic concepts by their efforts to operationalize them. The conclusions of these research methodologies have been seen as too general, too limited, or methodologically flawed to be immediately relevant for clinical practice. When these conclusions support psychoanalytic theory, they sometimes provoke the cynical remark that all this complicated research leads to findings that are self-evident to the experienced clinician. The analytic community at large tends to regard psychoanalytic research as a lengthy and expensive horse race with outcomes that are not dramatically different from those achieved by other treatment methods; such research, it is charged, has great limitations in providing evidence of the more specific and subtle effects of psychoanalytic treatment.

A third major type of resistance to psychoanalytic research focuses on the application to psychoanalytic practice of new theoretical models, such as those derived from Kleinian analysis, self psychology, object relations theories, the French psychoanalytic mainstream, or the intersubjectivity approach (Kernberg, 2004). In so far as adherents of these alternative psychoanalytic models have a sense that exciting developments are taking place in their theory and technique, and that there are mutual influences among theory, technique, and clinical interventions—particularly with the more difficult and marginal cases—there is pressure on clinical researchers to develop a particular model of psychoanalysis, increased competition and rivalry with other models, and the conviction that only sophisticated, "nondisrupted" clinical work will permit such creative competitiveness. Formalized research protocols, it is felt, could not possibly do justice to the differences between, say, a contemporary ego psychological and a contemporary Kleinian approach. The work of Bion, Green, Laplanche, Liberman, Loewald, Schafer, or Winnicott is experienced as more exciting than the research findings by empirical researchers in psychoanalysis.

A fourth factor is the concern of psychoanalytic clinicians, educators and theoreticians that the theoretical conclusions derived from empirical research such as, for example, infant observation may be "overstretched," yielding to the temptation to link

97

observable behavior patterns directly with assumed underlying neurological structures, and thus presenting an impoverished or superficial presentation of psychic reality and mental structures. For example, to many analysts, psychoanalytic infant researchers who demonstrate behavior patterns in infants that are clearly responsive to maternal behaviors underestimate the role of unconscious determinants of behavior, particularly unconscious aggressive and sexual drives. Because of the unconscious nature of these drives and the defensive operations directed against them, descriptive observation may provide only a partial view of infant development (Green and Stern, 2000).

A fifth factor derives from the nature of psychoanalytic education. As I have pointed out in earlier work (Chapter 3), psychoanalytic institutes, for a variety of historical and institutional reasons, are mostly geared to educating psychoanalytic practitioners and tend to emphasize the transmission of psychoanalytic theory and technique as practiced in the particular psychoanalytic center, to the relative neglect of the development of new knowledge. This emphasis on a particular approach as opposed to the alternatives favored in other centers or countries fosters an atmosphere of conformity rather than the questioning attitude research demands.

The institutional status of training analysts, their idealization as part of transference regression, and the institutional reinforcement of that idealization by the collective "anonymity" of the training analysts tend to restrict the examination of the analytic process to the candidates' treatment of patients. That juniors present to seniors but not vice versa leads to the tendency among candidates to idealize the (unknown) work of the senior analysts, perpetuates their insecurity about their work, and reinforces everybody's fear of external observations of the actual psychoanalytic process. At the same time, the questioning attitude required by a concerted effort to develop further theory and technique runs counter to the culture of idealizing transmitted knowledge and is all too readily identified as rebellious subversion. The perception of psychoanalytic research as a subversive activity, in turn, runs counter to candidates' wishes to avoid unnecessary conflicts during their training.

A related factor is the relative isolation of psychoanalytic institutes from university settings where ordinary research in scientific fields at the boundary of psychoanalysis is carried out. This contributes to an implicit, practical competition for time and dedication, with "outside" interests perceived as being in competition with psychoanalysis. Thus, for example, commitment to and research on psychoanalytic psychotherapy, group therapy, couples therapy, and sex therapy appears to be in potential competition with the study of psychoanalysis proper. In order to protect the focus on traditional psychoanalysis, the analytic institute may unwittingly inhibit an interest in research in fields of applied psychoanalysis. By the same token, alternative formulations regarding mental functioning, related to research in adjacent fields of knowledge, may be perceived as a challenge to traditional psychoanalytic theory, with the result that interdisciplinary research is discouraged.

A final and increasingly important factor is the social, political, and financial challenge to psychoanalysis that comes from psychiatry, clinical psychology, and commercial health systems. The socially sanctioned, cynical approach to the reduction of resources for mental health in the interest of cost effectiveness threatens psychoanalysis as a long-term treatment method, puts pressures on psychoanalytic institutions and the psychoanalytic community at large to demonstrate the cost effectiveness of analysis as compared to various other treatments, and creates resentment against research as an agent of the social rejection of psychoanalysis even among those analysts who realize that there is no shortcut to sophisticated outcome research. This drives a further wedge between psychoanalytic practice and the research endeavor.

## What needs to be done

I believe that a broad spectrum of research needs be carried out, from small projects limited to an individual candidate's scholarly investigation, to large institutional projects carried out among various institutes or between a psychoanalytic institute and a university setting. It is extremely important, I believe, to establish or reestablish the links of psychoanalysis to academia, particularly with university departments of psychiatry and clinical psychology, where interdisciplinary interests may facilitate interchange, and with the humanities and social sciences at large.

It may well be that the initial steps in such joint approaches require the recruitment and inclusion, as part of the psychoanalytic institute faculty, of scientists from other fields, not necessarily psychoanalysts, but open to and interested in collaboration with psychoanalytic researchers. Small institutes may have to invite a leading methodologist in research from another field as the first step to develop a solid research experience.

To foster and reward scientific work by candidates, institutes and societies should provide recognition and prestige for scientific contributions as well as for competence for clinical work. Prestige, for sure, should not derive from the unique ladder that leads to training analyst status within the present system. I believe that it is highly desirable that psychoanalytic institutes develop a department of research, directed by a psychoanalyst interested in such a development, or, particularly in small institutes where this may be less likely, by attracting a leading research methodologist although he may not be a psychoanalyst, who may help to transform questions raised throughout the stimulation of candidates to explore and write about controversial issues, leading to publications. This may have an energizing effect for the institute at large. Research on psychoanalytic psychotherapy is much more advanced presently than research on psychoanalysis proper (Fonagy, 2002). Psychoanalysis, making use of the development of methodology in the research on process and treatment techniques of psychoanalytic psychotherapy may advance much more rapidly than starting only from the traditional clinical situation. In the long run, the clear delimitation of psychotherapeutic technique from psychoanalytic technique, the instrumentalization of the corresponding criteria, the empirical confirmation of the specific effects of psychoanalytic psychotherapy and the institutional acceptance of its value in psychoanalytic institutes will permit to set up inter-institutional (multi-center) randomized clinical treatment outcome studies that compare the effectiveness of psychoanalysis and psychoanalytic psychotherapy. This step, in turn, should stimulate a new set of studies to focus more sharply on the therapeutic effects of specific process variables within psychoanalytic treatment.

An overall objective of psychoanalytic institutes should be to foster the development of psychoanalytic researchers among the candidates' body. The implication is not that every psychoanalyst should become a researcher, but, even if only one to three percent of all analysts in training become committed researchers, the field would be significantly better able to meet the challenges we currently face. The fact that Fonagy's *An Open Door Review of Outcome Studies in Psychoanalysis* (2002) published by the IPA (!), is not standard information forming part of psychoanalytic education everywhere, illustrates the enormous gap between what is actually being done to strengthen the scientific position of psychoanalysis by small groups of dedicated and enthusiastic researchers, on the one hand, and the painful ignorance of those efforts within our educational establishments at this point, on the other.

The very fact that present developments of alternative theoretical formulations and corresponding technical approaches within psychoanalysis are being actively explored clinically in many psychoanalytic institutes may foster the interest and commitment to develop research designs examining these questions. The supervisory situation, in which cases are discussed individually and in small groups also facilitates the activation of unconscious processes in the actualization of what is transferred from the individual psychoanalytic session to the supervisory situation. Within that situation, the possibility of systematic exploration of psychodynamic developments fosters the possibility of empirical research. The crystallization of contrasting conceptual formulations, with potential systematic observations available to discern the different consequences of their respective employment constitutes one first step into the direction of empirical research. The presence of scientists of boundary fields in neurobiology, the social sciences, philosophy, and developmental theory, should facilitate the explanatory confrontation of different viewpoints to look at the same phenomena, and stimulate the formulation of questions and a research approach to such alternative perspectives.

Neurobiology, I believe, needs psychoanalysis to advance the understanding of complex organization of symbolic functions, consciousness and its dissociation, and the impact of cognitive control over affect activation. And psychoanalysis needs the relationship with neurobiology to reexamine its theories in the context of the rapid developing knowledge of the biological basis of psychic functioning. In the social field, the understanding of fundamentalism, terrorism, fanaticism, may be powerfully enriched by psychoanalytic perspectives, and these current historical developments, in turn, may stimulate psychoanalytic development of the understanding of the expression of the unconscious in the social field. Freud's pathbreaking advances into this field should stimulate present day efforts in this direction.

I believe that, in the long run, research will contribute significantly to enrich psychoanalysis proper, broaden its applications, and provide important links with the neurosciences that should enrich and help psychoanalysis to develop further, but, simultaneously, psychoanalysis should enrich the knowledge in the complex areas of symbolic functions as an aspect of neurobiological functions and structures. I believe a parallel interchange may occur in the social sciences, and these interchanges will assure the position of psychoanalysis, not only within those sciences, but also within the social field and the cultural environment. A major precondition for this development, as I have stressed, is a radical change in our educational priorities and organization.

It is important to strengthen the dialogue between the small group of psychoanalytic researchers and the psychoanalytic community at large in an effort to moderate the intensity of the conflict between those who hold that only empirical research is of any value and that ordinary clinical research is old fashioned and irrelevant, and those who perceive naîveté, scientism, and unconscious resistance to psychoanalytic theory and methodology in any empirical research. Both viewpoints might come to be regarded as equally biased and unjustified.

The empirical research conferences of the IPA held annually in London demonstrate what can be achieved in focused dialogues to overcome the gap between researchers and clinicians. I believe it is an important task of the IPA to foster such small-scale conferences on particular areas in research that bring together specialists from world-wide psychoanalytic centers. This dialogue should be fostered in our professional publications as well as in the concerted efforts of psychoanalytic institutes to strengthen the relationship with the university in their geographic areas. The recent IPA volume on research in psychoanalysis (Fonagy, 1999) provides an encouraging example.

The understanding that psychoanalytic research needs to proceed simultaneously within the ordinary clinical setting, in applied analysis, in interdisciplinary research, and in empirical research should help to eliminate sterile and at times self-destructive discussions about what psychoanalytic research is, and whether psychoanalysis is a natural or a social science. So far, the most significant progress in our field has been achieved through understandings derived from the psychoanalytic situation itself, while naturalistic and empirical research is only beginning to deal with the growing complexity of theoretical formulations, clinical observations, and methodological challenges. We have to accept the fact that for quite some time to come, empirical research in psychoanalysis, in contrast to other, more mature sciences, will probably not contribute much to advancing our clinical methodology, and that the short-term achievement of research in terms of strengthening the relationship between psychoanalysis and related fields will precede a time when breakthroughs in research outside the clinical situation will influence that situation.

The political divide between empirical researchers and psychoanalytic theoreticians is damaging to our field and urgently needs to be overcome. It is important to provide opportunities and encouragement to theoreticians and clinicians interested in conceptual and "qualitative" research that follows the methodology derived from the use of psychoanalytic inquiry into the psychoanalytic situation as well as to empirical or "quantitative" researchers whose experience in systematic research is more advanced.

Meanwhile, a consistent educational process is required to acquaint psychoanalysts with research developments in related fields with important implications, if not for psychoanalytic technique, at least for (or against) the validity of psychoanalytic findings and psychoanalytic theory. For example, the demonstration of the mechanism of projective identification in a nonclinical setting, drawing on the research on affect expression by Rainer Krause (1988), constitutes, I believe, an important illustration of the possibility that methodologies derived from other scientific fields can contribute to research on psychoanalysis. Specialized programs in psychoanalytic institutes to train experts in other sciences to apply psychoanalytic theory to their own fields of knowledge should contribute significantly to research in applied psychoanalysis. For example, the contributions of Marcia Cavell (1993) in philosophy and of Ellen Handler Spitz (1985) in art theory—both of them graduates of the Columbia University Center for Psychoanalytic Training and Research—illustrate the effectiveness of this effort as part of psychoanalytic education. Psychoanalytic institutes need to invite leading scientists from related fields to participate in teaching the theory of mind. It is perhaps particularly in the fields of neurosciences, infant development, and social psychology that important contributions may fertilize psychoanalytic thinking.

Beyond these practical arrangements lies the need for a fundamental rethinking of psychoanalytic education. I believe that psychoanalytic institutes should conceive their mission as not simply the transmission of psychoanalytic knowledge but the development of new psychoanalytic knowledge, thus acquiring a university function regardless of their direct relationship to any particular university setting. Such a conception is a far cry from setting up isolated courses on methodology of research.

In the short run, intelligent and consistent political efforts will be required to protect psychoanalysis within the present climate of reduced resources for psychotherapeutic treatment. In the long run, the recognition of psychoanalysis as a basic science of mental functioning and respect for psychoanalytic treatment as a major, specialized treatment approach will depend largely upon the creation of an accepting environment in the university and in the culture. Ongoing psychoanalytic research and respect for research in boundary fields may provide a bridge to that environment.

## Note

1 Modified version of a paper published in *International Journal of Psychoanalysis* 87: 919–926, 2006.

## References

Bucci, W. (1997) *Psychoanalysis and Cognitive Science: A Multiple Code Theory*. New York: Guildford Press.

Clarkin, J.F. Yeomans, F.E. & Kernberg, O.F. (1999). *Psychotherapy for Borderline Personality*. New York: John Wiley and Sons.

Erle, J. & Goldberg, D. (1984). Observations on Assessment of Analyzability by Experienced Analysts. *Journal of the American Psychoanalytic Association,* 32(4): 715–737.

Fonagy, P. & Target, M. (2003). *Psychoanalytic Theories: Perspectives from Developmental Psychopathology*, Chapter 12, 270–282.

Kantrowitz, J., Paolitto, F., Sashin, J. & Solomon, L. (1987). Changes in the Level and Quality of Object Relations in Psychoanalysis: Follow-Up of a Longitudinal Prospective Study. *Journal of the American Psychoanalytic Association,* 35: 23–46.

Loborsky, L. & Crits-Christoph, P. (1998). *Understanding Transference: The Core Conflictual Relationship Theme Method*, (2nd ed.) Washington, DC: American Psychological Association Press.

Main, M. & Goldwyn, R. (1995). Adult Attachment Classification System. In: M. Main (Ed.), *Behavior and the Development of Representational Models of Attachment: Five Methods of Assessment*. Cambridge, MA: Cambridge University Press.

Mergenthaler, E. (1996). Emotion-Abstraction Patterns in Verbatim Protocols: A New Way of Describing Therapeutic Processes. *Journal of Consulting and Clinical Psychology*, 64, 1306–1318.

## Bibliography

Bateman, A. & Fonagy, P. (2004). *Psychotherapy for Borderline Personality Disorder: Mentalization-Based Treatment.* London: Oxford University Press.

Bucci, W. (1997). *Psychoanalysis and Cognitive Science: A Multiple Code Theory.* New York: Guilford Press.

Clarkin, J.F., Yeomans, F.E. & Kernberg, O.F. (1999). *Psychotherapy for Borderline Personality.* New York: John Wiley and Sons.

Erikson, E.H. (1950). Growth and Crises of the Healthy Personality. In: *Identity and the Life Cycle*, 50–100. New York: International Universities Press, 1959.

Erle, J. & Goldberg, D. (1984). Observations on Assessment of Analyzability by Experienced Analysts. *Journal of the American Psychoanalytical Association.* 32: 715–737.

Fonagy, P. (2002) ed. *An Open Door Review of Outcome Studies in Psychoanalysis.* London: International Psychoanalytic Association.

Fonagy, P. & Target, M. (2003). *Psychoanalytic Theories: Perspectives from Developmental Psychopathology*, Chapter 12, 270–282.

Freud, S. (1921). *Group Psychology and the Analysis of the Ego.* Standard Edition, 18: 65–143.

Green, A. (2000). Science and Science Fiction in Infant Research. In: *Clinical and Observational Psychoanalytic Research: Roots of a Controversy*, Eds. Sandler, J., Sandler, A.M. & Davies, R. Madison, CT: International Universities Press, 4: 41–72.

Kantrowitz, J., Paolitto, F., Sashin, J. & Solomon, L. (1987). Changes in the Level and Quality of Object Relations in Psychoanalysis: Follow-Up of a Longitudinal Prospective Study. *Journal of the American Psychoanalytic Association*, 35: 23–46.

Kernberg, O.F., Burnstein, E., Coyne, L., Appelbaum, A., Horwitz, L. & Voth H. (1972). Psychotherapy and Psychoanalysis: Final Report of the Menninger Foundation's Psychotherapy Research Project. *Bulletin of the Menninger Clinic* 36: 1–275.

Kernberg, O.F. (1998). *Ideology, Conflict, and Leadership in Groups and Organizations.* New Haven, CT: Yale University Press.

––––––– (2004). Recent Developments in the Technical Approaches of English-Language Psychoanalytic Schools. In: *Contemporary Controversies in Psychoanalytic Theory, Techniques and Their Applications.* New Haven, CT: Yale University Press: 18, 285–303.

Leuzinger-Bohleber, M. & Stuhr, U. (Eds.) (1997). *Psychoanalysen important Rückblick. Methoden, Ergebnisse und Perspektiven der neueren Katamneseforschung.* Giessen, Germany: Psychosozial-Verlag.

Luborsky, L. & Crits-Christoph, P. (1990). *The Core Conflictual Relationship Theme Method.* (2nd Ed.) Washington, DC: American Psychological Association Press.

Mergenthaler, E. (1996). Emotion–Abstraction Patterns in Verbatim Protocols: A New Way of Describing Therapeutic Processes. *Journal of Consulting and Clinical Psychology*, 64, 1306–1318.

Mitscherlich, A. (1963). *Aufdem Weg Zur Vaterlosen Gesellschaft: Ideen Zur Sozial-Psychologie*. Munich: R. Piper.

Moscovici, S. (1981). *L'Age des foules*. Paris: Librairie Arthème Fayard.

Panksepp, J. (1998). *Affective Neuroscience: The Foundations of Human and Animal Emotions*. New York: Oxford University Press.

Sandell, R., Schubert, J., Blomberg, J., Carlsson, J., Lazar, A. & Broberg, J. (1997). *The Influence of Therapist Factors on Outcomes of Psychotherapy and Psychoanalysis in the Stockholm Outcome of Psychotherapy and Psychoanalysis Project* (STOPPP). Paper presented at the Annual Meeting of the Society for Psychotherapy Research, Geilo, Norway.

Stephane, A. (1969). *L'Univers contestationnaire*. Paris: Petite Bibliothèque.

Stern, D.N. (2000). The Relevance of Empirical Infant Research to Psychoanalytic Theory and Practice. In: *Clinical and Observational Psychoanalytic Research: Roots of a Controversy*, Eds. Sandler, J., Sandler, A.M. & Davies, R. Madison, CT: International Universities Press, 5: 73–90.

Volkan, V. (2004). *Blind Trust: Large Groups and Their Leaders in Times of Crisis and Terror*. Charlottesville, VA: Pitchstone Publishing.

Wallerstein, R.S. (1986). *Forty-Two Lives in Treatment: A Study of Psychoanalysis and Psychotherapy*. New York: Guilford Press.

Weber, J., Bachrach, H. & Solomon, M. (1985a). Factors Associated with the Outcome of Psychoanalysis: Report on the Columbia Psychoanalytic Center Research Project (II). *International Review of Psychoanalysis*, 12: 127–141.

———— (1985b). Factors Associated with the Outcome of Psychoanalysis: Report on the Columbia Psychoanalytic Center Research Project (III). *International Review of Psychoanalysis*, 12: 251–262.

Weiss, J. & Sampson, H. (1986). *The Psychoanalytic Process: Theory, Clinical Observations and Empirical Research*. New York: Guilford Press.

# 7

# PSYCHOANALYTIC SUPERVISION

## The supervisor's tasks[1]

### The tasks of the psychoanalytic supervisor

A review of the literature on supervision in psychoanalytic psychotherapy and psychoanalysis indicates that the major emphasis is on what the supervisee needs to learn, how this learning can be achieved and evaluated, and what problems the supervisee needs to face and resolve in order to achieve competency as a therapist (Arlow, 1963; Blomfield, 1985; Greenberg, 1997; Junkers, Tuckett & Zachrisson, 2008; Martindale *et al.*, 1997; Target, 2002; Wallerstein, 1981). In what follows, I would like to focus on the tasks of the supervisor, what should be expected of him or her, and the difficulties one finds with supervisors rather than supervisees. Jacobs, David, and Meyer (1995) included this focus on the supervisor in their broad, systematic approach to supervision across the spectrum of psychoanalytically oriented treatments. Here I wish to focus particularly on the specific tasks of the supervisor of psychoanalytic candidates.

Tuckett (2005) and Szecsödy (2008) have contributed significantly to a review of the criteria involved in evaluating a candidate's psychoanalytic competence. It is generally agreed that a supervisor's responsibilities are to transmit to the supervisee knowledge of the application of psychoanalytic theory to psychoanalytic technique, with particular reference to the skills required to carry out the technical requirements of the supervised case. It is commonly accepted that a collegial attitude should be stimulated and maintained, with the avoidance of an authoritarian ambiance that conveys a supervisor's sense of seniority or superiority to the supervisee.

The simultaneous function of teaching and evaluating the candidate requires, of course, an honest assessment of the supervisee's work. Some supervisors find it difficult to combine teaching within a collegial atmosphere while critically evaluating the candidate, and yet that is an essential task of supervision (Junkers, Tuckett & Zachrisson, 2008). This dilemma is sometimes masked behind the façade of an analytic attitude, whereby the supervisor communicates relatively little to the supervisee, expecting him to guess the supervisor's views through carefully formulated hints. That, of course, runs counter to the mutual sharing of experience implied in a collegial attitude in which both participants learn in the process of supervision.

Beyond these commonly accepted tasks, I wish to stress the importance of an integrated view, on the part of the supervisor, of the field to be explored, communicated, and shared, so that the supervisor's concrete recommendations about technical interventions should be embedded in and reflect the application of his or her particular theory of technique. Some might argue, however, that an integrated theory of technique militates against free-floating attention and an intuitive response to the immediate situation that would capture the communication of unconscious meaning from patient to supervisee, from supervisee to supervisor, and from the supervisor to both supervisee and patient in terms of his or her countertransference reaction.

Nevertheless, I propose that there is no reason why such an intuitive process that absorbs, one might say, the total relationship of patient/supervisee and supervisee/supervisor could not be incorporated into a more general frame of reference that would permit the supervisor to transform an intuition into an interpretive remark. Such an implicit frame of reference, of course, is unavoidable as part of the selective focus of what the supervisor sees as essential at any point. The "selected fact" depends not only on immediate intuitive capture of the analytic situation, but also on the particular theory that orients the focus of the analyst's intention.

One can recognize psychoanalysts with different theoretical formulations in their apparently intuitive reaction to a supervisee's material. Intuition is a form of rapid processing of unconscious and preconscious components from within the theoretical frame of reference in which the supervising analyst has been trained. It might be argued that many supervisors have not formulated such an integrated view that underlies their own interventions, and some may even be reluctant to clarify such a view for themselves. My argument is that this formulation should become an ongoing task for the supervisor; carrying out such a task may become an important contribution to the supervisory process.

For example, a candidate whom I supervised presented a session with a narcissistic patient who had severe difficulties in his relationships with women, who were never good enough for him. In the first part of the session, the patient had criticized his girlfriend for her neglectful attitude toward her apartment, and what he considered her exploitiveness of him. Then he had talked in a desultory tone about a visit to a friend's house. His friend, he said, was happily married to a stupid woman and enjoyed a rather poorly paid job, but seemed happy with his lot. The patient then described his serious doubts about continuing the relationship with his girlfriend.

My supervisee had interpreted the patient's suspicious attitude about his girlfriend as a projection onto her of his own exploitive feelings, and the devaluation of his friend's life situation as a defense against the patient's envy of the friend's capacity for a satisfactory life and love experience. And the patient had listened to these interpretations with his habitual signaling of acceptance of them, but without any further emotional elaboration of this material. To my supervisee, it seemed an empty session.

I explored with my supervisee his sense of the session's emptiness, as well as the patient's conveying both apparent interest in the interpretation and a lack of emotional reaction to it, and then I suggested that the patient had enacted his defenses against unconscious envy of the analyst in the transference. The unconscious aspects of the conflict with his girlfriend were being enacted in the transference. The patient had been "learning" the meaning of his associations, rather than using the analyst's comments as a stimulus for his own associative processes. I used this session to go beyond the concrete analysis of feelings of emptiness in the countertransference to the analysis of the patient's mechanism of intellectualization and "cognitive learning" as an "appropriation," in replacement of an authentic dependency on the analyst. To this narcissistic patient, dependency on the analyst meant to accept needing him, to accept the analyst's freedom to work, and to establish a trusting relationship, all of which would cause profound and, so far, probably intolerable envy to the patient.

From here, we went into a more general discussion of the importance of conflicts around unconscious envy in narcissistic pathology and its impact on transference developments. This supervisory instance illustrates, I believe, the shift from a concrete exploration of the immediate situation to the more general theory of technique on which a concrete interpretation would be based.

From the viewpoint of the supervisor's task, such an integrated frame of reference is not to be rigidly "superimposed" on his or her intuitive reaction to the material, but consciously elaborated and formulated in the supervisor's mind so that it can be called upon to "explain" the reasons for the recommended intervention that, at first, seemed to be based on pure intuition. This integrated frame of reference requires knowledge and intellectual discipline, matched by an internal freedom for intuitive reaction to the material and its unconscious implications. Learning about the theory of technique that constitutes the organizing integration of the supervisor's intuitive listening and clinical formulations permits the supervisee to learn not only how to deal with a concrete situation, but also about the supervisor's way of thinking, the internal frame of reference from which he or she operates. This facilitates understanding not only of how to intervene in the concrete situation, but also of how to generalize that learning into a gradually expanding, integrated technical framework.

This viewpoint is critical of a not-too-infrequent situation in which the supervisor provides the candidate with wise comments or suggestions that seem to come from a position of profound understanding, without leading to the candidate's possibility of tracing such wisdom back to a general theoretical orientation from within which the concrete formulation would make eminent sense (although that theory might permit other interventions as well).

The supervisor's responsibility to articulate to the candidate his or her particular theory of technique may carry the risk, however, that the supervisor will end up presenting his position as "the only acceptable" one, or that, at any rate, the supervisee will reach such a conclusion, particularly if the supervisor's theory of technique corresponds to the dominant one at that training institute. The supervisor, while spelling out his or her personal views, should also keep in mind a responsibility to alert the supervisee of alternative ways of conceptualizing the issue under consideration, and related, alternative ways to intervene technically. In addition, the goal of stimulating the supervisee to explain his or her own ideas about how interpretations have functioned to move the analytic process forward should reinforce the supervisor's efforts to counter the authoritarian implication of imposing a particular theory of technique.

The supervisor's responsibility to articulate a clear, integrated theoretical foundation of his or her own requires active, ongoing work. It is a creative burden that forces the supervisor to critically review all interventions and recommendations made to the candidate, and to rework his or her theory of technique throughout time. I believe that the supervisor may be expected to grow and to continue developing a working understanding of psychoanalytic and psychotherapeutic techniques as supervisees present the infinite novelty of clinical situations that evolve in interactions between patient and candidate and between candidate and supervisor.

Related to this requirement is the importance of the supervisor's sharing with the candidate how the supervisor him- or herself would respond to the specific clinical situation being interpreted. While focusing on what the supervisor recommends that the supervisee do, the supervisor might often state what he or she would be thinking and doing under those same concrete circumstances.

## Institutional agendas

Supervision takes place, usually, in the context of an organizational institution, be it a psychoanalytic institute, a university outpatient department, a private or public mental health clinic, or a hospital setting, all of which have their own structural characteristics, institutional biases, and realistic expectations of learning on the part of the supervisee, as well as other, "hidden" agendas. Hidden agendas usually relate to problems around authority within the institution, legal or financial requirements that determine the boundaries of tolerance of atypical treatment situations and risk aversion, and/or idiosyncratic rules and regulations of individual supervisors. It might be trivial to refer to this fact were it not that these agendas may powerfully influence the supervisory process—determining, for example, a treatment approach that might be less than optimal, because what would be optimal would run counter to the institution's financial and/or political constraints, or implicitly activate ideological struggles within it.

For example, if a psychoanalytic institute has a predominantly ego psychological approach, but a supervisee is particularly interested in applying a self-psychology approach to a patient, the supervisor might support this, or not, according to the flexibility provided in the teaching programs of that institute and the supervisor's degree of willingness to depart from his or her own theoretical beliefs. The practical implication of this issue is that a parallel process evolves, not only in terms of the supervisee's unconscious enactment of a role reversal of experienced but not understood problems in his or her relationship with the patient, but also in the sense that the same process may be activated by the supervisor's subjectively experienced, unresolved conflicts with the institution in which the supervision takes place. In the latter situation, the supervisor enacts the conflict with the institution in a corresponding role reversal with the supervisee.

An example of this type of parallel process was seen in the case of a Kleinian–oriented psychoanalytic institute in which an intersubjective/relational approach had been adopted by a significant group of "rebellious" faculty members. A hostile interaction developed between one of the Kleinian supervisors and a supervisee who was interested in the intersubjective/relational approach, so that the institutional dynamic was replayed in the individual supervisory relationship.

The phenomenon of parallel process illustrates, better than anything else, the activation of unconscious relations in the supervisory process (Baudry, 1993). Unconscious countertransference reactions of the supervisee, usually related to an unconsciously registered but not consciously elaborated aspect of the patient's transference, are enacted in the supervisory situation. Such reactions are then "discharged" with a role reversal in which the supervisee unconsciously identifies with that aspect of the patient, while projecting the corresponding countertransference reaction onto the supervisor. The supervisor's alertness to this development, on the basis of the diagnosis of a specific distortion in the supervisory relationship, may help clarify the meaning of this transference–countertransference bind; but this process demands an open, honest, collegial relationship.

I believe it is very helpful for the supervisor, aware of institutional conflicts that may be affecting his or her subjective attitude toward the supervisee, to bring this out in the open. At the same time, the supervisor should feel free to point out the parallel process in the supervisor–supervisee relationship as possibly influenced by an unrecognized or unresolved countertransference problem in the supervisee's relationship with the patient.

In a group supervision at a Kleinian-oriented psychoanalytic institute, a candidate presented a case to me by starting with a recent session. He provided a minimum of preliminary information about the patient's earliest life experiences and went on to read his summary of the session. I interrupted him to say that I was interested in the patient's present difficulties, and, particularly, in a brief summary of the patient's present problems in the areas of sexual love, work, or social life. The group reacted quite strongly in reminding me of the recommendation to analyze "without memory or desire." I acknowledged their reaction and expressed my admiration of Bion (1967), but also pointed to some differences in my approach, and wondered whether we could work together in sharing both similar and dissimilar ways of reacting to the material of the session. The tension in the group decreased noticeably, and I believe we were able to learn from each other; I had the opportunity to illustrate my view about the potential relationship between presently dominant life conflicts and the predominant transference development.

Such an open exchange in the supervisory process may bring about an honesty that reduces the highly prevalent paranoid fears of the supervisee, particularly in authoritarian organizations, and in turn fosters honesty of communication regarding the psychotherapeutic or psychoanalytic process, and facilitates countertransference analysis of the supervisee in a non-threatening, non-intrusive way.

## Countertransference exploration

In this connection, the exploration of the supervisee's countertransference is an important yet delicate aspect of the supervisory process. I believe that it is very important to generate a collegial atmosphere in which the supervisee may feel free to openly explore his or her countertransference reactions, including those to the supervisory process of that particular patient. The supervisor may use countertransference analysis to explore aspects of the nature of the patient's transference that may have impacted the supervisee's subjective experience, but have not been fully understood and elaborated by the supervisee.

The analysis of how the patient contributes to the countertransference reaction of the supervisee is what is important here, while maintaining a tactful respect for the boundaries of privacy regarding deeper aspects of the supervisee's conflicts that may have been activated in the supervisory situation. Supervision should not become a psychotherapeutic process; conflating the two usually leads to regression in the supervision, tends to blur the clarity of the supervisory process, and may interfere with the collegial aspects of the relationship. It may also foster transference displacement and acting out by a supervisee in relation to his or her personal psychoanalysis.

For example, I supervised a candidate for the treatment of a severely narcissistic patient who presented unstable object relations, sexual promiscuity, and an unconsciously envious and derogatory behavior toward women. After telling me that her patient had expressed sexual fantasies about her in a clearly seductive way, the candidate—a highly intelligent woman who was usually secure and open—told me that this had made her feel very insecure, and in fact she had difficulty dealing with the patient. We explored this further, and she finally said: "I have to confess that if I met this man one evening in a bar without any prior knowledge of him, I would be tempted to go to bed with him."

I commented that she was making it clear he was attractive to her as a man, but what was it in him that made her afraid of him? This led us into a discussion of the controlling aspects of his seductive behavior: his implicit attempt to undermine her authority as an analyst and to transform her into his image of a desirable and unavailable woman whom he would be tempted to "conquer," which was his usual behavior pattern—unconsciously motivated by envy and hatred of women, whom he perceived as teasing him. I expressed appreciation of the candidate's capacity to talk honestly about her feelings with me, but focused on the meaning of the patient's induction of those feelings, and I respected the candidate's privacy regarding the particular unconscious tendencies that might have made her feel particularly attracted to this man.

Some degree of idealization of the supervisor on the part of the supervisee is probably unavoidable under conditions of a good supervisory experience, particularly if the supervisee is simultaneously experiencing regressive reactions in a psychoanalytic treatment. The supervisor needs to keep in mind that, in all interpersonal situations in which there is a role distribution between one who "knows" and one who "needs to know," an implicit deskilling of the latter may occur, with the consequent attribution of all knowledge and skills to the supervisor and a self-devaluation of the supervisee. Efforts to maintain a collegial attitude through direct, open, "non-oracular" communication of the supervisor's knowledge and experience may modify the idealization into a creative, warm professional relationship, in contrast to an idealized one that fixates the supervisee's conviction that the supervisor will always know better and will always be superior, and a permanent hierarchy will remain in their relationship.

Such a negative fixation at an idealizing level is not infrequent, particularly in institutions with highly prestigious, powerful, and even guru-like figures, whose own narcissistic needs may foster a tendency to surround themselves with admiring students. The encouragement of mutual or peer supervision by groups of trainees who already have some years of experience is one helpful countermeasure; in the process of "intervision," in contrast to "supervision," trainees may become aware of possessing more understanding and skills than they have been conscious of in supervisions with revered elders.

## The dynamics of group supervision

This leads me to the process of group supervision, which may be very helpful in integrating the developing experience and knowledge of supervisees, while also providing them with a more realistic awareness of the limitations of the supervisor's knowledge. In a group situation, there is an opportunity to examine the clinical aspects of a case from many different perspectives, thereby providing a richness and diversity of understanding that does not privilege any one line of thought over another.

It is helpful for the supervisor to acquire a knowledge of group dynamics, which will permit him or her to utilize the supervisory group situation itself as a teaching instrument. I am referring here to the role distribution that automatically occurs in groups as an expression of the parallel process characteristic of the individual supervisory relationship. In practice, an unresolved transference–countertransference fixation in a case presented to the group may elicit a range of responses in the group—responses that correspond to conflictual or split-off aspects of transference and countertransference in that case. Joint analysis by the supervisor of these different reactions to the material may provide an in-depth analysis of the dominant transference–countertransference situation that the presenter "discharges" in the group, without being fully aware of the issues that he or she is implicitly communicating.

Naturally, this process tends to be obscured when the supervisor acts as though he or she were the only source of knowledge regarding the problems presented in the case under review. In fact, such an assertion of the "last word" by the supervisor may inhibit communications in the group and, therefore, the learning process itself.

An interesting expression of institutional dynamics occurs when the members of a supervision group each have individual supervisors of the cases that they present to the group. (The same dynamics are also present in continuous case seminars in a psychoanalytic institute in which only one candidate presents a case in treatment—as long as that candidate's individual supervisor is not also the group leader.) Under these circumstances, significant differences in the approaches of the individual supervisor and the group supervisor may rapidly emerge to challenge the candidate—and the group supervisor—in many ways. Rivalries between the two supervisors may implicitly color group interactions, and the trainees' shared anxieties over these discrepant views may emerge either timidly or openly. This is an excellent opportunity to point out that to be exposed to different viewpoints has an enormous educational advantage, in that it forces the student to consider alternative frames of reference, compare them, and develop his or her own synthesis.

I supervised a candidate who presented a patient with a marked hysterical personality disorder and strong masochistic features, both in her relationship with her husband and in the transference. I helped the candidate see the patient's chronic fights with her husband as the unconscious expression of profound oedipal guilt and related submission to a dominant but also deeply frustrated mother, whose own marriage had been a very unhappy one. At one point, the supervisee presented the patient to a group supervision conducted by another training analyst at my institute. After a few weeks it became clear that, in that group, the patient's marital conflicts were seen as expressing the profound frustration of her oral-dependent needs in her relationship with her mother, now reenacted in her relationship with her husband.

The candidate was tense and troubled: she told me that the group supervisor had questioned her interpretive approach, and that much of what was being suggested in the group supervision made sense to her. My countertransference reaction included a sense of irritation with the candidate, a sense of competition with the group leader, and, as I also recognized, a complex condensation of my oedipal rivalry with the group leader with the candidate's enactment of her patient's masochistic pattern with me. And, at a different level, I was frustrating the candidate's dependency wishes on me. . . .

I decided to share with the candidate these interpretations of the institutional situation and their relevance to the understanding of her patient's transference situation. I invited her to elaborate this situation in her own mind while feeling free to discuss all of it with me, and to reach her own conclusions in further exploring her experience with the patient. I said that I felt "a lot of competition was in the air." Her presentation to the group, I noted, at first brought about a potential competition between her view identified with mine, and that of the group supervisor. Then she felt identified with the group supervisor and in competition with my view.

One might say that—leaving the objective analysis of the patient's treatment situation open—the candidate had been afraid to oppose the group supervisor, subordinated her view to his, and now was afraid of disagreeing with me, asking for my help in dealing with this situation. In fact, I added, I too had felt in myself a sense of competition with the group supervisor, and a slight sense of corresponding irritation with her (my supervisee). The situation could also reflect an institutional discussion, I commented, around the relative importance of oedipal and pre-oedipal conflicts. I thus replicated in my countertransference the same activation of feelings of the "danger of aggression" in this competitive situation, and I was running the risk of threatening the supervisee's helpful dependent relationship with me.

I wondered whether, if I was right, this entire situation might unconsciously repeat the transference–countertransference situation: the patient's inducing in the candidate-analyst a wish to respond positively to the patient's demand for understanding and help in dealing with her "impossible" husband, while the analyst was struggling with confronting the patient with her provocative behavior toward her husband out of unconscious guilt over the "forbidden" sexual relationship with him.

My intervention, I believe, calmed the supervisee and opened the road to further exploration of her understanding and management of the treatment situation. She thoughtfully reflected on her internal conflict between her wish to assure the patient of her empathic understanding, and what she saw as a need to confront the patient about generating unwarranted fights with her husband, as though to maintain a good mother–daughter relationship at the cost of the marital one.

In fact, as has been pointed out by various authors (Galatzer-Levy, 2004; Levin, 2006; Shane & Shane, 1995), the exposure of trainees to

117

alternative viewpoints in the context of a non–authoritarian institution fosters the learning process as well as professional maturation. It may be argued that, to the contrary, exposure to such contradictory views may lead to chaos and confusion; this may be true, particularly when there is no forum in which different viewpoints can be aired and compared, and instruments provided to the students with which to arrive at their own synthesis. Psychoanalytic institutes today may be facing a major challenge in determining what basic "common theory of technique" may be available to provide a solid ground for students that will permit them to reach educated decisions regarding alternative approaches.

One test of the extent to which a trainee has achieved a reasonable ability to internally evaluate different viewpoints is to assess the trainee's ability to develop an integrated frame of reference for his or her own technical understanding and approaches. The trainee's understanding and approaches should not rely on a chaotic, eclectic mixture of different approaches in different situations that do not give evidence of a common, integrative framework as the basis for which a move into alternative techniques can be justified.

## Professional responsibility

An important issue that is often not fully clarified is the question of who carries the responsibility for the patient. The ideal situation between supervisor and supervisee is one in which both parties are clear that the supervisee ultimately carries this responsibility. The supervisor has the freedom to recommend a way of handling a situation, while the supervisee has the freedom to accept or reject that recommendation, using his or her own judgment, with awareness that the ultimate professional, legal, and personal responsibility for the patient rests with the supervisee.

In many educational institutions, however, the ultimate responsibility may lie with the institution, particularly from a legal standpoint, and this then limits the degree of freedom that both parties have in relation to the treatment approach. When the supervisor, in representing the educational institution within which he or she supervises, carries the responsibility for the well-being of the patient, his or her responsibility to the patient, the supervisee, and the institution must all be carefully weighed. In most cases, this does not impinge on the supervisory process; but when there are serious problems in the functioning of a supervisee, or "impossible" clinical cases that create high-risk complications for the institution, the distribution of these responsibilities must be spelled out clearly and openly, with the understanding that the supervisee, under certain circumstances, may have to comply with the supervisor's instructions.

The extent to which this is a problem naturally depends on the particular ideological and legal culture in which the educational institution operates. In the United States, with its highly litigious culture, this issue becomes very important with problematic cases. My main point here is that the extent to which responsibility for the patient rests in one or another professional, or is shared by them and an institution, should be clearly communicated.

A psychoanalytic candidate treated a patient with a severe personality disorder in analysis as part of his practice within a university hospital. At one point, the patient became acutely suicidal. It seemed to me, the supervisor, that this suicidal tendency was not linked to a depressive reaction, but was part of a characterological pattern that needed to be analyzed rather than treated with a preventive hospitalization. However, I was concerned about who was responsible for making that decision. I could have documented the reasons for my recommended approach, but the patient was not my patient. The candidate was part of an institutional system—the hospital—that had a very conservative view of such situations.

After clarifying the various responsibilities involved, the supervisee and I decided that he would consult with his administrative supervisor in the hospital on this case. The supervisee would then make the decision about the strategy to follow in the light of that consultation. I committed myself to helping him regardless of his course of action.

This leads to the issue of limitations in the candidate's professional functioning, and the responsibility of the supervisor in circumstances where this is problematic. The supervisor's honesty is essential with trainees who, for a variety of reasons, are not able to achieve the minimal level of skills required. Situations in which a supervisor internally gives up on a supervisee—without honest and courageous communication about it, directly to the supervisee—are not infrequent. The supervisor has a responsibility to the institution and the profession, as well as to the supervisee and the patient. Following are examples of cases in which such painful moments of truth emerge.

119

## Candidates' psychopathology

First, there is a great reluctance to acknowledge the possibility that—particularly at advanced stages of psychological and/or medical training—a supervisee who has been able to reach the point of specialization in psychotherapy or psychoanalysis may not have the intellectual capacities to carry out such work. It is, of course, difficult to differentiate a lack of emotional introspection or awareness of the depth of human feelings as an expression of character pathology from cognitive factors per se, and the supervisor, without the availability of psychological testing or alternative sources of information, may not be in a position to make this differential diagnosis. The usual assumption is that the supervisee is emotionally incapable of achieving adequate competency. The safest way to reach such a conclusion, of course, is to provide the supervisee with ample opportunities to learn in the supervisory sessions, patiently repeating the same information while evaluating to what extent a learning process is taking place.

The supervisor is responsible for remaining alert to what happens to his or her contributions: to what extent they function as seeds planted that grow and flourish, or, conversely, whether they resemble young plants that perish in the desert. Individual supervisors may disagree on the length of time that is reasonable for a supervisee to begin to demonstrate certain core competencies, but there comes a point when a failure to learn may have to be addressed. When it becomes evident that repeated clarifications in the supervisory situation do not bring about change, and that the same problems emerge again and again, this should, of course, be shared openly with the supervisee.

The following case was one of the most painful experiences in my functioning as a supervising analyst. The candidate had been able to obtain a full education in medicine and psychiatry, helped to achieve this goal, it must be said, by the efforts of a particular agency, throughout her life. She was a warm, responsible, engaging person who was received with open arms at an international institution that was particularly interested in fostering the higher education of members of a minority group, including psychoanalytic training.

I was one of three visiting supervising analysts (from a different country) at the international institution that supervised the candidate's work, and my impression from her interaction with me was

120

that she was not capable of achieving further learning. Although she had had almost two years of supervision, I felt that I had to repeat the same suggestions over and over again, and that, while she almost desperately tried to use what I had said in the following sessions with her patient, no long-term traces of our discussions were evident. I spoke with her openly about the situation, more and more frequently as time went on, and she was straightforward in conveying her difficulty in transferring general principles from one situation to another.

I could not identify any major characterological difficulties in the candidate, and after a time, I consulted with two other supervisors about her situation. All three of us had exactly the same experience: we all wanted to help her but could not. We studied her past records and discovered that she had had significant learning difficulties all along, and was able to reach this advanced stage of her professional career only through extremely hard and consistent work. She had a fine memory, which had helped her through all her educational experiences, including medical school. Our conclusion was that she had some kind of cognitive limitation or impairment, and, finally, we recommended a shift in her career direction, as well as a neuropsychological examination if she were interested, and we suggested a suspension of her psychoanalytic training at that institution.

A frequently encountered situation that may lend itself to confusion with the previous one is the case of a candidate with significant narcissistic pathology who, although eager to learn whatever new knowledge is offered, soon becomes convinced that he or she has absorbed it all and that there is nothing new the supervisor can offer. This type of supervisee tends to show an excessive degree of idealization at the beginning, followed by subtle devaluation of what he or she has received. Such trainees seem to absorb what the supervisor offers as simple or clever formulas that are useful only as such, but lack the capacity to authentically expand the supervisee's own elaboration and development of the material.

Sometimes severe narcissistic pathology manifests in the form of an excessive enthusiasm for some new, "original" development that seems to be offered by a certain supervisor, but this is followed by the trainee's disappointment or disillusionment, and then by the search for another new, magical approach with someone else, leading to surprisingly radical shifts in approaches by the candidate that, in the end, reveal a superficial acquisition of each new theory of technique.

Supervisees with significant emotional immaturity, whose personal chaos not only distorts their capacity to listen to patients but also does not permit them to integrate new learning in a significant way, constitute another source of frustrating supervisory situations. However, the gradual resolution of conflict and personal growth achieved in the trainee's psychoanalytic or psychotherapeutic treatment may improve the supervisory experience significantly.

The key challenge in all limitations to learning is to determine the cause. To what extent is the supervisor, his or her attitude or approach, part of the problem? To what extent is the supervisee's personality or intelligence a significant factor?

We must acknowledge that significant psychopathology on the part of the supervisee may sometimes remain undetected even by very experienced supervisors. Simultaneous supervision of each trainee by several supervisors significantly improves the likelihood of diagnosing serious difficulties and resolving them in the educational process. Such an arrangement, of course, is not possible in the private supervision of an independent mental health professional by another one, but should be possible in institutional settings, particularly in departments of psychiatry, and even more so in psychoanalytic institutes, where the educational structure is so focused on supervision. Regular meetings of supervisors to discuss supervisees, particularly those who seem to present problems, may help clarify issues that, for the individual supervisor working alone, may take much more time to fully appreciate.

For example, I once supervised a fourth-year (!) psychiatric resident who was treating a very ill borderline patient. I found it impossible to get a clear view of this patient, in spite of the fact that the supervisee seemed very clear in what he was saying, seemed to have a good understanding, and was quite open. But the patient was getting worse by the day, with all kinds of complications emerging, in the patient's life, in the patient's relationship with the therapist, and in the therapist's relationships with other mental health personnel connected with the treatment. I was tempted to see the patient myself in order to find out what made it so difficult to get a live picture of the patient throughout the supervisory process.

I decided to discuss the situation with the supervisory group connected with this supervisee's progress. I found out that, not only did other supervisors have the same difficulties with him, but there were also very serious questions about his ethical behavior. In the middle of our discussions, this supervisee disappeared from the map, abandoning his functions as a resident without formal resignation, and had to be formally dismissed from the program.

Another fourth-year resident was invited to continue the treatment of the patient whose care I had supervised, and, after a few weeks of supervision with the new trainee, not only did I have a clear understanding of what kind of person the patient was and of the main conflicts to be explored, but all the complications in the patient's relationships with other professional staff and in the patient's life began to resolve as well. A transference–countertransference bond established with the new therapist could now be meaningfully explored in the supervisory sessions. In short, I had missed the first trainee's severely antisocial features and his capacity to convey a pseudo-mature understanding that in fact reflected consistent distortions of the information I had been receiving from him.

## Supervisory material

It is helpful for the supervisor to show flexibility in letting the supervisee choose in which form he or she wishes to present case material to the supervisor, with the agreement that, in turn, the supervisory material selected can be flexibly chosen as well, incorporating information on tactical and strategic interactions and interventions.

In this regard, it is interesting to note that studies of a brief segment of one session, of an entire session, of a sequence of sessions, and of development in the treatment over a period of weeks typically reveal the same structure; in other words, the same transference–countertransference pattern and dominant defensive operations throughout those very different time spans. The macrocosmos of the session reproduces the microcosmos of the interaction in a brief segment of it. The shift from studying segments of a session to studying what happens over weeks, and vice versa, provides a third dimension to the evaluation of the clinical material and of the trainee's learning process. Many supervisors insist on receiving no written notes, but only subjective information on the basis of brief summaries the supervisee has made for him- or herself, while other supervisors require detailed process notes of verbal interactions in their natural sequence. Again, flexibility and shifts in approach in this regard, over time, seem optimal.

Informal, verbal communication on the part of the supervisee provides rather imprecise information about the concrete therapeutic dialogue, but excellent information about the supervisee's general understanding, attitude, and parallel process. Detailed written material, drawn from written notes or audio recording during the hours, provides a more accurate reflection of the dialogue and of the therapist's interventions, but may miss some of the subtleties of emotional interactions that are communicated by means of the parallel process. Listening to audiotapes of sessions conveys more clearly the emotional interaction and gives a very full sense of what has been happening in the session, but, because of the slowness of the process of replicating the timing of development in the sessions, it is usually necessarily limited to listening to segments of a particular session.

Viewing videotapes of psychotherapy sessions provides maximum information of content and attitudes, and permits judgments regarding transference and countertransference by means of the shifting non-verbal behavior of patient and therapist. A limitation, of course, is the difficulty of building videotaping into the therapy in a natural enough way so that it does not significantly distort the therapeutic process. Videotaping also reduces evidence of the parallel process in the supervisory sessions: the supervisee is cast into a passive spectator role. However, all in all, videotaping may be the best source of information about the overall functioning of the therapist, and often there are surprisingly marked differences between what the therapist reports and what one sees on video.

Perhaps the main problem with videotaping is that, in the case of psychoanalytic treatment, most of the information is gained through the patient's verbal communication of subjective experience, with relatively little non-verbal, visually observable interaction occurring in the sessions, which makes videotaped psychoanalytic sessions extremely boring to watch, to the extent that the supervision may become a self-defeating process. In contrast, in the case of psychoanalytic psychotherapy, particularly with severely regressed patients, where intensive behavioral, face-to-face interactions between therapist and patient are registered, videotaping—in our experience at the Personality Disorders Institute at Cornell University—is by far the most effective way of facilitating the supervisory process.

In this connection, it must be recognized that the bias against videotaping psychoanalytic sessions is so strong in many psychoanalytic circles that even the exploration of this medium as a potential contribution to the supervisory process may shock some psychoanalytic colleagues. This is not the place to address this issue in the contrasting light of experiences in various research-oriented organizations that have confirmed the feasibility of psychoanalytic work under such circumstances. But I will mention that, on the basis of clinical and research experience spanning thirty years, it is clear that patients quite readily accept ongoing video recording if they have been appropriately informed and assured of the confidentiality of those recordings, and the psychotherapeutic process is remarkably little affected by such arrangements. In our experience at Cornell, therapists who are just beginning their professional careers have significant initial difficulty with video recording due to their own self-consciousness, but they, too, quickly forget that the camera is there.

## General characteristics of competence

A research finding regarding the competence of therapists carrying out psychoanalytic psychotherapy may be relevant. Although this finding applies to psychotherapy rather than psychoanalytic supervision proper, I believe it may also be relevant in the latter.

Our work at the Personality Disorders Institute at the Department of Psychiatry at the Weill Medical College of Cornell University and the Westchester Division of the New York Presbyterian Hospital has provided us with important learning regarding the overall desirable personality qualities of therapists and the development of therapeutic skills in psychoanalytic psychotherapy with severe personality disorders. In the present paper, I shall limit myself to pointing out our conclusion that four relatively easily evaluated qualities of therapeutic interventions in psychoanalytic psychotherapy define the quality of psychotherapeutic work on the part of our trainees (namely, third-year psychiatric residents and beyond, and first-year postdoctoral psychology fellows and beyond).

These four determining factors of therapeutic interventions are:

- the relevance of the therapist's comments to the dominant affective issue evolving in the session;
- the clarity with which interpretive interventions are formulated;
- the depth to which those comments penetrate into the patient's dominant conflicts, particularly the unconscious layers of defense and impulse involved in the conflicts activated in transference and countertransference; and
- the speed with which the trainee is able to carry out such interventions.

125

This last feature may seem surprising, but the dissociative nature of patients' communications in severe personality disorders, the prominent role of enactment and acting out in sessions, and the prevalence of non-verbal behavior over what is communicated verbally about the patient's subjective experience combine to bring about rapid shifts in the content of the hours. These shifts require correspondingly rapid interventions, rather than patiently waiting for the material to clarify itself over time.

When everything goes well, it should be possible, over time, for the supervisor as well as for the supervisee to construct in their minds an integrated picture of the patient's personality, including a three-dimensional awareness of the present vicissitudes of the patient's conscious and unconscious life experiences and his or her relationship to significant aspects of the past. Supervisor and supervisee should also be able to experience directly which areas that have to be approached are now affectively dominant in the sessions, and which areas of the patient's life experience are glaringly absent in the treatment situation and therefore require an active focus. Mutual learning may occur as supervisee and supervisor freely express their views and questions about the patient.

For the supervisor, seeing the supervisee's growing independence in doing good work, supported by his or her capacity to convey new information and to provide new leads to the supervisor, is a gratifying experience of knowing one has contributed to the supervisee's autonomous growth. I have found it very helpful to vary the intensity and rhythm of my contributions to the supervisory process, ranging from periods in which I might very actively try to convey information and influence the therapeutic process, to those in which I might sit back and position myself on the receiving end as I listen to what is going on with the patient, and to what new contributions the therapist may make.

Good supervision becomes an extremely interesting learning process for both participants; a supervision that is failing can be a trying experience for the supervisor, one to which he or she should not react masochistically (or sadistically!). Over time, it will become clear to what extent the trainee is developing his or her own frame of reference, integrating knowledge received from the supervisor without there being a process of "surface imitation" that is often misread as identification with the supervisor.

A senior candidate would present her case to me with general reflections about what struck her most in a particular session or over a particular period. She might reflect on alternative ways to handle the material that she presented, and she very openly expressed uncertainties or doubts. She was able, in looking back at a set of sessions over a more extended time period, to venture hypotheses about where the analysis was going, or in what way she was changing her view about a particular development.

I had the growing feeling during that supervision that an experienced colleague was presenting a case to me. Not infrequently, I was surprised and stimulated by the originality of her interventions. I was learning in the process, and I told her so. Not surprisingly, she wrote a series of papers on the technical issues this case presented, making an original contribution to our field.

Körner (2002) defined the objectives of psychoanalytic education as the development of candidates' knowledge, technical skills, and analytic attitude. All three can be observed over time in the course of the supervisory process, and they facilitate a realistic evaluation of that process—an evaluation that, as mentioned earlier, must be shared fully and openly with the candidate, and the supervisor must remain open to the candidate's reactions to the supervisor's views. The supervisor's self-reflective function may be shared with the supervisee to an increasing degree over time, so that the supervisor's speculations, uncertainties, and possible alternative formulations regarding the patient can be made available in more direct and open ways, facilitating the supervisee's identification with the supervisor's self-reflective attitude. Transmission of this attitude, in turn, broadens and deepens the supervisor's pleasure in the supervisory process.

Last but not least, the supervisor may convey to the candidate the need to be very patient in tolerating the repetition of severe problems again and again, and the same transference developments over time, without losing patience, while maintaining an attitude of alertness and therapeutic "impatience" in every session. And of course, this also holds true for the supervisory process: there is a need to be patient over time, but also to attempt to maximally utilize every supervisory hour, while remaining alert to the defensive operations and obstacles that may block that process.

## Note

1 Published in the *Psychoanalytic Quarterly Volume* LXXIX, Number 3, 2010.

## References

Arlow, J.A. (1963). The Supervisory Situation. *J. Amer. Psychoanal. Assn.*, 11: 576–594.

Baudry, F.D. (1993). The Personal Dimension and Management of the Supervisory Situation, with a Special Note on the Parallel Process. *Psychoanal. Q.*, 62: 588–614.

Bion, W.R. (1967). Notes on Memory and Desire. *Psychoanal. Forum*, 2: 271–280.

Blomfield, O. (1985). Psychoanalytic Supervision: An Overview. *Int. Rev. Psychoanal.*, 12: 401–409.

Galatzer-Levy, R. (2004). Chaotic possibilities: Toward a New Model of Development. *Int. J. Psychoanal.*, 85: 419–441.

Greenberg, L. (1997). On Transference and Countertransference and the Technique of Supervision. In *Supervision and Its Vicissitudes*, ed. B. Martindale, M. Mörner, M.E.C. Rodriguez & J.-P. Vidit. London: Karnac, 1–24.

Jacobs, D., David, P. & Meyer, D.J. (1995). *The Supervisory Encounter: A Guide for Teachers of Psychodynamic Psychotherapy and Psychoanalysis*. New Haven, CT: Yale University Press.

Junkers, G., Tuckett, D. & Zachrisson, A. (2008). To Be or Not To Be a Psychoanalyst: How Do We Know a Candidate Is Ready to Qualify? Difficulties and Controversies in Evaluating Psychoanalytic Competence. *Psychoanal. Inquiry*, 28: 288–308.

Körner, J. (2002). The Didactics of Psychoanalytic Education. *Int. J. Psychoanal.*, 83: 1395–1405.

Levin, C.B. (2006). That's not Analytic: Theory Pressure and "Chaotic Possibilities" in Analytic Training. *Psychoanal. Inquiry* 26, 5: 767–783.

Martindale, B., Mörner, M., Rodriguez, M.E.C. & Vidit, J.-P., eds. (1997). *Supervision and Its Vicissitudes*. London: Karnac.

Shane, M. & Shane, E. (1995). Un-American Activities and Other Dilemmas Experienced in the Supervision of Candidates. *Psychoanal. Inquiry*, 15: 226–239.

Szecsödy, I. (2008). Does Anything Go in Psychoanalytic Supervision? *Psychoanal. Inquiry*, 28: 373–386.

Target, M. (2002). Psychoanalytic Models of Supervision: Issues and Ideas. Paper presented at the Training Analysts' Colloquium of the European Psychoanalytic Federation in Budapest, Hungary, November.

Tuckett, D. (2005). Does Anything Go? Towards a Framework for a More Transparent Assessment of Psychoanalytic Competence. *Int. J. Psychoanal.*, 86: 31–49.

Wallerstein, R.S., ed. (1981). *Becoming a Psychoanalyst: A Study of Psychoanalytic Supervision*. New York: Int. University Press.

# 8

# SYMPTOMS OF FAILURE AND EARLY EFFORTS TO MODIFY PSYCHOANALYTIC EDUCATION[1]

## The Eitingon and the French model: an overview

### Introduction

Psychoanalysis is currently under powerful attack within our culture, and within the university, particularly from the viewpoints of a strong biologically oriented psychiatry and a cognitive/behaviorally oriented clinical psychology. Governmental and health delivery systems are questioning the efficacy and cost-effectiveness of psychoanalytic treatment. In some countries, the external demands for research-based evidence regarding the efficacy of psychotherapy and our own concerns as to whether we possess research methods appropriate to the study of psychoanalysis have brought about intense controversies and soul searching in our midst. Questions as to the applicability of psychoanalytic concepts and techniques to psychotherapy and the competition of other psychotherapeutic models with psychoanalytic approaches have combined to raise basic conceptual, clinical, educational and political questions.

In this context, an issue emerges that has not received sufficient attention. I am referring to the responsibility of psychoanalytic institutes to go beyond transmitting psychoanalytic knowledge and methodology to new generations of candidates, and take a major initiative in fostering development of new knowledge about analysis while strengthening the relationship between psychoanalysis and our academic, intellectual, and cultural environment. The role and functions of psychoanalytic societies, of course, are also intimately involved in these questions and these tasks. Thus the scientific activities of psychoanalytic societies must be integrated with those of their institutes if we are to maximize the impact of psychoanalytic thinking upon the surrounding cultural and social environment. That environment's interest can be aroused and sustained if psychoanalytic institutes maintain an exciting ambiance of scientific discourse, ongoing systematic development of knowledge, and the collegial collaboration of institute faculty with creative candidates so as to invigorate the scientific and professional presence of the psychoanalytic endeavor. Finally, we must acknowledge that analysts become passionate defenders of the system in which they were trained, and sometimes passionate detractors of other systems. Perhaps this paper can serve to facilitate a more dispassionate scrutiny of the assets and liabilities of different systems of analytic training and thus facilitate modifications in the direction of improving the ambiance and effectiveness of analytic training everywhere, whatever the dominant system may be in any particular locale.

## The traditional Eitingon model

From this viewpoint, I believe, a concerned critique of psycho-analytic education is warranted. Our educational methodology has actually changed very little since the inauguration of the Eitingon (1923) model in the years 1920 to 1926, at the Berlin Psychoanalytic Institute, which established the tripartite model of (1) training analysis, (2) supervision of control cases, and (3) theoretical and clinical seminars that still prevails in most institutes worldwide. While fundamental shifts in educational methodology have taken place in the academic world surrounding us, a cautious conservatism has dominated psychoanalytic education. Spurred by dissatisfaction with the Eitingon model, the French system of psychoanalytic education underwent fundamental changes thirty years ago. But the International Psychoanalytic Association (IPA) maintained an official stance of benign tolerance rather than undertaking the systematic, unbiased analysis of the advantages and disadvantages of the two major models as would seem indicated. This essay is intended as a prologue to such an investigation.

It has clearly been an enormous advantage for the IPA to have developed a standard, relatively uniform model of psychoanalytic education (that is, the Eitingon model) throughout all the regions of the psychoanalytic community, thus preserving the unity of the scientific field of psychoanalysis. But the disadvantages of standardization seem to have become more prominent as such stability of training has been effectively achieved; the time for re-examination of our educational methods seems to have arrived.

What follows is an effort to focus on the major problems of psychoanalytic education as they have evolved in the context of relative uniformity and stability over the past sixty-five years. While Eitingon's tripartite model has guaranteed the thoroughness of psychoanalytic education and provided a proven, time tested method for maintaining minimal common standards, the shortcomings of this model deserve further attention, particularly, in view of the urgency of the challenges from our external social and intellectual milieu.

What have been the major shortcomings of the classical Eitingon model? Regarding the *training analysis*, the training analysts were originally meant to be selected as the elite of psychoanalytic practitioners to whom the analysis of candidates could be entrusted. It is by now quite evident that the role of the training analyst has gradually been incorporated into an organizational status system as part of an oligarchic administrative structure that controls psychoanalytic institutes and contributes to their authoritarian atmosphere. That authoritarian atmosphere has often been actualized in a monolithic theoretical orientation determined by the leading training analysts of the respective institutes, the inordinate influence of controlling political groups in determining who would have the right to teach, and the creation of an institutional arrogance that antagonized many professionals in the boundary disciplines from which candidates potentially emerge. The result has been an active isolation, throughout the world, of self-contained psychoanalytic institutes from their academic university and cultural environments. The selection of training analysts (like that of society members) as part of the ruling elite has often been a secretive, political process, geared to protect and strengthen a group in power as much as to assure a high quality of professional performance in providing an optimal personal analysis for candidates. In some cases oligarchy became a gerontocracy of training analysts, and fostered the politicization of the educational process in the sense that competing groups of training analysts tried to reinforce their lines by selective appointments to institute faculty.

Training analyst status also confers economic advantage, by assuring a source of analytic cases, a significant consideration in geographical areas where such cases would otherwise be scarce. A major problem of the training analysis, of course, was the "reporting" training analyst, a radical deviation from the clinical requirements of technical neutrality. The system of reporting analytic progress to the institute inevitably stimulates non-analyzable submissive behavior in the candidates, as well as varying degrees of dishonesty (acknowledged by some former candidates who sought a second analysis "for themselves").

The teaching of *seminars* has typically been reserved for training analysts as well, implying the same monopoly of theory that influenced analytic technique and implicitly interfered with the questioning attitude and creativity of the candidates. Case presentations and ongoing process groups are carried out by candidates and junior members under the consistent supervision of training analysts and senior members of the psychoanalytic community, who never presented their own analytic work. Thus the candidates never have the opportunity to familiarize themselves with the actual clinical work of the training analysts, with all its normal difficulties and shortcomings. The result is a reinforcement of the idealization of the supposedly perfect training analyst, and the confusion of technical neutrality with the concept of "anonymity."

Anonymity rationalizes the veil cast over the personal idiosyncrasies of the training analyst, as a means of permitting the full deployment of the transference by the candidate-analysands. On a deeper level, however, the emphasis on anonymity implicitly protects idealizations that can never be analyzed, and reinforces the essential paradox in the training analysis formulated by Arlow (1969, 1970, 1972) and Roustang (1982): as mentioned before, the explicit purpose of the analysis is the resolution of the transference, while an implicit purpose of the training analysis is the candidate's identification with his analyst, a paradox intrinsic to the training analysis. It is no coincidence, I believe, that the height of the insistence on the anonymous quality of the training analyst, both within Ego psychology and the Kleinian school occurred during the late 1950s through the early 1970s, the time of the height of power, prestige, institutional autonomy and isolation of psychoanalytic institutes, particularly in the United States and Great Britain.

Regarding the *supervision* of candidates by training analysts, the intrinsic problem of idealizing teachers whose concrete clinical work is unknown is complicated by the tendency of supervisors to assume an elusive attitude that forces the psychoanalytic candidate to gradually learn and adjust to the technical views of the supervisors without a full and explicit communication of their ideas. Meanwhile the supervising analysts lack a sense of their responsibility to link individual case supervision with the approach to psychoanalytic technique being taught in the seminars. The candidate is supposed to develop such an integration by himself, in an atmosphere in which it is implied that an optimal methodology exists, without being fully and explicitly taught or communicated. Clinical seminars typically begin with the works of Freud, presented not as history but rather implicitly and reverentially as if a model for current practice. At times such teaching was carried out by senior training analysts accompanied by junior faculty who aspired to training analyst status, and whose subservient behavior toward the seminar leader was easily captured and integrated in its implications by the group of candidates.

The psychology of the "silent" psychoanalyst that influences supervision pervades the relationship between the institute and the candidates as a student body as well: The institute, too, is "silent," failing to provide clear information about requirements for acceptance, admittance to seminars, criteria for assigning control cases and graduation. This stance contributed to an atmosphere of mystification of the entire educational structure of the psychoanalytic institute. Not knowing how and where decisions were made, and by whom, affected graduates as well as candidates. The selection of training analysts often occurred by "delicate tapping on the shoulder" of the happily elected, while those who were "untapped" searched in vain for an explanation of their exclusion.

The development of a three-tiered class system in psychoanalytic institutes and societies throughout the world was an inevitable consequence of this educational system. The "ruling class" of training analysts enjoyed a sense of power and security, while having to be concerned with protecting their power base against potentially challenging groups of other training analysts. Many "splits" of psychoanalytic societies derived from the power struggles among competing groups of training analysts. Others arose from the final rebellion of the "second class," namely, the graduates without training analyst status, who were excluded from educational functions and deprived of a major source of prestige within the psychoanalytic institution. "Farming out" of post-graduate courses and popularization of psychoanalytic knowledge to the general public were the consolation prizes for society members who did not make it as training analysts, while typically the most senior training analysts would generously refuse to take such tasks reserved for the second class.

In all fairness, it needs to be pointed out that most training analysts were unaware of the social and political consequences of their conscious efforts to maintain anonymity in order to protect the transference analysis of their candidates within the social structure of the institute. The natural wish to protect themselves and their candidates from the potential acting out of transference and countertransference within the boundaries of the educational institution they all shared, was a powerful motive for shifting technical neutrality into social anonymity.

The "third class" was constituted by the candidates. Some were well protected by their submissive and passive allegiance to their training analyst group within what Greenacre (1959) described as the "convoy system." Others had to struggle against the paranoid feeling that their development was threatened, that ominous failures or shortcomings had been or might be discovered, that would threaten their eventual graduation. The candidates were isolated from each other by the system of "unhooked telephones," that is, the danger that if candidates were to reveal to their training analysts the critical comments about them expressed by other candidates, there would be punishing consequences for the latter indiscreet souls. The resulting climate of protective distancing among the candidates reinforced a paranoid atmosphere among them, or at least led to paralysis and impotence regarding any joint action involving their concerns about the educational process (Dulchin & Segal, 1982a, 1982b; Lifschutz, 1976).

I believe that it is no coincidence that one of the most creative psychoanalytic institutions in the 1940s and 1950s was the British Psychoanalytic Society where the clashing Kleinian, Anna Freudian, and middle group analysts (the Independents) engendered an atmosphere of open controversy, scientific stimulation, and competition that fostered, throughout those years, an enormous scientific curiosity, creativity and productivity. Here, in spite of the negative aspects of the Eitingon model, such an atmosphere of open scientific exploration of alternative theoretical and technical models counteracted the stifling effects of intellectual monopolies. For the most part, throughout the world, however, the educational process became increasingly sterile. For example, in many societies candidates were implicitly or explicitly excluded from scientific meetings so as not to contaminate the transference with premature and inappropriate exposure to the personality of their training analysts. The stultifying atmosphere of psychoanalytic institutions when the monopoly of scientific thinking is at a height, is also reflected in the prevalent "cross sterilization" characteristic of the society meetings, where the subservient repetition of the ideas of the local leading lights with some minor variations will be warmly applauded, while any "deviant" viewpoint is sharply criticized, often in a formally gentle and intellectually savaging way. Psychoanalytic parochialism was painfully apparent in international psychoanalytic congresses where opposing viewpoints were aired without leading to authentic dialogues, so that scientific progress was hardly possible. In short, the nature of the educational structure of psychoanalytic institutes cast a wide shadow over psychoanalytic societies and the entire scientific life of the psychoanalytic community (Keiser, 1969).

Over the years concerned psychoanalysts pointed out the destructive nature of the combination of training analysis, supervision and seminars as the system had evolved (Bernfeld, 1962), but they were isolated voices within a generally self-congratulatory atmosphere at conferences and congresses dealing with psychoanalytic education. It was only in the 1960s that the radical change of the French model arose to challenge the Eitingon system, but that French model itself has been institutionally ignored until practically the present time. I shalll examine this model in a later section of this paper. Meanwhile, within the Eitingon model, a growing questioning of the shortcomings I have summarized gradually became more vocal (Bruzzone, 1985; Giovannetti, 1991; Green, 1991; Infante, 1991; Lussier, 1991; Wallerstein, 1993), and led to important efforts to correct some of its most negative features while maintaining the basic model. In all fairness, it needs to be said that, while nowadays probably most analysts agree with the critique of the negative consequences of the Eitingon model mentioned, the common assumption that "these are problems of the past" is not accurate. In my experience, throughout all three regions, many of these problematic features are still present in many institutes.

## Corrective modifications of the Eitingon model

The first important modification of the Eitingon model was the elimination of the "reporting" training analyst. It is heartening that, in contrast to the rather critical reception of my critique

135

of the atavistic nature of the "reporting" training analyst when I first presented it in the United States (see Chapter 3), the majority of psychoanalytic institutions in all the geographic regions following the Eitingon model have by now abandoned reporting by the training analyst. Some of them have made it explicitly unethical for the training analyst to provide any information about his candidate (other than the day when the training analysis started, the frequency of sessions per month, and the day the analysis would be concluded or interrupted). The few institutes throughout the world that still tolerate the "reporting" training analyst are no longer proud of it, and it may be expected that this serious distortion of the psychoanalytic process will totally disappear in the near future.

A second significant change has been the recognition of the divisive and corrupting features of the traditional selection of training analysts, and the need to depoliticize that process as much as possible. Here, unfortunately, the lack of understanding of administrative theory by authorities in many psychoanalytic institutes has led to new complications: more about this later on.

Ideally, the development of functional criteria and processes for the appointment of training analysts should go a long way towards eliminating the problem. In one institute within the American Psychoanalytic Association, for example, all graduates from the institute who have completed five years of experience beyond their graduation are routinely approached and asked whether they would be interested in becoming training analysts. If they respond positively, the Education Committee (I am using the term Education Committee for what in many institutes is also the task of the Executive Committee), then appoints an Ad Hoc Committee of two or three training analysts to meet with the applicant over a number of sessions. These meetings serve to explore professional activities since graduation, participation in psychoanalytic seminars, supervision, scientific publications, etc., interest and plans for future psychoanalytic career, and to hear the applicant present one or two cases, to be discussed in detail. On this basis, the Ad Hoc Committee then makes a recommendation to the Education Committee for either acceptance or rejection of the applicant as training analyst. This recommendation is discussed by the entire Education Committee. If it reaches a decision against appointment at this time, the director of the institute is charged with communicating this to the applicant, together with the reasons for not being appointed, discussing with the applicant what if anything he/she may do to change this decision. If there are conflicts or controversies of any kind, the director appoints one other member of the Education Committee for a second review. The obvious advantage of this system is that it is potentially fair and functionally reasonable, and provides assurance of information regarding how the decision was made, why, and by whom; it has satisfactorily eliminated in that particular institute the politicization of the process of selecting training analysts along with the conflicts and emotional regression that formerly characterized the process. In some other institutes, the ad hoc examining committee for the appointment of training analysts is constituted by members of other institutes, not their own.

By contrast, many societies in Europe and Latin America have tried to eliminate the authoritarian way of selecting training analysts by instituting a democratic process whereby members are elevated from recent graduates to associate members, from associate members to full members, and from full members to training analysts by means of universal secret votes. These societies have confused political with functional decision-making. The latter involves a mechanism that corresponds to the task, is transparent, logical and fair, and not subject to the vagaries of a political process (Kernberg, 1998, Chapter 8). The secret vote shifts the locus of control from the psychoanalytic institute proper to the political currents of the psychoanalytic society. These, in turn, are linked to the political currents within psychoanalytic institutes, so that, in short, sometimes the treatment is as bad as the illness.

Another significant change in the Eitingon system throughout all three regions has been the opening of seminars, in the sense that candidates may choose elective seminars as well as participating in obligatory seminars, and opening up to institute faculty or even to the entire membership of the society, the possibility of offering such elective seminars as part of the psychoanalytic institute structure. This is significant progress toward broadening the content of the psychoanalytic curriculum, with the potential for bringing in controversial subjects or orientations.

In addition, the development of candidates' organizations that participate in the educational process by providing feedback regarding their educational experience, evaluate their teachers, participate in the curriculum committee, and maintain a direct, ongoing channel of communication with the institute director or executive committee, may change the atmosphere of psychoanalytic education, particularly when it is matched with a concerted effort on the part of the faculty to provide ongoing, clear and complete information regarding all educational issues. Continuous case seminars in which senior analysts, particularly training analysts, present a case they are currently treating, and seminars for supervisors that help them link their supervisory function with overall teaching of technique at the institute, and mutual sharing of what the cognitive, academic functions are that should be included in supervision contribute to demystifying the supervisory process.

There are some particular developments stemming from the Eitingon model that can serve as experiments in nature and hence as a background for addressing its various problems, and the new problems that emerge as old ones are dealt with. The Argentinean Psychoanalytic Association (APA) has developed a point system by which candidates as well as members of the society may accumulate points for progression, promotion, and advance in institutional tasks. While one might criticize the "mechanical" nature of these procedures, in this very large institution, the advantages of a method that decreases potential beaurocratic complications are significant. That Association also combines the principle of "freedom of teaching" with "freedom of curriculum," meaning that, as far as the courses offered are concerned, any member of the psychoanalytic society may teach any type of seminar, as long as a sufficient number of students elect it to make it worthwhile. All students have the freedom to select their own curriculum as long as they attend an established number of both obligatory and elective seminars.

The advantages of this model include a remarkable absence of ideological struggles between groups with different theoretical orientation, the opportunity to learn from a broad variety of faculty members with very different viewpoints, and a refreshingly tolerant atmosphere at seminars and supervisions. A potential disadvantage of this model, however, is the loss of quality control when seminar teachers are reluctant to criticize their students for fear that attendance at their seminars might drop. Also, some charismatic teachers are able to "collect" students around them without much regard to the quality of their teaching. Furthermore, some candidates, when left to their own choices, may experience the many different approaches offered to them as fostering an uncritical eclecticism. In general, all educational enterprises face the problem of constructing a functional education system that maintains quality control while maximizing creativity; psychoanalytic education is not exempt from this dilemma.

Another psychoanalytic society, RIO II, of Rio de Janeiro, devised a system of "accompanying psychoanalysts" in which a limited group of training analysts and candidates work together over a period of two years, in both seminars and individual supervision. The group spirit that develops during this experience permits great freedom of interchange of information, shared knowledge of the development of each candidate, and open communication among all those involved. I believe, however, that the problem of quality control may also affect this structure, because the attachments among members of these faculty/candidates' educational groups make it more difficult for the faculty to be critical of members of their own collegial group. We obviously need educational research to study our original advances as well as our problems.

In short, significant changes are developing within the Eitingon system in the attempt to correct its most striking shortcomings. The increased communication within the International Psychoanalytic community has also contributed indirectly to improving the atmosphere of psychoanalytic education. As contrasted to the rigid intellectual barriers that separated, for example, Ego psychology and Kleinian analysis from each other, French psychoanalysis from Anglo-Saxon and German Psychoanalytic approaches, etc., the growing awareness of the problems of monolithic institutions has led to active efforts to establish contacts and invite analysts from different orientations to participate in educational activities of psychoanalytic institutes. The tradition of teaching about "deviant schools" in order to subject them to preventive downgrading, prevalent in psychoanalytic institutes of the United States until fifteen years ago, has shifted into a growing effort to learn about alternative approaches with open minds (Cooper, 1990).

Perhaps, at this point, the greatest shortcoming of the effort to reduce the problems of the Eitingon model is reflected in the democratization of the process of advancing in psychoanalytic status via secret votes of the entire membership. In several European and Latin American countries where the psychoanalytic societies have more control over the functioning of their corresponding institutes than is the case, say, in the United States, this process of "democratization" tends to produce more political distortions, of what, in essence is an educational function, than in the United States, where the greater independence of psychoanalytic institutes from their societies tends to reduce this kind of politicized decision-making (Kernberg, 1998).

## *The French model of psychoanalytic education*

This model emerged in the 1960s and is dominant in French language psychoanalytic societies, particularly the French Psychoanalytic Association (APF), the Psychoanalytic Society of Paris (SPP), the Belgium Psychoanalytic Society, and it has a strong influence on the organizational functioning of the Francophone Branch of the Canadian Psychoanalytic Society, and the Swiss Psychoanalytic Society. The basic common features and underlying rationale of this model, which has undergone significant changes and is still presently being modified in several of these Societies, have been pointedly spelled out by Green, (1991), Lussier (1991), and Wallerstein (1993). The French model attempts to eliminate those authoritarian and regressive aspects of the Eitingon model that led to distortion of the psychoanalytic process and infantilization of psychoanalytic candidates. What follows are the essential characteristics of this radical critique of the Eitingon system.

To begin, the French model rejects the concept of the *training analyst*. It attempts to keep the candidate's analytic experience totally uncontaminated by institutional complications. In its ideal form, this model proposes that the personal psychoanalysis should predate the formal entrance into psychoanalytic training, and that an aspiring candidate should feel free to select any psychoanalyst he feels deserves his trust. The admission process into the psychoanalytic institute takes place only after a sufficient number of years of analysis to enable the future candidate to experience the influence of the unconscious mind, and in this process to acquire an analytic attitude.

Thus the selection of candidates takes place not at the start of their training, but after an analytic experience that can provide the faculty members who examine the prospective candidate with more realistic and tangible evidence of the potential candidates' capacity for analytic work, his analytic attitude, capacity for insight and introspection, intuitive grasping of unconscious material, and the extent to which potential "blind spots" have been resolved.

In the original model, the future candidate could enter into analysis with whomever he might choose, including analysts who did not belong to the society to which he was applying. In practice, over the years, the tendency has been to restrict analysts of future candidates to those of the same society to which he seeks admission, and even further, only to the full members of that society: in this regard, there are differences among the societies that follow the French model. It almost goes without saying that this has been a strictly "non–reporting" model from its very inception, and that the French model has repudiated the analyst's judgments of an analysand as an influence upon the latter's progress in the psychoanalytic institute.

The French model also criticizes the implicitly authoritarian nature of the Eitingon model's *seminar structure*, the typical arrangement of seminars by years, with classes that ascend a hierarchically organized curriculum like that of an elementary or high school. In its ideal form, the French model proposes complete freedom for the candidate to participate in the seminars that interest him/her, and conceives of these seminars as gatherings in which knowledge is not simply transmitted, but new knowledge generated in the context of the study of psychoanalytic literature. Such seminars, therefore, include faculty, candidates, and members of the society. The interest and excitement of such seminars determines their attractiveness to candidates, as well as fostering a learning process without the submissiveness and indoctrination that are potential by–products of the Eitingon model.

In practice this aspect also has been modified to the extent that, while candidates are encouraged to participate in post–graduate seminars of the society, they are also expected to attend seminars specifically geared to the candidates' group. The individual freedom, however, to choose, the number and sequence of the required seminars is such that each candidate determines his progression through the seminar structure rather than being subjected to a rigid, year by year regimen. Evaluation of the candidates "performance" in the seminars (including group supervision: some French analysts offer continuous supervision in small groups, often in connection with a specific topic) is brushed aside, as part of the overall stance toward the candidates as mature individuals whose learning is determined by their motivation and responsibility.

In so far as no evaluation of the candidates derives from their seminar participation, the major weight of the quality control function of the psychoanalytic institute is given to the supervisors. The *individual supervision* within the French model is a highly specialized process, within which the candidate is expected to acquire a methodology for observing and understanding unconscious processes. This emphasis on learning of the unconscious process activated in the transference/countertransference bind is reinforced by the exploration of the unconscious processes activated in the supervisory experience itself.

This model, therefore, maximizes the utilization of "parallel process," in which the situation of the candidate and the control case is seen as reflecting and being reflected by unconscious processes generated in the supervisory relationship. Supervision thus becomes a very intense, private and emotionally charged experience within which the experiential function dominates strongly over the academic one.

In the ideal French model, psychoanalytic supervision thus acquires characteristics similar to the psychoanalytic process that is being explored. The ideal Francophone model as proposed by Lussier (1991) contemplates the supervision of four to five cases over a period of at least four to five years each, but in practice the number of cases and the duration of the supervisory experience has decreased to approximate the usual frequency and duration of supervision of the Eitingon model. It needs to be mentioned that, in contrast to the Eitingon model that prescribes four or five sessions per week for both the training analysis and the supervised control cases, the original French model accepts a minimal frequency of three sessions per week for both the training and the supervised control cases. An unintended demonstration of the differences of supervision within the Eitingon and French model was given by the conflicts that emerged during the 1997 pre-Congress on Training at the Barcelona International Psychoanalytic Congress. A proposal arising from institutes based on the Eitingon model to study the supervisory process in the light of the exploration of actual supervisions raised a strong protest from European psychoanalysts working within the French model, who became sharply critical of what they considered the inappropriate public exploration of the highly private nature of individual supervision.

### A critical review of the French model

In practice, some of the problems of the Eitingon model have tended to emerge within the French model as well. To begin, the tendency to restrict the selection of analysts for pre-candidates to full members of the psychoanalytic society where a candidate applies, has promoted the politicization of the advance from associate to full members. A two class system has emerged involving full members, invested in maintaining some obstacles for associate members to become full members, and the class of associate members struggling to eliminate these barriers. Here the bureaucratization, and democratization of the decision-making process regarding who has the right to analyze future candidates introduces once again the politicization of what essentially should be an educational process, and tends to activate authoritarian pressures. In addition, the relative freedom and independent decision-making of the candidates as to how to select, in what order, and with what intensity, the seminars that they will take part in, produces a relative isolation of the candidates from each other, as the group processes involving each candidates' class typical for the Eitingon model do not develop.

In small psychoanalytic societies where everybody knows everybody else, this may not be a problem, and collegial processes evolve between candidates and society members. In large societies, however, or societies that control psychoanalytic education over several cities, it tends to lead to an isolation of candidates, a sense of being neglected or that nobody is watching over their interests; and this fosters dissatisfaction, disorientation, and a sense of drifting. However, because the candidates in French model institutes usually are older than those in the Eitingon model institutes, this relative isolation may be less of a problem: The candidates may be mature, autonomous professionals in other fields, who are accustomed to independent functioning. At the same time, because there is very little centralized control of the candidates' progress, the evaluation of their readiness to graduate tends to be pushed toward the termination of their training. At this point they are usually expected to present a graduation paper evaluated by the entire group of full members of the society. Here, instead of the "pre-selection" process typical of the Eitingon model, by which candidates are selected before they start their training analysis, the French model has evolved in some societies into a "post selection" model in which critical judgment is applied only at the very end of the training.

This "final judgment," combined with the anonymous nature of a secret vote inevitably provokes anxiety and stimulates regressive trends in the candidates, not to mention the possibility of arbitrariness of a once and for all decision-making process on the part of a large number of society members who really may not know the candidate at all. If that society, in addition, is constituted by groups with very different and contrasting ideological commitments, the termination paper may have to be a truly political document in which the candidate has to avoid offending one or the other groups of his judges. This may lead to a significant distortion of what should be an exercise in scientific and professional thinking. It fosters passive resistance, paranoid fears, and dishonest formulations, and casts an authoritarian shadow over the entire educational process. In small psychoanalytic societies such a problem does not evolve, but there, given the intimate professional contacts between candidates and members as part of the efforts to avoid the infantilization of the academic work of candidates, joint professional endeavors of candidates and members may lead the institution to select candidates who espouse the institution's particular idiosyncrasy or ideology. An elitism is thus fostered that may acquire provincial qualities as well: "we select only those we feel we can get along with."

While the French model is quite efficient in selecting supervisors from those society members who have given observable evidence in group supervisions of their educational capacity, (and thus is potentially much more reliable than the Eitingon model in selecting training analysts), it has the disadvantage of a regressive idealization of the supervisory process. As an illustration of this point, it is an open secret (or myth?) in Paris that, in order to be accepted as a candidate by the smaller and more "elitist" French Psychoanalytic Association (APF), it is a definite advantage to have a personal analysis with one of the supervisors of that society.

Finally, a major problem with the French model is the lengthening of the training by the time required for the personal psychoanalysis that precedes ordinary institute training. This leads to a more advanced age of the graduation of psychoanalytic candidates, and therefore, to the exacerbation of a problem common to all psychoanalytic training, namely, that people in the most productive years of their lives remain students, not fully authorized to contribute originally to their own science and profession, with an implicit reduction of creativity and contributions to our field. It may be argued that this older age range is an advantage in terms of the candidates' life experience and maturity. I believe, however, that the extended duration of the training itself may foster an unhealthy regression.

## General problems common to both educational systems and some solutions

• *Infantilization of the psychoanalytic candidate*

The regressive effects of the personal psychoanalysis, potentially reinforced by those of personal supervision, are, obviously, an unavoidable feature of psychoanalytic education, and influence the entire educational process. In theory, this regressive pressure may be counteracted and reduced by the stress on the academic aspects of psychoanalytic education, including, first of all, the theoretical and clinical seminars and second, the academic and collegial functions of personal supervision. However, as I shall point out, there are regressive features in both models that reinforce this regression and weaken the academic aspects of the training.

To begin, institutes tend to disregard the past scholarly accomplishments of candidates, many of whom have had distinguished careers before turning to psychoanalysis. One of the more painful and striking problems of psychoanalytic education is that, instead of utilizing the knowledge and experience our candidates bring from other fields, we treat their extra-analytic contributions with indifference, depreciation and even suspicious rejection. It is as if to learn about the unconscious would require that the mind be cleansed of all interest in "conscious" knowledge and experience.

Candidates' hopefully analyzable tendency to idealize their training analysts and the group or ideology to which they belong activates splitting mechanisms and paranoid attitudes toward alternative psychoanalytic groups or ideologies. Such tendencies are reinforced by psychoanalytic institutes' critical rejection of alternative psychoanalytic models, and by fostering a quasi religious attitude toward certain basic psychoanalytic texts or masters that a candidate can question only at his peril. Here we must talk about the idealization of Freud's work, which takes different characteristics in the Eitingon and French schools.

Idealization of Freud's work, in the Eitingon model, takes the form of presenting Freud's texts for study without connecting them with contemporary thinking or with developments in other fields which, had they occurred during Freud's lifetime, would have influenced his formulations. Within the French model, to the contrary, a tendency exists to study Freud's methodology of thinking while not necessarily accepting his conclusions, so that, in this regard, independent and critical review of Freud's contributions is encouraged. At the same time, however, insistent reference to Freud's thinking as the basis for all new contributions, also ends up conveying a dependency on the work of the original formulator of psychoanalysis that lends itself to idealizations and their split off counterpart.

Within both models there is an implicit tendency to discourage candidates from participating creatively in the development of psychoanalytic science. One illustration of the generally shared devaluing

145

of candidates scientific contributions is illustrated by the psychoanalytic candidates' pre-Congresses, at the time of the International Psychoanalytic Congresses. Here candidates present papers to each other relating to their common educational experience, as well as to general areas of psychoanalytic endeavor. This seems a strange split in the activities of our profession: what would we think if the cardiologists in training presented scientific papers on cardiology in a pre-congress for residents and not to the Congress of cardiology proper? The fact that both candidates as a group and analysts as a group feel comfortable with this strange arrangement illustrates, I believe, this issue.

The presentation of a "scientific" paper at the end of training with the decision by the majority of members whether the author should graduate and be accepted into the society, is another illustration of the regressive distortion of scientific work by hierarchical and political pressures of the psychoanalytic society and institute. It is of course of great interest that psychoanalysts should learn how to carry out scientific work and write a scientific paper. However, such a paper is often an isolated activity within an educational process that does very little to foster a scientific attitude or kindle interest in the acquisition of research methodology appropriate to the psychoanalytic process. The association of the "graduation" paper with the implicit disappointment, disillusionment and loss of motivation connected with the paranoid fears around graduation often leads the candidate to abandon scientific work entirely once accepted into the society. In some societies, the candidates' graduation papers are judged by a group of senior psychoanalysts who have written very little in their professional life, which conveys the message that scientific work is for students, not for those who are safely established in the power structure of the psychoanalytic organization. The fact that such graduation papers often have to be written with careful attention to quoting the right authors from the same society and to avoiding quoting authors who belong to other or "deviant" schools contributes to making a mockery of what ideally could be part of the scientific education.

*Scientific isolation and ignorance*

A good number of psychoanalytic institutes throughout the world implicitly ignore psychoanalytic contributions from other approaches

146

or schools. Here the cultural and linguistic barriers that affect psychoanalysis at large have a particularly powerful impact. French candidates often ignore significant contributions from Anglo–Saxon psychoanalysis; English speaking psychoanalytic candidates systematically ignore key contributions from French psychoanalysis; both French and Anglo–Saxon candidates ignore significant contributions from Spanish, Italian or Portuguese language contributions. The mutual ignorance of French and German speaking psychoanalytic institutions is proverbial, although the general ignorance of German contributions in other language psychoanalytic communities is even more impressive. This linguistic problem transcends psychoanalytic education, but, from the viewpoint of the particular tasks of psychoanalytic institutes to provide a broad scientific perspective, it would seem that it reflects a passive renunciation of the task of expanding psychoanalytic knowledge that properly belongs to our institutions of learning.

Psychoanalytic institutes remain highly reluctant to introduce relevant information from sciences bordering on our field into their seminars and discussion groups. For example, in studying the psychoanalytic theory and treatment of depression the important contributions from the neurobiology of depression are largely ignored (except, perhaps, the discussion of tolerance or intolerance of psychopharmacological treatment, and its relevance for the psychoanalytic treatment of depression). Discussions of drive theory that neglect important shifts in the conceptualization of instinct theory in biology, and the important contributions of the neuropsychology of affects to the study of the relationship between affects and drives, are another illustration of this point. While controversies surround the question to what extent infant observation has relevance for psychoanalytic theory, the very discussion of these implications and this controversy is avoided in many institutes' seminars. Perhaps the most striking avoidance of developments in related sciences is that regarding the sociology of small and large groups, the possibility of expanding Freud's analysis of mass psychology, and updating it with the evidence gathered in sociological and historical analysis.

In many psychoanalytic institutes throughout the world there is a distrust of the university, and of clinical psychiatry and psychology; psychiatrists and psychologists who spend significant time in academic endeavors are suspected of not being true psychoanalysts. "Psychiatrist" is a denomination that has particularly pejorative connotations when pronounced within the French and some Latin-American psychoanalytic approaches.

The systematic neglect of research training and of developing a research attitude is a major problem of contemporary psychoanalytic education, reflecting a dangerous lack of concern for the scientific standing of psychoanalysis in the world that surrounds us. It needs to be stressed that psychoanalytic research includes a broad spectrum of investigation, ranging from clinical research in the psychoanalytic situation to scholarly critique of psychoanalytic concepts; from hermeneutic research regarding the clinical application of conceptual models, to empirical research within and outside the psychoanalytic situation. Research as a broad spectrum of systematic thinking and activities fosters the progress of psychoanalytic knowledge and its acceptance in the intellectual world. Isolated courses on scientific methodology, or isolated discussions of the controversy regarding psychoanalytic research are a far cry from a systematic building into psychoanalytic education of a dimension that fosters concern and commitment to the development of new knowledge.

### Irresponsibility regarding candidates' educational experience

This is perhaps a more subtle point, that refers to the attitude of the psychoanalytic institute, not toward any particular individual candidate, but toward the candidates as a body, and the responsibility the institute takes upon itself in accepting candidates for psychoanalytic education. Perhaps the most well-known aspect of this problem is the reluctance of individual supervisors and seminar leaders to confront candidates with serious problems in their functioning, or to face in a timely fashion the incapacity of a candidate to deal with psychoanalytic material. Supervisors as well as seminar leaders tend to be reluctant to express their criticism to candidates, and often do it only indirectly, in communication to other members of the faculty, so there develops a less than totally honest atmosphere surrounding candidates who have problems in the course of their education. It takes courage to confront a candidate, or to be critical in a seminar within a social structure where candidates' freedom of choice may mean that teachers who are demanding will be shunned for others who do not carry out a quality control function.

In this regard, there are differences between the French and the Eitingon models. One of the advantages of the Eitingon model is the potential availability of the entire group of seminar leaders and supervisors who jointly may provide clear feedback regarding the candidate's functioning. Within the French model, the supervisor's exclusive responsibility for this function makes the supervisory process much more difficult and fosters a regressive ambiguity of the evaluation process. In addition, the concerted effort, within the French model, to protect the autonomy of the candidate in his learning psychoanalytic theory, methodology and applications, may reinforce a relative neglect of his progress, abandonment being the price paid for avoiding the risk of infantilization. Therefore, the tendency toward "post-selection" (to select out at the end of the training) is very strong in the French model, in contrast to the dominance of "pre-selection" (whomever is admitted, is likely to graduate) in the Eitingon model.

The problem with the "pre-selection" model, that is, of selecting candidates before they have started their training analysis or after only a very brief period of previous analysis is that it limits our ability to predict which candidates will actually become good psychoanalysts. I believe the pre-selection model may be quite adequate in a majority of cases, but it tends to fail with some candidates who have severe personal psychopathology that is only unmasked in the course of the psychoanalysis proper. On the other hand, the unusual and eccentric candidate who may actually be a great potential contributor to the field, or even more so, a distinguished, professionally productive professional from another field who wants to attain psychoanalytic training, is often regarded with suspicion and rejected in what sometimes amounts to true institutional masochism: not too infrequently, we reject highly original, creative scientists, whose understandable resentment is all too likely to extend from the rejecting institute to psychoanalysis in general, and whose loss to our field may be far more detrimental to analysis than we may recognize.

On the other hand, the "post-selection" model, when combined with an institute's laissez-faire attitude toward candidates' progress may result in candidates drifting for ten to fifteen years, without clearly being aware of what is preventing them from graduating. Meanwhile their institutes are faced with "eternal students" who may express a collective unconscious protest against an educational process in which they have been abandoned to waste the potentially most productive years of their lives. Not graduating is their revenge. Some institutes of the Eitingon model have attempted to correct the regressive effects of psychoanalytic education by the appointment of special mentors or ombudsmen to provide feedback and foster the candidate's professional development.

At the bottom, a paradox exists between a tight educational structure that tends to foster regression in the candidates, and an excessively loose one that may produce regressive features through its very lack of structure and support, which increases candidates' anxiety, adding to the regressive potential hidden in the supervisory process. From the viewpoint of a functional educational experience, I believe that the ideal quality control should take place not in the form of pre- or post-selection, but an ongoing selection by means of appropriate feedback and quality control within a respectful and collegial atmosphere that contains conscious efforts to reduce the regressive effects of psychoanalytic education: more about this later.

### Authoritarianism and arbitrariness

Because of the regressive features that are largely unavoidable within both the Eitingon and French model, the unfortunate possibility exists of isolated manifestations of arbitrary assault on psychoanalytic candidates' professional development, self-esteem, and survival in the training program. There are candidates who, for various institutional reasons, become the favorites in the training institution, while others are held back or punished, with implicit messages to the entire body of candidates as to what behavior patterns foster progression and which ones are risky for survival within the institution (Kernberg, 1998, Chapter 13). The more authoritarian the institute, the more such selected "black sheep" experiences become part of the legends of psychoanalytic education. In one European institute, the obsessive and authoritarian quality of a leading training analyst had lengthened the entire educational process to the extent that graduation, full membership, and training analyst status would take an inordinate number of years. An entire cohort of candidates abandoned their training in frustration and became part of the lore of that institution. In another, a Latin American psychoanalytic institute, a small number of training analysts prevented the appointment of new training analysts over many years, accumulating a large list of "pre-candidates" in a waiting list while their charges per session for personal psychoanalysis reached astronomical proportions. Several psychoanalytic institutes in Europe and Latin America tolerated the inappropriate sexual involvement of training analysts with candidates over an extended period of time, reflecting the hierarchical power exerted by those particular psychoanalysts. The corrective interventions by the local society or the International Psychoanalytic Association came about belatedly as a painful corrective process.

Influential training analysts have been able to postpone the graduation of "rebellious" candidates for many years, in an action correctly perceived by the entire psychoanalytic community as a demonstrative punishment. In one North American institute, the arbitrary behavior of the leader of that institute was practically expressed in almost public demonstration of his power. "Rebellious" behavior on the part of candidates might include a candidate's refusal to take a particular patient recommended to him for analysis by a powerful training analyst; an allergic candidate's insistence that his training analyst not smoke during their sessions; a training analyst's rejection of a candidate who differed with him politically (a rejection, in a Latin American institute, that placed the candidate's professional future at risk during a profound political division of their country). The fact that psychoanalysis cannot survive in totalitarian political systems has been amply confirmed by the painful experience of the twentieth century. One might say, of course, that in all academic institutions, in fact, in all social organizations with hierarchical power structures, arbitrariness and mistreatment are unavoidable. I believe, however, that these cases are too frequent within the psychoanalytic educational system to be dismissed as part of ordinary institutional functioning, and point to the powerful authoritarian pressures generated in the course of psychoanalytic education.

### Denial of external social reality and its effects on psychoanalytic education

In many countries, psychoanalysis is faced with powerful challenges and social and financial restrictions that affect the life of candidates as well of the faculty of psychoanalytic institutes. These realities are rarely discussed and integrated into an adjustment of the institute's educational policies. A major issue is the lack of control cases around the world in the current climate of rejection and distrust of psychoanalysis proper along with proliferation of competing psychotherapies and of the availability of many professionals offering therapy at low intensity and low cost. This climate obviously affects the psychoanalytic community at large, but is of particular relevance to the psychoanalytic institute, where candidates have difficulty getting control cases in time, and have to reduce the fees for control cases in order to maintain the desired four times a week frequency, at the price of severe reductions in their income.

Psychoanalytic candidates must pay for their analysis, their supervisory experience and seminars, while enduring a significant reduction in income because of the low fees for their control cases. This is an objective constraint that requires, I believe, active consideration on the part of psychoanalytic institutes of ways to help the candidates as a body to obtain patients. There are institutes that do not perceive that as their responsibility.

Training analysts, as mentioned before, are relatively protected from this social reality by the very fact that they have a number of candidates in analysis. This constitutes an often subtle pressure toward restricting the appointment of training analysts, and toward a lack of concern among training analysts as a group for the difficulties of their juniors in obtaining patients. These difficulties are related to the disconnection of the institute from the university, from clinical psychiatry and psychology, and from medicine. Intellectual isolation contributes to reducing the prestige of psychoanalysis in the scientific community, adding significant weight to the criticism in the culture at large of psychoanalysis as an elitist, subjectivist, impractical, expensive procedure. Many institutes fail to explore the relationship between psychoanalysis and psychotherapy, the indications, contraindications and limitations of psychoanalysis, and of modified techniques. Candidates learn only a standard psychoanalytic technique, while in their practice most of their work consists of *ad hoc* psychotherapy, for which most of them have had little or no systematic preparation. In fact, in some places in Europe and Latin America, institute leadership is quite happy to see Societies of Psychoanalytic Psychotherapy develop independently in their city or region, seeing it as their own mission to preserve the "purity" of psychoanalytic education. They thus ignore the potential complications and challenges to psychoanalysis that may derive from competition between well-trained psychotherapists, on the one hand, and analysts unfit to practice anything but standard psychoanalysis, on the other. Psychoanalytic institutes are in a position to provide psychoanalytic candidates with training in the most sophisticated and specific psychoanalytic psychotherapy. In failing to do so, they are missing out on effective competition with alternative schools and the strengthening of the psychoanalytic identity by defining an integrated theoretical frame for analysis and psychotherapy. The fact that, in many places, around the world, the brightest and most motivated psychiatrists and psychologists in training in their respective specialties are not interested in psychoanalytic education, I believe, is not only a reflection of popular attacks on analysis, particularly the hostility in many departments of psychiatry and psychology, but also of the lack of excitement conveyed by many psychoanalytic institutes regarding what they have to offer.

## Proposed solutions

It should be clear from what I have said so far that I think neither of our two major models or their modifications offers an ideal solution to the problems I have outlined. Psychoanalytic education, as I have pointed out earlier, is an explosive, "radioactive" procedure. What we can hope is to reduce the regressive, authoritarian and infantilizing features of psychoanalytic education by an ongoing effort to maintain and develop the best of our experience, while modifying and discarding what has proven to be counterproductive and damaging to the mission of psychoanalytic institutes. Perhaps the most important conclusion that I draw from what I have said is that we have to accept that there is no ideal model, that we need to experiment with alternative educational methods, and that psychoanalytic education can no longer assume that it is immune to the changes in the social, professional, scientific, and educational culture that surrounds us.

We need to investigate the effects, the strengths and the shortcomings of alternative models. That, in fact, is the mandate under which the Committee on Psychoanalytic Education of the IPA (COMPSED) is operating at this point, replacing the exclusive focus on the redefinition and maintenance of "standards" of an earlier time, with concern about progress in educational methodology and evaluation of its outcome as a major task of our institutes. I believe that the redefinition of the task of psychoanalytic institutes as generating new psychoanalytic knowledge may bring about significant changes in the direction of reducing the infantilizing of candidates, increasing the scientific openness and outreach of psychoanalytic education, and concentrating on the stimulation of the creativity of candidates in the context of an inspiring atmosphere of excitement, security, and collegiality of their training. Such a redefinition, to my knowledge, has not yet been carried out by any specific psychoanalytic institute, and the effects of such an institutional change that I am proposing still need to be tested.

The stress on a functional organizational structure—in contrast to authoritarian models or the defensive democratization and bureaucratization of psychoanalytic education as reaction formations against authoritarianism—is another key aspect of my proposals. I believe that it is important to provide an intensity of experiential as well as academic learning, with interactive feedback that provides candidates with appropriate knowledge of their strengths and weaknesses, quality control together with stimulation for improvement. As mentioned before, I believe that the ongoing, step by step evaluation of the candidates' performance—rather than attempting to maintain quality control by either pre- or post-selection, is an optimal educational approach. It implies a flexible and open admission of candidates, with an intensity of teaching and supervision that permits the selection of those who really are able to become analysts, and facilitates their development at a reasonable speed in order to help them graduate and become full-fledged members of our profession while they are still young adults. We need to select supervisors who are knowledgeable, clear and direct in their interactions with candidates, able to be critical without becoming sadistic, respectful and open to different views, honest in their criticism and in being able to say no. Obviously, seminar leaders need to show similar qualities; in all cases, we need to avoid contradictions between what is communicated to the candidate and said about him behind his back.

Perhaps one of the most destructive phrases frequently heard in the context of efforts to change, improve, or become more flexible is: "What's the hurry?" Candidates need individualized attention, particularly during the early phases of their analytic education: An ombudsman or mentor assigned by the institute to provide the candidate with feedback and advise, knowledgeable regarding the candidate's specific professional background and expertise, willing and able to provide advise and orientation regarding all academic matters, can make an enormous difference, and limit the regressive effects of the personal analysis on the total educational experience of the candidate. Obviously, like all other educational experiences, this one can also be perverted, for example, if the ombudsman is obtaining confidential information from the candidate and communicating it, without his authorization, to the institute authorities. The function of the ombuds-man as the candidate's "lawyer" need to be differentiated from that as his mentor, taking responsibility for guidance in his studies. If the ombudsman function leads to an increase in paranoiagenetic effects on the candidate, its purpose has clearly failed or been perverted.

The discussion of "standards" of training is often reduced to considering whether three or four or five sessions per week are required for adequate training or control analyses. This is an important theoretical and clinical (and also political) question that concerns the psychoanalytic community and demands appropriate research. Unfortunately, this issue tends to decrease the attention to the problems I have outlined regarding training analysis, super-vision, and seminars. As part of our need to experiment with new educational models, we probably have an excellent opportunity for doing so when expanding psychoanalysis into new regions such as Eastern Europe, the Far East, the Middle East and the African Sub-Continent. We cannot assume that introducing psychoanalysis into completely different cultures will not affect the educational pro-cess, and we may make use of the opportunity that such expansion provides for trying out new methods of psychoanalytic education. The recent approval of Concentrated Analysis by the Executive Council of the IPA, that is, the possibility that candidates who have to travel enormous distances to get to their analyst may have two sessions on the same day, within a total of two or three days of the week, may permit psychoanalysis to become available to other-wise extremely distant and isolated communities, while avoiding the negative consequences—and masochistic temptations—for candidates who might otherwise obtain psychoanalytic training only at the cost of severe disruption of their personal, family, and professional life. Preliminary clinical evidence, provided particu-larly by Brazilian institutes, would indicate the feasibility of the Concentrated Analysis Model, and further experience in this regard is being gathered by them at this time.

Above all, the regressive idealization and split-off paranoiagen-esis that haunt psychoanalytic institutes need to be reduced by a functional administrative structure and functional approaches to the major tasks of psychoanalytic education. In what follows, this general principle is illustrated with concrete examples.

Regarding the question of training analysis as a function, a profes-sional status, and an essential aspect of the Eitingon model, I believe that there are two major alternatives to be followed. On the one hand, if the psychoanalytic education of an institute is of such high quality that it can assure a high level of graduates, and if they become full members of the psychoanalytic society upon graduation, then there would be no need for the title, and status of "training analyst" in such an institute. Any members of such a society who would express an interest in analyzing candidates after say, five years of experience, would be able to carry out this function if he/she found a candidate trusting this member for his/her personal analysis.

If, on the other hand, the psychoanalytic institute cannot provide an assurance of excellence of its graduates to the general satisfaction of the entire society, the selection of training analysts as the members most capable or best prepared to provide a good analytic experience to candidates may be a transitionally optimal method, as long as that selection is a truly functional one, until the institute has become an honestly effective educational institution. Again, a five year minimum experience as a graduate analyst may be a reasonable requirement, in addition to the specific criteria of professional maturity, the combination of emotional and intuitive subtlety, knowledge in depth of theory and method, and an openness to his/her unconscious matched with intellectual clarity and openness. In this connection, I strongly believe that all "military" ranking of analysts should be eliminated, particularly the problematic classification into "associate" and "full" members. All graduates from the institute should be eligible for immediate full membership. The presentation of a scientific paper should come after acceptance, as a joyful welcome, and not one more initiation ritual. The pleasure of scientific contributions should not be spoilt by making it a pre-condition for hierarchical ascendance in the society's power structure.

I believe that the total separation of the personal analysis from the rest of the candidate's educational experience is absolutely essential, and that reporting should definitely be eliminated and considered as unethical behavior. Information about the dates of beginning and ending the analysis, and the total number of sessions of psychoanalysis would seem an acceptable exception to that rule. The training analyst should maintain complete distance from any decision-making process involving the candidate who is in analysis with him/her. I also believe that this personal analysis should come to a natural end, disconnected from all other educational experiences of the candidate, whether before or after his/her graduation. The expectation, in some institutes around the world, that the candidate must continue in a personal analysis until the day of graduation runs against the very spirit of the psychoanalytic encounter.

Kächele and Thomä (1998) have recommended recently to replace the triad of training analysis, supervision, and seminars with the triad of "teaching, treatment and research." Psychoanalytic institutes, they suggest, should only request a strictly limited number of sessions—for example, 200 sessions—of training analysis with a training analyst. Then the candidates should be free to decide whether and with whom they would want to continue in a therapeutic analysis. Kächele and Thomä stress the importance of senior analysts' presenting their case material in continuous case seminars, and point to the importance of research training as an essential aspect of psychoanalytic education. I fully agree with their stress on the importance of research training and on the presentation of senior analysts' case material in continuous case seminars, but I wonder whether a regimented restriction of the number of hours of training analysis (or personal analysis with an analyst authorized by the institute) can do justice to the complexity of personal psychoanalytic experience. Candidates with significant narcissistic character pathology, for example, may require more than two or three years of personal analysis to overcome their narcissistic defenses, and the artificial separation of the training and therapeutic functions of the personal analysis seems problematic. I agree, however, with Kächele and Thomä, and with Sandler (1998) in questioning the excessive duration of many training analyses. I believe that both bureaucratic restriction and bureaucratic extension of the personal analysis are problematic approaches to the dilemma of the training analysis.

Regarding the organization of psychoanalytic seminars, the combination of obligatory and elective seminars, and the flexible opening up of society seminars at which candidates may participate, in the same way as society members are invited to participate in institute seminars if they so desire, is one of the positive contributions of the French Psychoanalytic model that deserves further exploration. The educational culture surrounding the psychoanalytic institute, particularly, how university education is organized in that country, probably influences more of the corresponding local psychoanalytic education than we are aware of, and it would seem perfectly appropriate that such general, culturally dominant educational models be replicated in psychoanalytic institutes as well. The main point here

157

is to provide an atmosphere of excitement and freedom, to avoid indoctrination, and foster questioning and original work within the institute seminar structure. At the same time, the provision of a basic frame of reference may protect the candidate from what, at an extreme, may become a chaotic eclecticism. It may be helpful for the institute faculty to familiarize themselves, to begin, with the theories and contributions of outside academics invited to teach in interdisciplinary seminars and to convey the developments in boundary fields that need to be integrated as part of a sophisticated scientific education. I am proposing what may appear to be a paradox: an enriched, intensive, challenging curriculum combined with a flexibility of approach that gives a high degree of responsibility and autonomy to the candidate for structuring his learning; an integrated, basic frame of theory, technique, and applications, with a questioning and challenging attitude to all dogmatic assertions, and an ongoing concern over the risks of indoctrination and passive receptiveness.

It would seem extremely important to enrich psychoanalytic seminars with a *multiplicity* of academic methods geared to stimulate excitement and creativity, ranging from informal discussion groups to formal lecture series, from inviting leading theoreticians from alternative schools to meet with the candidates, to developing seminars by experts in other scientific disciplines that are related to psychoanalytic exploration, thus providing a broad scientific education in those areas where interdisciplinary study is most crucial. The seminar structure of psychoanalytic institutes should provide the opportunity for observing the pedagogic talents and attitudes of teachers, thus facilitating a functional selection process for supervisory status, and for mutual feedback of teachers and students, while preserving the possibility of quality control regarding specific learning.

There are pros and cons as to whether seminar performance should be part of the candidates' evaluation process, and we do need to study the extent to which a purified French model of quality control carried out exclusively through supervision may be preferable over one where seminar participation is also evaluated. I believe that, in a functional academic atmosphere, an evaluation of candidates' academic learning in the seminar structure is appropriate and feasible without generating a regressive, dogmatic and infantilizing atmosphere. Obviously, if such an evaluation of quality control is combined with an indoctrination of theory and suppression of critical thinking, quality control may simply become a method of thought control. I believe that the emphasis on the personal evaluation of a candidate's work by means, predominantly, of the supervisory process, and the emphasis on the seminar work and scientific development by means of the intensity yet flexibility of the curriculum are mutually complementary, and not in contradiction. The message is that all candidates need to be well grounded clinically, while those who are interested and effective in their scientific development will be particularly rewarded by the institute's intellectual climate and their personal recognition and stimulation.

I believe that the effort to develop an explicit, detailed, specific, basic methodology or theory of psychoanalytic technique is an advantage, in so far as a common frame of reference then permits the evaluation of alternative technical approaches. The fear that learning a "theory of technique" reduces the psychoanalyst's freedom to intuitively grasp the unconscious expressed in the psychoanalytic situation is unfounded. An explicit theory of technique can support an analyst's efforts to understand and manage chaotic countertransference responses to the patient's material, while a theory of interpretation may provide a background that is general enough to allow for a wide variety of intuitive approach to the patient's material. The same is true for psychotherapy: having incorporated a psychoanalytic theory of technique facilitates learning psychoanalytic psychotherapy, enormously enriching the technical capabilities of candidates, and helping psychoanalysis scientifically and professionally in a social environment often characterized by undisciplined "wild psychotherapy."

I believe it is important that the content of the psychoanalytic curriculum vary over time. The teaching of Freud's work—regardless of whether it is explored from a historical viewpoint or a theme oriented viewpoint, whether the content of his conclusions or his methodology of thinking are underlined—needs to be integrated with an analysis of contemporary developments within psychoanalysis as well as in the surrounding scientific world. In other words, we have to avoid teaching Freud's work as "bible reading," and prevent unanalyzed idealization processes from infiltrating psychoanalytic education.

As mentioned before (Chapter 6) psychoanalytic candidates should be stimulated to carry out research as part of their analytic training experience. I agree with Cooper (1999) that "the development of a cadre of dedicated researchers and scholars" is "our

159

most pressing task." This implies the setting up of specific research departments within psychoanalytic institutes, the development of experts in appropriate research methodologies as part of this research department, and their availability as consultants to psychoanalytic seminars, study groups, and particularly to individual candidates and faculty members on an ongoing basis. The effects on the morale of the candidates' group of their peers' work being published in leading psychoanalytic journals cannot be overrated. In my experience, psychoanalytic institutes fostering such scientific contributions on the part of candidates, and their presentation of this work at society meetings, has an immediate positive effect on the commitment, excitement, and creativity of the entire candidates' group. The inhibition of the creativity of psychoanalytic candidates, in my view, is one of the major problems of present day psychoanalytic education, and one of the most damaging features for the development of psychoanalysis as a science. The additional support in regard to research expertise given to selected candidates who can be motivated—or come with such a motivation—to carry out specific research projects may stimulate indirectly the questioning attitude and creativity of the entire candidates' group.

The curriculum should be a curriculum in evolution, with on-going testing of the effectiveness of the seminar program as a whole, along with on-going testing and critical exploration of the contents of each particular seminar. It is important that certain senior members of the faculty do not become chronic monopolizers of key seminars, and that appropriate rotation of teachers provide candidates with a broad spectrum of educational experiences.

Regarding the function of supervision, it emerges as the essential quality control measure, a learning experience that optimally may combine academic with experiential features. The fact that training analysts and supervising analysts are usually selected in the Eitingon model as if they were two functions of the same person illustrates, I believe, the lack of sufficient consideration of how important the pedagogical qualities of the supervisor really are. The selection of supervisors and the assurance of the quality of their work is perhaps the most essential aspect of the psychoanalytic institute's responsibility. Appropriate selection criteria for supervisors are usually missing or underemphasized in the Eitingon model. The French model of supervision, however, creates its own problems stemming from its regressive features, and its often excessive focus on the experiential aspects of the process to the neglect of the responsibility to teach directly. For different reasons, the same problem may affect supervision within the Eitingon model if the supervisor imitates psychoanalytic "neutrality" and "anonymity."

As mentioned before, supervisors should have a good knowledge of the general theory of technique that the candidate acquires in his seminars, and be able and willing to refer back to that general theory of technique and its relation to the practical interventions warranted in the control case under supervision, thus gradually bridging the gap between theory of technique and concrete clinical interventions. They should feel free to explore the consequences for the treatment of the patient of countertransference dispositions in the candidate, while respecting the candidate's privacy and avoiding the transformation of supervision into a psychoanalytic treatment situation. Supervisors should be able to both identify with overall institute educational objectives, and yet preserve a sufficient degree of autonomy so that philosophical differences they may have with how various issues are taught may be shared candidly with the candidate. In other words, the exploration of "parallel process" applies not only to the explicit analysis of the transfer of the candidate's experience in the treatment of a patient into the supervisory situation, but also the supervisor's self-reflection on the transfer of his/her relationship with the institute into the concrete supervisory relationship with the candidate.

In short, much should be expected from the supervisor. The observation of group supervision may provide important information about supervisory talent, together with the evaluation of the supervisor's knowledge and emotional capabilities for supervisory work. Supervisors definitely need to evaluate their candidates, thus providing quality control, and it is important that supervisors be expected to have the courage to discuss candidates' difficulties directly with them rather than holding back and conveying their criticisms only to third parties.

It would seem extremely important that the supervisors communicate among each other, evaluating jointly how their candidates are functioning with their various control cases, and that this information reach the candidate, ideally through the supervisors themselves and/or via an ombudsman designated to help the candidate explore such feedback and work it through. The supervisory experience should be a collegial one of which periodic mutual evaluation of candidates and supervisors may be an important aspect. The extent to which candidates should be free to select their supervisors is an open question. Probably a mixture of personal selection and assignment may help candidates to avoid "blind spots." This is an area for experimentation and for potential cultural variation from institute to institute.

Regarding the overall structure of the psychoanalytic institute, it is important that the methods and criteria for selecting faculty members, training analysts and candidates, for the progression of candidates, graduation, etc. be transparent, public information. The organization of psychoanalytic candidates into an administrative structure, the leadership of which is in on-going contact with the psychoanalytic institute's director and/or Executive Committee can enable the candidates to participate responsibly in the educational process, and provides individual candidates with a channel for redress of grievances. Obviously it is possible to develop such formal structures without delegating any real authority to them, and it is one of the tasks of the institute to analyze honestly the extent to which its structures correspond to their functional purposes.

Many of these measures are being developed at this very time in different psychoanalytic institutes throughout the three regions of the International Psychoanalytic Association. What happens, however, is that many changes are in response to particular problems within a particular institute, rather than arising from an overall evaluation of the basic tasks of the particular institute, the basic constraints to these tasks, and the optimal administrative structure that would do justice to those tasks and constraints.

A well-devised organizational structure can probably protect an institute against excessively regressive organizational features, but it cannot assure its optimal development without creative and inspired leadership (Kernberg, 1998, Chapter 13). It is important that a mechanism for selecting inspired educational leadership be built into the structure of psychoanalytic institutes, and that institute directors be given sufficient authority over a sufficient time span to be effective, as it takes at least several years to provide an innovative organizational leadership. An Institute whose directors change on a routine basis every year may be indicating that it is not interested in change or progress.

Periodic meetings of the entire faculty, and faculty retreats with combined meetings of faculty and candidates or their representatives may contribute to ventilating problems obscured in the daily management of the educational enterprise. One indication of a functionally adequate or optimal institute may be that the scientific contributions of its faculty and students and the ability of its teachers to inspire the candidates are its most important sources of pride, while professional prestige is no longer dependent upon attaining the position of training analyst status on the hierarchical ladder.

To conclude, I have 15 questions that may quickly indicate how far a psychoanalytic institute has progressed with the work of educational innovation: I trust, in the light of everything said so far, they are self-explanatory.

1  Is research methodology and concern built into the program?
2  Are multiple psychoanalytic theories and clinical approaches respectfully taught?
3  Is there a functional candidates' organization in place?
4  Are candidates participating in making scientific contributions to the field?
5  Are scientific developments at the boundary of psychoanalysis taught?
6  Is there a functional, non-political method for appointing training analysts or for assigning the authority to analyze candidates?
7  Are candidates stimulated and helped to accelerate their training?
8  Is there a functionally changing curriculum in place?
9  Is there an integration of pre- and post-graduate seminars?
10  Are candidates evaluated in an on-going, step by step process, with appropriate feedback?
11  Do supervisors communicate with each other and with seminar leaders?
12  Is the institute actively courting, engaged in, collaborating with the local university settings, and participating in training mental health professionals?
13  Are junior faculty invited, developed, and functionally integrated into the institute?
14  Is the personal analysis of the candidate totally separated from the rest of the educational experience?
15  Is there a functioning mechanism in place that helps to deal with candidate or faculty break-down or incompetence in a humane yet responsible way?

## Note

1 Originally published as: A Concerned Critique of Psychoanalytic Education. *The International Journal of Psycho-Analysis*, 81:97–120, 2000.

## References

Arlow, J.A. (1969). Myth and Ritual in Psychoanalytic Training: A Report of the First Three Institute Conference. Ed. Charlotte Babcock. *Training Analysis*, 104–120.

_____ (1970). Group Psychology and the Study of Institutes (unpublished manscript).

_____ (1972). Some Dilemmas in Psychoanalytic Education. *J. Amer. Psychoanal. Assn.*, 20: 556–566.

Bernfeld, S. (1962). On Psychoanalytic Training. *Psychoanl. Q.*, 31: 453–482.

Bruzzone, M. *et al.* (1985). Regression and Persecution in Analytic Training: Reflections on Experience. *Int. Rev. Psychoanal.*,12: 411–415.

Cooper, A.M. (1990). The Future of Psychoanalysis: Challenges and Opportunities. *Psychoanal. Q.*, 59: 177–196.

_____. (1999). Psychoanalytic Education: Past, Present and Future (unpublished manuscript).

Dulchin, J. & Segal, A.J. (1982a). The Ambiguity of Confidentiality in a Psychoanalytic Institute. *Psychiat.*, 45: 13–25.

_____ (1982b). Third–Party Confidences: The Uses of Information in a Psychoanalytic Institute. *Psychiat.*, 45: 27–37.

Eitingon, M. (1923). Report of the Berlin Psychoanalytical Policlinic. *Int. J. Psycho-Anal.*, 4: 254–269.

Giovannetti, M. de Freitas (1991). The Couch and the Medusa: Brief Considerations on the Nature of the Boundaries in the Psychoanalytic Institution. Fifth IPA Conference of Training Analysts, Buenos Aires (unpublished).

Green, A. (1991). Preliminaries to a Discussion of the Function of Theory in Psychoanalytic Training. Fifth IPA Conference of Training Analysts, Buenos Aires (unpublished).

Greenacre, P. (1959). Problems of the Training Analysis. In *Minutes of Training Analysts' Seminar*. Chicago Institute for Psychoanalysis, November 21.

Infante, J.A. (1991). The Teaching of Psycho–Analysis: Common Ground. Fifth IPA Conference of Training Analysts, Buenos Aires (unpublished).

Kächele, H. & Thomä, H. (1998). *Memorandum about a Reform of the Psychoanalytic Education* (unpublished manuscript).

Keiser, S. (1969). Report of the Outgoing Chairman of the Committee on Institutes to the Board on Professional Standards. *Bull. Amer. Psychoanal. Assn.*, 25(2): 1168–1169.

_____ (1996). Thirty Methods To Destroy the Creativity of Psychoanalytic Candidates. *Int. J. of Psycho-Anal.*, 77(5): 1031–1040.

_____ (1998). *Ideology, Conflict, and Leadership in Groups and Organizations.* New Haven, CT: Yale University Press.

Lifschutz, J.E. (1976). A Critique of Reporting and Assessment in the Training Analysis. *J. American Psychoanal. Assn.*, 24: 43–59.

Lussier, A. (1991). Our Training Ideology. Fifth IPA Conference of Training Analysts, Buenos Aires (unpublished).

Roustang, F. (1982). *Dire Mastery: Discipleship from Freud to Lacan.* Baltimore, MD: Johns Hopkins University Press.

Sandler, A. (1998). *On the Transmission of Psychoanalysis Today.* Bulletin of the European Psychoanalytic Federation, 50: 62–74.

Wallerstein, R.S. (1993). Between Chaos and Petrification: A Summary of the Fifth IPA Conference of Training Analysts, *Int. J. Psycho-Anal.*, 74: 165–178.

# 9

# THE COMING CHANGES IN PSYCHOANALYTIC EDUCATION

## Part I[1]

### *Totschweigen* [to kill by silence]: a review of relevant psychoanalytic literature

Mary Target (2001), in her comprehensive review of the literature on psychoanalytic education, points to a recent increase in papers on this issue in contrast to earlier times, attributing this change to an inhibition that gradually was overcome. While highly critical analyses of psychoanalytic education emerged from the very beginning (Bálint, 1948; Bernfeld, 1962), a majority of the early papers were descriptive, and usually affirmed the validity of the Eitingon training model prevalent throughout the international community related to the International Psychoanalytic Association (IPA), as highlighted by the classical work of Lewin and Ross (1960) and Joan Fleming (Fleming, 1961; Fleming & Benedek, 1966). It was not until the 1970s that critical analyses of the organizational structure implicit in the Eitingon model and of the educational programs of psychoanalytic institutes began to dominate the respective literature: a critique that is now, by far, the dominant trend in the corresponding contributions: Arlow, 1969, 1972; Bruzzone *et al.*, 1985; Davidson, 1974; Dulchin & Segal, 1982; Greenacre, 1966; Kairys, 1964; Keiser, 1969; Lifschutz, 1976; Szasz, 1958.

From early on, criticism of psychoanalytic education focused on dysfunctional aspects involving the selection of candidates, the criteria for graduation, the nature of psychoanalytic seminars and supervision, and particularly the authoritarian consequences of the training analysis system and the excessive bureaucratization of training. In the 1980s and 1990s this critique turned its focus to the underlying structural and organizational problems in psychoanalytic education and their historical antecedents (Bruzzone *et al.*, 1985; Cooper, 1990, 1997; Dulchin & Segal, 1982; Giovannetti de Freitas, 1991; Green, 1991; Infante, 1991; Kernberg, 1986, 1996, 2000, 2001a, 2001b; Köpp *et al.*, 1990; Lussier, 1991; Roustang, 1982; Wallerstein, 1993). Analyses from a historical and organizational, but predominantly from a psychoanalytic perspective proper have pointed to the stultification of candidates leading to inhibition of creativity, professional impoverishment, and scientific standstill. Major changes in psychoanalytic education have been proposed to remedy this situation (Auchincloss & Michels, 2003; Bartlett, 2003; Berman, 2000a, 2000b; Cupa *et al.*, 2003; François-Poncet & Lussier, 2001; Garza-Guerrero, 2002a, 2002b; Gomberoff, 2001, 2002; Kernberg, 2001a, 2001b; Kirsner, 2003; Levine, 2004; Meyer, 2003; Szecsödy, 2003; Thomä & Kächele, 1999).

There are, of course, contributions that, basically, defend the present psychoanalytic educational structure, while proposing some changes that, they believe, may reduce shortcomings without changing the essential structures of psychoanalytic education (Amati-Mehler, 2000; Butterfield-Meissl & Grossman-Garger, 1996; Calef & Weinshel, 1973; Orgel, 1982; Shapiro, 1974; Weinshel, 1982).

In an effort to draw some general conclusions about the impact of this bibliography, and what it reveals about the self-reflection of the psychoanalytic community regarding its educational structures, I propose several tentative generalizations. To begin, problems in our educational structures were sensed very early. Bernfeld (1962) originally gave his pathbreaking paper on analytic training in 1952, and, although it was not published until after his death in 1962, its critique is relevant to this day. Together with Bálint's (1948) early critique, and the papers that followed in the 1960s and 1970s, these papers were largely ignored by the psychoanalytic community. In fact, what appears to me most impressive is the extent to which the nature of serious problems in psychoanalytic education, clearly emerging in the psychoanalytic community of all three regions (Western Europe, Latin America, North America), was ignored at the organizational level. Even as evidence of grave problems of an institutional, professional and ethical nature rocked the boat and threatened psychoanalytic education in several countries, the official attitude was dismissive. Discussions of these problems at meetings and congresses were noticeably absent or tepid at best.

I believe that powerful resistances emerged against self-reflectiveness in this domain, this tendency to protect or defend the status quo illustrating, in the process, the very problem that was being signaled by those early critiques. This resistance was overcome, finally, in the 1980s, as external reality contributed to put into sharp focus the inflexibility of the psychoanalytic community's failure to respond quickly and effectively to the new challenges. We must also bear in mind that this myopia coincided with a period of ascendance of psychoanalysis from the 1950s through the 1970s in some European countries, as well as Argentina and the USA.

As long as psychoanalysis flourished, and psychoanalytic institutes were being solicited by large numbers of highly trained and qualified applicants, while psychoanalysis was accepted as a prestigious treatment within academia and in the community, the critique of psychoanalytic education could be ignored. Such lack of a self-critical stance proved costly, however, as threats to psychoanalysis emerged from alternative psychotherapeutic approaches, short-term treatments driven by managed care, improvements in psychotropic medications, the self-help movement and other cultural factors. I believe that a recognition of the urgent need to innovate psychoanalytic education, together with needed investments in outreach and research, for the protection and development of the psychoanalytic profession and science, has become too evident for the previous inhibition and denial to succeed.

Following this general overview, I wish to highlight a few contributions that have been particularly relevant to various sections of the analysis and proposals that follow. Bernfeld (1962), criticizing the excessive bureaucratization of psychoanalytic education, providing the historical background for the Eitingon system, and pointing to the institutional infantilization of candidates, alerted the psychoanalytic leadership to problems in the training analysis system. There are four papers by psychoanalytic candidates (Bruzzone *et al.*, 1985, from Santiago, Chile; Köpp *et al.*, 1990, from Berlin; François-Poncet & Lussier, 2001; and Cupa *et al.*, 2003, from Paris) that are of particular interest because they describe, respectively, the paranoiagenic atmosphere in a psychoanalytic institute from a candidate's perspective, and the confusing paradoxes in psychoanalytic education provided by the total educational structure. It is interesting to observe that Bruzzone *et al.* and Köpp *et al.* were training within an Eitingon system institute in Chile, and Germany, while the Paris candidates' papers, obviously, reflect the French educational system. We can see that problems of authoritarianism affect very different educational models, from diverse geographical and cultural settings.

Cooper's (1997) sharp critique of the destructive discouragement of psychoanalytic research which prevails points to one of the problems of the present educational system. In many locales, not only does there not appear to be any interest in fostering the development of psycho-analytic scientists and researchers, but, to make matters worse, some institutes adopt a frankly negative attitude toward research in general.

Körner (2002) has given us, I believe, a most important overview of the road to objectifying the criteria for psychoanalytic compe-tence on the basis of knowledge, technique, and psychoanalytic attitude. Cabaniss *et al.* (2003) at the Columbia University Center for Psychoanalytic Training and Research, on the basis of empiri-cal research, provide evidence of specific problems in psychoanalytic education with regard to the striking uncertainty and confusion about the requirements for graduation characteristic of the member institutes of the American Psychoanalytic Association (APsaA).

Proceeding from the question "How can we objectify and do jus-tice to our global subjective judgments of a candidate's competence?", Tuckett (2005) has proposed three parameters that jointly may permit such an objectifiable assessment of competence. They are:

1   the participant observational frame, the candidate's capacity to sense relevant data, affects and unconscious meanings;
2   the conceptual frame, the candidate's capacity to link the observed data meaningfully with relevant unconscious dynamics;
3   the interventional frame, the formulation of an interpretive inter-vention communicating effectively the candidate's understanding, and the related sensitivity to sensing the patient's reaction to this interpretation. This approach may be an important beginning towards the task of transforming subjective clinical judgments into objective standards.

A symposium on "Problems of Power in Psychoanalytic Institutions," with contributions by six authors has been published in *Psychoanalytic Inquiry* (Kernberg, 2004), and provides important relevant informa-tion. A contribution by Target (2002), on "Psychoanalytic Models of Supervision: Issues and Ideas" presents an aspect of her work as Chair of the European Psychoanalytic Federation's Working Party on Psychoanalytic Education, and provides interesting perspectives on supervision, particularly the learning expectations of the supervisee and how the interaction with the supervisor might influence it. It does not however, focus on the requirements for the supervisor as such (!). In this connection, Bartlett (2003)—a candidate at the now combined Philadelphia Institute—wrote a critique of the dispirited nature of seminars in psychoanalytic institutes.

Meyer's (2003) analysis of the distortion that the very status of "training analyst" inevitably introduces into the analysis of candidates, interfering as it often does, with the possibility of full transference analysis and resolution is a thought-producing contribution to the literature. He designated this situation as "subservient analysis." The final report from Rocha Barros (2001) from the Pre-Congress on Training at the IPA Nice Congress reveals how this issue—the nature of the training analysis—clearly split the participants, and in parallel to the endless discussion of whether psychoanalysis should be required on a four to five time basis or on a three to four time basis, that has characterized so many self-limiting discussions on methodology of psychoanalytic education. Garza–Guerrero's (2002a, 2002b, 2005) contributions provide a highly critical perspective regarding what should be aspired to, in the long run, for psychoanalytic education. Berman (2004) has described the Israel Psychoanalytic Society's struggle to overcome its own institutional rigidities over an extended period of time. In addition, the analysis of the historical roots of authoritarianism in psychoanalytic education by Cremerius (1986, 1987), and the narrative of the book by Reeder (2004), have contributed significantly to the contemporary discourse on the training analysis system.

Finally, with regard to the subject of selection of psychoanalytic candidates, the comprehensive overview of this issue by Kappelle (1996) supports the conclusion of the Commission on the Evaluation of Applicants for psychoanalytic training (CEA) of the IPA. This commission summarized its findings, stating,

> At present we question whether it is possible with any certainty to say more than the following: that a person who seems analyzable, says he wants to be an analyst, and has accomplished in life enough so far to give promise that he can carry out what he intends to do or wants to be, should be acceptable.

My own contributions to the analysis of problems in psychoanalytic education started with explorations of the relationship between the goals of psychoanalytic education and the administrative structure of psychoanalytic institutes.

I concluded that severe discrepancies between educational goals and administrative structures were influential in determining authoritarian features in psychoanalytic education, and outlined the corresponding symptoms. I later described the influence of different psychoanalytic cultures and the personality of leadership in the distortion of administrative structures, then illustrating the consequences of excessive rigidity and fear of change in an ironic description of the experiences of psychoanalytic candidates. I began to suggest possible changes in various aspects of psychoanalytic education in several contributions (Kernberg, 2000, 2001a, 2001b), that constitute the background for the present integration of such proposals into a comprehensive administrative structure, reasonably free of the consequences of the traditional training analysis system. What follows is that integrated set of proposals, and the theoretical and practical discussion of their implications.

## Paranoiagenic aspects of psychoanalytic education

As president of the IPA, I was also privy to individual concerns, complaints, and revelations of a broad variety of difficulties faced by members and candidates. What came as a shocking surprise was the discovery that seemingly isolated cases of mismanagement, mistreatment, unethical behavior, or gross unfairness as causes of individual and group complaints in various societies and institutes throughout the three regions proved to reflect more general, chronic ways of institutional malfunctioning that seemed detrimental to the tasks of psychoanalytic education, to the morale of the corresponding institution, and to the professional and scientific creativity of both faculty and candidates. Anne-Marie Sandler's (2004) dramatic, tactful and concerned analysis of a long-lasting tolerance within the British Psychoanalytic Society and Institute of a notorious case of corruption of psychoanalytic principles and ethics, unfortunately, is not about an isolated incident: I have been involved in similar situations in all three regions. While in all human institutions it is unavoidable, I believe, that such situations emerge, the question is, to what extent

171

is a dysfunctional institutional structure contributing to trigger them and to prevent their correction.

I have suggested earlier that an organizational analysis of psychoanalytic education leads to the conclusion that the administrative structure of psychoanalytic institutes is discrepant with its professed primary tasks. While the explicit objective of psychoanalytic education is the development of scientific knowledge, and an artistic, personal skill to apply this knowledge to psychoanalytic treatment—the objective of a university college and an art school—the administrative structure corresponds in practice to the combination of a technical school and a religious seminary. I also have proposed that the origin of this discrepancy is the very nature of the "product" handled by psychoanalytic institutes, namely, the dynamic unconscious as revealed in transferences and countertransferences of all participants, in the context of an institutional setting that does not permit the ordinary "dispersal" of unconscious material in between sessions as in the case of patients being psychoanalyzed in a private relationship with a psychoanalyst. The combination of this major etiological factor with a dysfunctional administrative structure determines a heightened paranoiagenic atmosphere, typical of all social organizations whose administrative structure does not correspond to their primary tasks (Jacques, 1976). This paranoiagenic tension may take different forms and crystallize around different subject matters, but is a common, major indicator of organizational failure.

## The non-functional authority of the training analyst

As mentioned before, a growing literature examines the pros and cons of the present training analysis system, ranging from an older defense of that system to more recent efforts to modify it radically in order to reduce its negative effects, to the proposal of abolishing it altogether. In what follows, I shall explore the dysfunctional organizational consequences of the present training analysis system, and express my own conclusions regarding what to do in the section on "Some concrete suggestions."

It needs to be stressed that there are significant differences among the structural arrangements of psychoanalytic institutes and societies, and regarding their mutual relationships. In fact, in response to the very critique of authoritarianism in psychoanalytic education, institutes in various countries have modified their structures, changed the methods of selection of training analysts, and granted candidates some participation in the administrative committee structure of the institute. In this regard, the degree of "paranoiagenic temperature" varies significantly from institute to institute.

At the same time, however, the basic problems of the Eitingon model generated by the training analysis system—and the corresponding problem of the French analytic system where power is concentrated at the level of supervision—persist in remarkably resilient ways. From that viewpoint, it is helpful to outline the basic common features that maintain the dysfunctional characteristics of present-day psychoanalytic education. "Power elites," of course, may emerge in any social organization, and universities are no exceptions; but all dysfunctional organizational structures tend to maximize the danger of institutional distortions of authority and power, and psychoanalytic education, I propose, suffers from such structural abnormalities, that cause functional arrangements to be transformed into authoritarian ones.

In most institutes the appointment to "training analyst" often carries with it an appointment as supervisor, seminar leader, and potential member of the administrative leadership of the institute. This represents an accretion of power that runs counter to the reality that these various capacities—to analyze, supervise, teach, and to be a good organizational leader—are not necessarily related skills found in the same person, and their monopolistic combination represents simply a "power grab" by a privileged minority. In addition, scientific research is usually undervalued if not frankly suspect, and applied psychoanalysis, both in terms of psychoanalytic psychotherapy and the theoretical application of psychoanalysis to other fields of knowledge, is clearly perceived as peripheral. This contrasts to the highly idealized notions of the personal psychoanalysis, the transmission of standard psychoanalytic technique, and the career ladder of the training analyst. These facts contribute further to accentuate the power and hierarchical status of the training analyst. A hierarchical ladder is established that runs from "pre-candidate" to candidate, to recent graduate, to associate member of the society, to full member, to non-training analyst faculty, to training analyst, and, within the training analysts' group in large psychoanalytic institutes, to the executive committee or the education committee. As a result of this concentration of power, graduates who aspire to become members of this elite have to adjust themselves politically to the training analysts' group of their institution, which fosters an institutional atmosphere of submissiveness and opportunism. Such dynamics are often displayed openly in psychoanalytic seminars co-taught by training analysts and non-training analysts.

Differences in theoretical viewpoints may be one source of conflict within the training analysis system, apparently reducing the internal bonding of the power elite, and, potentially, even leading to organizational splits. In practice, while such divisions within the training analyst group might lead to an opening of intellectual discussions and scientific inquiry, given the methodological difficulties in carrying out psychoanalytic research and the fear of questioning basic psychoanalytic theories that intuitively seem to support the structure of the psychoanalytic institute as it has traditionally evolved, such theoretical divisions usually evoke the search for support by sympathizers rather than scientific inquiry. The potential division among training analysts thus may lead to a division within the institute, that then opens up a channel of expression of the conflict between submission and rebellion. Theoretical disputes indirectly provide an outlet for the conflict between unquestioned idealization of some training analysts on the part of the faculty and student body, and displacement of the repressed, dissociated, or projected counterpart to this idealization—fearful hostility and devaluation—on to one of the groups fighting for dominance within the institute.

Naturally, when a strong ideological current dominates a particular institute, the aggression is projected outside, to competing psychoanalytic ideas and institutions, such as we saw in the historical, mutual suspiciousness and devaluation between Kleinians and ego psychologists from the 1940s to the 1970s. As a graduate from a South-American Kleinian-oriented institute and a visiting fellow to an ego-psychological institute and a Sullivanian leaning Institute in the USA in the early 1960s, and training analyst at ego-psychological institutes in the USA from the late 1960s on, I was able to personally experience these different institutional cultures. The contemporary stress on plurality of approaches to psychoanalytic theory and technique would seem to ameliorate this situation, leading to a more open and questioning atmosphere. However, that very position of plurality may also assume the characteristic of a dominant ideology, passively accepted as such without raising challenges to the incompatibility of alternative models, or, in the absence of any empirical research, the apparent theoretical openness may lead to self-congratulations regarding the "scientific attitude" that simply replaces one theoretical edifice with an eclectic one.

The final authority of psychoanalytic institutes, in practical terms, resides with the executive committee or education committee, typically constituted either by training analysts only, or, with representation from the faculty and/or the psychoanalytic society, by a group in which training analysts have an overriding decision-making power. The non-training analysts who may become part of such administrative structures are not immune from the hierarchical nature of the relationships in the institution, aware that prospects of eventually joining the training analysts' group may depend on the extent to which they accommodate to the rulings of that elite. In joint meetings of candidates and faculty members as part of the curriculum committee and other committee structures, the overriding authority of the executive committee becomes apparent, as does the unwillingness of the non-training analyst faculty to challenge such authority.

Orientation to the hierarchical structure of the institute on the part of candidates, as well as junior society members, also derives from an additional fact: the economic dependence of junior members and candidates on referral of desirable patients (inclusively financially viable patients) from senior analysts and, particularly, training analysts. This is a painful fact of life in many countries, especially at the present time with fewer patients seeking psychoanalysis. Institutionally favored candidates may develop a significantly different practice from those who have fallen in disfavor.

In short, an inordinate atmosphere of submission to the established authority acts as a disincentive to innovative endeavors in psychoanalytic institutes, and reinforces a climate of unanalyzed idealizations of the training analyst. As Roustang (1982) suggested many years ago, the idealization that affects candidates, who, in their personal analysis, are supposed to resolve their transference, while, at the same time, they are expected to identify themselves with their analyst, creates a double bind for candidates. Thus, a basic contradiction in the individual training analysis and the distorted administrative structure of psychoanalytic institutes powerfully reinforce each other. One of the consequences of this state of affairs is the unconsciously motivated isolation of psychoanalytic institutes from their social and cultural environment, our next point.

175

# The motivated isolation of
# psychoanalytic institutes

The history of the psychoanalytic movement is marked by the emergence of early dissidents, who, based upon their charismatic personalities or a disappointment within the psychoanalytic community, decided that major or minor differences in theory or technique warranted their setting up an independent psychoanalytic group. As Bergmann (2004) has pointed out, during Freud's life, his personal relationships played an important role regarding whether different viewpoints could be incorporated into the evolving psychoanalytic theory or would lead to dissidence. At times, dissidence opened up an area of psychoanalytic theory that was later explored by Freud himself. The organizational threat that dissidence signified related to the very subjective and intimate nature of the new knowledge acquired through psychoanalytic exploration, not verifiable by external, "objective" means, so that new discoveries could easily be challenged. The decision regarding what was acceptable derived from an organizational consensus that, therefore, could be challenged and throw the delicate nature of the new science into disarray (Kerr, 2004). The effort to control this threat led to the institutionalization of psychoanalytic education, which provided the boundaries of what was psychoanalysis and psychoanalytic technique proper. These boundaries were historically fixed and changed historically, so that what at one point appeared as an impossible dissidence might appear at another time as a modification in theoretical perspectives.

It is painful to say so, but, in many institutes throughout the three international regions, an exclusive concern with psychoanalytic theory and technique, totally divested of any contact with other disciplines, evolved as the ideological counterpart to the authority of training analysts, while suspiciousness of sources of knowledge from university settings led to critique and organizational rejection of psychoanalysts who were dedicating a significant part of their lives to such university endeavors. To illustrate this point practically, in the immense majority of psychoanalytic institutes, before the end of the twentieth century, there was no study or in-depth reference to the new developments in instinct theory in biology, in affect theory in the neuropsychological and neurobiological field, and in the biology of depressive disorders. Candidates who, in their professional commitments outside their training activities, would get in touch with those specific developments were at times treated as if they questioned basic principles of psychoanalysis. The training analysis system derived apparent strength from its exclusive focus on a restricted psychoanalytic theory and technique, and mistrust of external scientific challenges. To this day, many psychoanalytic institutes do not inform their candidates about—let alone use for educational and research purposes—the *Open Door Review of Outcome Studies in Psychoanalysis* (Fonagy, 2002), an updated report on empirical research on process and outcome, published by the IPA.

The self-destructive isolationism of psychoanalytic institutions in the USA, leading to the separation of psychoanalysis from most psychiatric university settings in the 1970s and 1980s (similar developments took place later in Germany and Scandinavian countries), was largely a consequence of the monolithic assertion of psychoanalysis by psychoanalytic institutes, and their rejection of the scientific, educational, and research requirements of university settings to explore critically all developing areas in the broad field of the mental sciences. In all fairness, restrictive policies in university settings, such as in Germany, limiting professorial activities not directly related to their official tasks, made the integration of academic and psychoanalytic activities more difficult. But the psychoanalytic institutes, in turn, exploited this situation by marginalizing further academicians who could only maintain a limited psychoanalytic practice. This isolation, retreat or expulsion from university settings reinforced the narrowing of intellectual pursuits in psychoanalytic institutions, and was a setback to the impressive developments of psychoanalytic knowledge that had taken place in the 1940s and 1950s, particularly in Great Britain. During this period, radically divergent theories and techniques within the British Psychoanalytic Society generated a period of intense scientific and creative inquiry. Then the cultural impact of French psychoanalysis—in significant part motivated by Lacan's dissidence and its impact on French culture—led, in turn, to a cultural interchange with their environment on the part of French psychoanalytic institutions that had maintained their identity within the IPA. This development provided French psychoanalysis with an opening to cultural and political currents that compensated for the relative isolation of psychoanalysis from university settings in a strict sense. The British case illustrates the positive effects of a break-up of ideological monopolies, and the French case the positive effects of an open interchange with the surrounding culture.

My main point is the stress on the defensive nature of intellectual isolation of psychoanalytic institutes, related, I am suggesting, to the effort to maintain their hierarchical structure in the light of a changing social, scientific, and educational environment. In recent years, the growing concern expressed within traditional institutes about the threat to the "identity" of the psychoanalyst involved with professional and scientific activities outside the narrow boundaries traced for themselves by traditional psychoanalytic institutes is a symptom, I believe, of this defensive retrenchment (Beland, 1983; Thomä, 2004). I propose that the concern with the "identity" of the psychoanalyst is an expression of fear to use psychoanalytic knowledge and technique for exploring new challenges presented by the nature of the broad spectrum of patients that we are seeing nowadays, and by dramatic developments in the neurosciences and the social sciences. Practically, the concern expressed in many—if not the majority of—psychoanalytic institutes over the threat to their psychoanalytic identity when candidates and graduates appear seriously interested in developing the theory and technique of psychoanalytic psychotherapy, or psychodynamic group processes, or couple's therapy illustrates this issue. A professional identity depends on the professional work one is committed to, what one does, the conviction about what one does, and the correspondent knowledge, technical skills and specific attitude. To assume that this identity is at risk when the work expands into new areas, when new interests and knowledge enrich it, reflects a biased, timid conservatism. Even the esoteric debates within psychoanalysis about "what is science" and "what is research" seem to be more geared to protect the status quo than addressing the philosophical and methodological contributions that these questions may stimulate.

One consequence of this general state of affairs has been the heavy-handed conservatism and the slowness with which institutes have reacted to the dramatic changes in the field. The membership of the psychoanalytic societies who do not have "training analyst" status have experienced a reduction in the number of patients in analysis in their private practice for a significant period of time. Training analysts, by virtue of a steady stream of candidates seeking analysis, have been relatively protected from the full impact of changes in the social environment. Psychoanalytic institutes only began to react to these changes when they were threatened with fewer psychoanalytic candidates from departments of psychiatry and from medicine in general, and in response to the shift of the candidate's body to clinical psychology and other professions, including social work and the humanities. Finally, the tendency to withdraw behind institutional walls may be seen in the curious rejection of the easy transfer of candidates and training analysts from one psychoanalytic institute to another, especially in the component institutes of the IPA where the high uniformity of educational procedures would seem to support easy transfer of educational status and functions among these psychoanalytic institutes of different cities.

## The bureaucratization of criteria for training vs the development of true professional standards

I have pointed out in earlier work (1998) that two fundamental mechanisms employed by organizations to reduce group regression and a paranoiagenic ambience under conditions of dysfunctional organizational structures are ideology formation and bureaucratization (Jacques, 1976). Ideologies are shared systems of thinking and beliefs that unite a certain social group in terms of its functions, purpose, and past history. Psychoanalysis, as a belief system, has qualities of an ideology regardless of the fact that it constitutes, at the same time, a bona fide scientific theory and method of treatment. The monopoly of thinking characterizing traditional psychoanalytic institutes, including the presently fashionable "pluralism" (also based on the deciding influence of leading psychoanalysts rather than on objective confrontation by empirical evaluation of alternative psychoanalytic theories), has a protective function in maintaining the cohesion within the institution, and in protecting institutes by such commonality of thinking from the risk of internal fragmentation or the loss of boundary control.

Bureaucratization refers to an excessive stress on rules, procedures, and regulations; practically, in the case of psychoanalytic institutions, the procedures that determine the acceptance, progression, and graduation of candidates, as well as the acceptance of members of psychoanalytic societies, their advances in membership, and the appointment of training analysts. No organization can function without administrative procedures, so that bureaucratic arrangements are an indispensable part of the functional process of the relationship of task groups and task systems within an institution. However, when a dysfunctional organization experiences a threat to its basic fabric, bureaucratic arrangements may proliferate in an attempt to protect the institution from insecurity and excessive mutual suspiciousness. Here bureaucratization provides a certain security and predictability in the face of the feared arbitrariness related to distorted power relationships (in contrast to functional authority).

The lack of scientific research in psychoanalysis also affects psychoanalytic education. The lack of clear criteria of competence in psychoanalytic work, the fact that these criteria are left to the judgment of the training analysts rather than being objectively verifiable, has resulted in the bureaucratic nature of the discussions regarding the required frequency of sessions, the number of supervision hours of control cases, the presentation of papers for graduation and advancement, in short, in the trend to transform educational concerns into a system that permits easy "counting." As a result, the controversy over the number of weekly sessions (four in the USA, five in the UK, three in France) illustrates how an arbitrary number has become a battle cry for the assumed maintenance of "standards."

What can be done to reduce the development of high paranoiagenic tendencies in psychoanalytic institutes, with the corresponding idealization processes split off from devaluation and hostility, passive submissiveness, and provocative rebelliousness? What can be done to reduce the subtle, well-concealed sadistic and masochistic forms of acting out that punctuate psychoanalytic education, that are a source of much unhappiness, complaints and even lawsuits? What follows are some concrete recommendations for changes in the administrative structure and related educational approaches in psychoanalytic institutes, geared to transform the organizational structure into a more functional one, and to reduce the high level of paranoiagenesis. Having made several suggestions regarding many issues that I refer to in earlier work, here I shall integrate them systematically, and propose additional solutions to provide an integrated frame for a new educational structure. Thus, for example, changes in the functions of the training analyst proposed before (Kernberg, 1986, 2000) will now be subsumed in the recommendation for transforming the current training analysis system altogether; criteria for the function of supervision, methods of selection, progression, and graduation are spelled out within a coherent overall educational frame; and functional faculty organizations and relationships between institute and psychoanalytic society are explored.

## Some concrete suggestions

*Changing the training analysis system*

The wish to assure that the personal psychoanalysis of candidates be carried out at a high level of expertise is reasonable, and one might even say that it is a responsibility of psychoanalytic institutes to assure the quality of the personal analytic experience of their candidates (Sachs, 1947). In fact, it is the professional responsibility of psychoanalytic institutions to assure that all graduates are competent in carrying out psychoanalytic work. One might raise the question whether it is ethically justified that a special "high-quality" group be selected for analyzing candidates in contrast to a "lesser quality" accepted for the analysis of patients in general. The recognition of this disparity was addressed within the French psychoanalytic system, where any full member of the psychoanalytic society may carry out the personal psychoanalysis of candidates, and, after vigorous protest by the associate members of the Paris Psychoanalytic Society, they too are eligible to carry out the personal analysis of psychoanalytic candidates.

The practical question is whether requiring a certain number of post-graduate years of experience, combined with a specially devised objective examination would be adequate to assure a high quality of competence, and, at the same time, decentralize the distribution of power by broadening the "training analyst" base within the psychoanalytic society. This examination would be available to all graduates, with the implication that it would automatically assign authority to analyze psychoanalytic candidates. It seems reasonable that such an advanced degree of competence in psychoanalytic practice be instituted, but with solid guarantees that this does not serve the purposes of a particular power elite in psychoanalytic institutes, and that the monitoring participation of the psychoanalytic society in such a process or of a university structure, for institutes functioning in such a setting, or of outside entities trusted by all those concerned, be involved. Alternatively, one might argue that optimal standards of training in institutes themselves should assure such a competence of all graduates, but this may be an idealistic stance. A special examination after a certain number of years of post-graduate experience, say five years, may be reasonable as long as it is routinely available to all graduates and members of a psychoanalytic society.

The question of whether the training analysis system should be abolished or modified presents strong arguments on both sides

(Amati-Mehler, 2000; Denzler, 1995; Garza-Guerrero, 2002a, 2002b; Gomberoff, 2001, 2002; Greenacre, 1966; Kairys, 1964; Keiser, 1969; Kernberg, 1992, 2000; Kerr, 2004; Kirsner, 2003; Levine, 2004; Lussier, 1991; Meyer, 2003; Michels, 1999; Orgel, 1982; Reeder, 2004; Sandler, 2001; Shapiro, 1974; Thomä, 1993; Thomä & Kächele, 1999; Torras de Beá, 1992; Virsida, 2004; Weinshel, 1982). Garza-Guerrero (2004), in a strongly-worded overall synthesis of his critique of the present psychoanalytic educational system in a lead article of the *IJP* presents the case for radical changes. In a rejoinder to his article, Laufer (2004) presents a conservative critique of it. This debate illustrates again the growing awareness of our educational problems, and the openness with which they are beginning to be discussed by the international psychoanalytic community.

In summary of my assessment, I believe that the toxic effects of the present training analysis system and its stultifying and, in the long run, destructive consequences for psychoanalytic education are beyond doubt. The following arguments support a modification of the system in the direction of providing specific assurances regarding the clinical excellence of psychoanalysts authorized to carry out the analysis of candidates. The development of a candidate's knowledge of, and personal experience with, the dynamic unconscious, essential for a psychoanalyst, also helps reduce "blind spots" that might interfere with their analytic work and warrants the assurance of excellence of their analysts.

In addition, there is general agreement that psychoanalytic experience continues to grow significantly after completion of the formal psychoanalytic institute training. Thus, for example, a five-year period between graduation and eligibility of an analyst for the analysis of psychoanalytic candidates, with the provision of evidence of sufficient immersion in psychoanalytic practice throughout that time, would seem evidently reasonable. An objective, general certification process might also be relevant, and here we touch on the problematic issue of psychoanalytic certification in general, which I explore later. For the time being, given the present unavailability of objective standards of competence, the process of appointment to "training analyst" may have to remain in large measure the subjective judgment of examining committees that, in turn, may present the danger of perpetuating a self-selected elite with authoritarian functions and control of a particular institute.

On the other side of the argument—proposing to abolish the present training analysis system altogether—is the question of the subjective and politicized process of the present ways of selecting training analysts (and its related corruption) that has been prevalent in all three regions, and the fact that some candidates and recent graduates may be functioning at a much higher level, revealing much talent for psychoanalytic work, than many graduates with more years of experience and institutional "presence." Here the argument goes in the direction of candidates being free to find out for themselves who are the desirable and respected psychoanalysts in the community, or psychoanalysts sufficiently distant and independent from the psychoanalytic institute for the candidate to feel "safe" from any mutual interference between personal psychoanalysis and psychoanalytic training. The main argument on this side is the danger that, whatever the process of selection for those authorized to carry out the psychoanalysis of candidates, it will unavoidably perpetuate the pathological power structures presently stultifying psychoanalytic education.

Also, in the view of those who propose to abolish the system, ideally, our educational processes should be such that, when we do graduate a psychoanalyst, we should be able to trust his capacity for further development of professional competence, and, in this context, abandon the old method of "compassionate graduation": in short, the solution would be a better quality control in psychoanalytic education, so that every graduate should be able to analyze candidates.

I believe that there is an advantage in maintaining a specific quality control for psychoanalysts authorized to analyze candidates, reflected in the requirement of a certain number of years of experience, say five, and the assurance of immersion in psychoanalytic work, with flexible criteria regarding alternative professional functions that equally may represent very well an important commitment to the application of psychoanalytic principles and techniques. An objective assessment by means of a committee constituted of faculty members of the psychoanalytic institute, and also of non-faculty members of the society, should make it possible to keep this an honest process, open to the society's scrutiny of the institute or of any specific "power group" within it.

The general policy of the institute and of psychoanalytic societies at large should be, I propose, that all graduates be encouraged to obtain a second, high level of confirmation of professional competence, and that institutes should be evaluated critically in terms of the proportion of their graduates who successfully apply for this qualification. Needless to say, that qualification should, by itself, be no guarantee or license for any other educational tasks in the institute, or for any organizational representation, and be totally disconnected from all other educational processes affecting the candidates. The total separation of personal analysis from the rest of psychoanalytic education can only be guaranteed when the analyst carrying out a training analysis, in addition to not having any influence over his candidate's personal career as a student, clearly does *not* represent the authority of the psychoanalytic institute in a symbolic function as its representative (Garza-Guerrero, 2002a, 2002b; Meyer, 2003; Reeder, 2004; Roustang, 1982).

It may be argued that many analysts who have obtained the second level of certification, and, therefore, are authorized to analyze candidates, would also be interested in obtaining faculty positions as supervisors, seminar leaders, researchers, or accepting administrative functions in the institute or society. It makes an enormous difference, however, if these are roles independently and selectively obtained rather than reflecting the "anointment" of the analyst as the representative of the analytic ideal of the institute and carrier of the power of a defined, professional elite.

In effect, here we reach a fundamental argument presented by Roustang, Garza-Guerrero, Meyer, and Reeder that deals with the contradictory nature of the present training analysis system: the psychoanalytic candidate is expected to resolve the transference in the course of the treatment, while, at the same time, identifying with his psychoanalyst as his institutional ego ideal. Obviously, this issue cannot be eliminated totally, but the separation of the personal analysis from all institute educational structures provides a much better chance to reduce the negative effects of the institutionally fostered idealization of the training analyst on the candidate's attitude regarding technical and theoretical issues and psychoanalysis in general. At the same time, it would seem highly desirable to strictly limit the number of candidates at one time that any psychoanalyst may analyze, in order to avoid, not so much the "convoy" system (Greenacre, 1966), but the very de-skilling of the psychoanalyst who would see mostly such "special" cases, and whose narcissism may be significantly affected by the prestige that analyzing candidates now brings with it. I believe no analyst should be authorized to analyze more than three candidates at the same time.

It may be argued that, regardless of how committees are set up to certify the acceptable experience and quality of work of a graduate analyst who is seeking "training analyst" status, this process would inevitably also be contaminated by political influences, theoretical bias, grudges against any particular graduate on the part of his training institution, etc. Obviously, if there existed serious evidence for incompatibility with such a promotion because of malpractice, ethical problems, incapacitating illness, etc., this would have to be documented, and a mechanism for the redress of grievances put in place for anybody feeling prejudiced against. Still, the question of political considerations and bias may not be eliminated altogether.

The present system of purely subjective evaluation of applicants for training analysis status, before more objective, generally agreed-upon criteria are in place, is obviously imperfect. It is, however, preferable, I believe, to use this imperfect approach to offer the possibility to all interested graduates to be certified at a higher level of expertise and to be authorized to analyze candidates than to maintain the present, restrictive training analysis system. Such a certifying process, generally available as a second level of evaluation to all graduates, would eliminate the tightly controlled power elites from many institutes, and demystify the symbolic function of the training analyst as a representative of the institute's ego ideal and supreme exponent of psychoanalytic practice. The percentage of graduates who would apply and be certified at this second level would also provide an indication of the extent the local institute is a truly functional educational institution rather than a politically overshadowed one: the extent to which a low percentage of such certifications takes place, might indicate the acknowledgment of failure of the educational process in that society's institute.

If this proposed system were too complex, ridden with bureaucratic complications, inordinately absorbing resources of the psychoanalytic community, I believe that the alternative process would still be preferable, that is to authorize all graduates from the institute to psychoanalyze candidates as well. This "worst-case" scenario would be compensated immediately by the awareness of future candidates that it is in their interest to select from among the locally available analysts, those with a certain number of years of experience and recognized professional expertise.

This "worst-case" scenario, however, has also been considered a "best-case" scenario by those who propose to abolish the training

185

analyst category and function altogether. It may be argued, in support of this proposal, that, if the potential responsibility for analyzing candidates were delegated to all institute graduates, this would reinforce the institute's commitment to their optimal training, and to good quality control for graduation. It also would increase the pressure for optimal training and quality control of the supervisors. And, last but not least, it would assure the abolition of the training analysis system more clearly than the alternative proposal of several years of postgraduate experience, immersion and certification. It would demystify radically the personal analysis in terms of the idealization of the analyst as a member of an "anointed elite."

Against these considerations, however, are the facts that analytic expertise continues to increase after graduation with years of immersion in analytic work, and that a specialty examination offered to and expected to be undertaken by the large majority of graduates may become an objective, public process, with explicit expectations and procedures, and protected from bureaucratic sterility by its linkage with explicit educational goals of the institute and the profession. The percentage of graduates who obtain this certification certainly would reflect on the quality of the respective institute. The establishment of control mechanisms in the form of channels for redress of grievances should assure the objectivity of the corresponding examination. And a graduate psychoanalyst should be able to tolerate taking an examination.

One solution that seems to me unacceptable and yet, in the light of past experience, a dangerous temptation would be to assert that all is well with these proposals, except that, before a new method is put into place, research must be carried out regarding the desirable objective criteria for certification that would confer the authorization of all satisfactory graduates who apply after a certain number of years from graduation: "No change before we have completed such a research." This argument has been applied to other proposed institutional changes in psychoanalysis and usually masks a cynical effort to maintain the status quo, and mocks the terminology of research for this purpose (sometimes by the same persons who have serious reservations about the value of empirical research in the psychoanalytic realm). If the analysis underlying my recommendations is correct, the urgency of our need to innovate psychoanalytic education is such that endless delay in changing the training analysis system may be further aggravating the difficult situation that psychoanalytic education experiences at this time. Research on this process should go on in parallel to change.

The authorization to analyze psychoanalytic candidates should not carry with it any other authority in the psychoanalytic institute, be it of a supervisory, seminar leadership, or administrative nature. As mentioned before, the personal analysis of psychoanalytic candidates should be disconnected completely from the rest of psychoanalytic training, as is already the case in the French system. It would seem reasonable, however, that the analyst who will carry out such an analysis of a candidate should confirm to the psychoanalytic institute that he or she is, indeed, carrying out this analytic treatment, and notify the institute regarding either the completion or the suspension of the analysis.

It is desirable that a significant overlap takes place between the personal analysis and the analysis of control cases on the part of the candidate. This could be assured by an early assignment of as many control cases as possible to the candidate, rather than the "one by one drop" system still prevalent in many institutes. The custom of forcing psychoanalytic candidates to stay in personal analysis until their graduation is an illustration of the arbitrary and authoritarian misuse of psychoanalytic treatment for bureaucratic purposes.

Should a minimum of sessions per week be required for such a psychoanalytic experience? From the point of view of optimal exposure to a psychoanalytic experience, a high frequency is desirable, but may have to be limited by individual considerations as well as different models of psychoanalytic education. I believe it would be reasonable to put an absolute minimum at a three sessions per week basis, recommending the experience of one or several periods of higher frequency of sessions, which would incorporate all the different psychoanalytic traditions, and certainly leave open the possibility for training analysts within different educational systems to recommend a higher number of sessions per week that corresponds to their convictions and experience. And it needs to be kept in mind that analysands with significant narcissistic pathology require a higher frequency of sessions than those where this is not a significant aspect of their character structure. On the other hand, a more radical model, that places the entire responsibility for the psychoanalytic experience in the hands of the analyst and his analysand, would leave it to the analysts and their analysands themselves to decide the pace of their analysis. This would require a conviction about the professional responsibility and trust in our graduates, and confidence in the educational methods of the institute in realistically assessing the level of the candidates' work: in my view, that does not correspond to contemporary reality. Such a delegation of authority requires an institutional maturity and level of educational efficacy that may appear utopian at this time, but would not seem out of the question in the future, if everything goes well with psychoanalytic education.

By the same token, the relationship between the personal psychoanalysis and all other aspects of training would be reduced to a minimum, with the understanding that the analyst may terminate a psychoanalysis of a candidate that he or she believes is not viable, but without any communication to the institute other than the fact of this interruption or termination. Any other communication about a candidate to the psychoanalytic institute should be considered an ethical violation of the principle of confidentiality, and possibly disqualify the analyst from further assumption of such responsibilities.

## Supervision

The selection of supervisors would become the main concern of psychoanalytic institutes, and should be carried out on the basis of evidence provided by members of the psychoanalytic society that they are proficient in the skills implied in psychoanalytic supervision. This proficiency may be demonstrated in group supervisions within the institute as well as in the post-graduate activities of the society, in the presentation of clinical work that conveys a sense of knowledge, capacity to transmit such knowledge, and personal qualities commensurate with an empathic, sensitive, and totally incorruptible attitude toward educational responsibilities. The supervisor's functions should include the capacity to spell out to the candidate a general frame of psychoanalytic technique as the background against which concrete interventions suggested in each case are warranted, and to help the candidate link such a general theory of technique with the practical interventions in clinical work. It may seem trivial to state this: but, in practice, a lack of such an integrative frame of psychoanalytic technique is quite prevalent among supervisors, a reflection of the equally frequent absence, in psychoanalytic education, of a concerted effort to provide such a frame. The supervisor should be able to transcend such a lack, if it existed.

Undoubtedly, there are different roads toward proficiency in psychoanalytic supervision. Some supervisors proceed from an intuitive attitude ("a preconscious grasp of cognitive issues") to cognitive clarity, while others proceed from a cognitively clear intellectual frame, moving gradually into a more intuitive range (Arlow, 1963; Baudry, 1993; Blomfield, 1985; Greenberg, 1997; Levy & Parnell, 2001; Martindale *et al.*, 1997; Target, 2002, 2003; Wallerstein, 1981). An empathic, introspective grasp of clinical material, in any case, should be translated by the supervisor into a formulation that reflects the application of a theoretical frame to that material and of a theory of technique related to it. The supervisor's denial of the relationship between concrete interpretive interventions and an implicit theory of technique, attributing all analytic interventions to purely "intuitive" understanding, may not only create the danger of an excessive tendency to engage in the supervisee's countertransference exploration, with a corresponding distortion of the supervisory relationship, but also in disparate interpretations that may make it very difficult for the supervisee to grasp the underlying principles that determine the interventions being suggested by the supervisor.

In short, I believe that it is the supervisor's responsibility to link concrete interventions with a communication of his underlying theoretical frame. He or she should be able to help the supervisee not only with the concrete interpretation of the material at any particular point, but with developing an internal frame that permits him to creatively apply his theory of technique to different circumstances. The supervisee should be encouraged to integrate his own theoretical frame while acquiring the freedom to integrate his knowledge, his intrapsychic exploration, and his attentively listening to the patient and observing his behavior into one pool of information that needs to be understood and prioritized ("the selected fact"). It may appear trivial to spell this out, but such a technical skill on the part of the supervisor requires a clarity of thinking on his part, the capacity for clear communication, and a willingness to share his thinking, including his doubts and uncertainties regarding the concrete issues at hand, with a candidate. The demand on the supervisor, therefore, is of a comprehensive understanding of psychoanalytic technique and, at the same time, knowledge of the spectrum and depth of the candidate's exposure to teachings about technique in seminars and other supervisions, in order to clarify different approaches, reduce discrepancies, provide enrichments, while still respecting the candidate's autonomy to develop his own theoretical frame, rather than insisting that the candidate think and analyze as the supervisor does.

The supervisor's willingness to illustrate his explanations with experiences from his own cases may be very helpful, in contrast to a quite prevalent attitude as part of which the supervisor says very little and maintains an atmosphere of "anonymity" that imitates the style of psychoanalytic treatment. This stance may cause regressive and paranoiagenic effects in the supervisee. The supervisor's awareness of the advantages and disadvantages of reviewing entire sessions, segments of them, or an entire period of analysis; the advantages and disadvantages, in short, of the supervisor's exploring macro- and microstructures, his sophisticated knowledge of the literature of psychoanalytic technique: all should be assumed as included in the responsibilities and skills of the supervisor.

It may well be that one of the requirements for becoming a supervisor may be a certification process of professional competence as described before, with the clear understanding that a large majority of all graduates of an institute would be motivated for such a certification and that, therefore, the certification process would not become a political obstacle in the way of appointing supervisors. In addition, supervisors may be authorized by a set of criteria for selecting supervisors, objectified by the demonstration of these skills in group supervisions or supervisors' training sessions. I believe it is realistic to establish objective criteria for assessment of the quality of the supervisor, by identifying explicit criteria and instituting a means of monitoring adherence to good supervisory practice.

The lack of concern with the standards of psychoanalytic supervision is a major problem of contemporary psychoanalytic education, resulting in incompetence in some cases, and even in corruption of the educational process, as candidates submit, at times, to incompetent supervisors, and some irresponsible supervisors avoid taking an active stance regarding candidates' difficulties. Supervisors should be clearly aware of their educational and non-therapeutic functions. For example, they should respectfully explore countertransference issues only to the extent to which they affect the psychoanalytic process of the candidate's treatment of his patients, and not engage in a pseudo-therapeutic attitude that imitates psychoanalytic encounters and blurs the boundary between personal analysis and an educational experience.

Supervision should be a collegial experience between colleagues of different levels of knowledge and experience, and promote the autonomous development of the candidate, at the same time as the supervisor carries out a monitoring function that includes the quality control of the candidate's work. In fact, I believe that, clinically, supervision is the very centerpiece of psychoanalytic training, and, both in the form of individual supervision and group supervision, should provide optimal learning opportunities for the candidate as well as an ongoing monitoring of the candidate's development. In some places, it has been suggested that it is impossible to combine the task of helping the candidate in the treatment of his patient "to be supportive" with the task of an objective evaluation of him. I believe that this is an absurd assumption. Every teacher has the combined task of teaching and evaluating the student. If a supervisor cannot combine these two essential functions of supervision, he should not carry out this task.

One important aspect of the supervisor's work is the utilization of his knowledge of "parallel process" (Arlow, 1963; Baudry, 1993; Kernberg, 1992) and of its limits. The understanding that unresolved problems in the transference/countertransference constellation of the supervisee's work with a patient may show up as a distortion of the immediate interpersonal relation with the supervisor has been a valuable contribution to the possibility to clarify such introjected yet "non-metabolized" aspects of the transference/countertransference bind. The supervisee now unconsciously reflects this unresolved issue in the supervisory session, often with an unconscious identification with that aspect of the patient that the supervisee has not understood while yet intuitively sensing it, and projecting on to the supervisor aspects of himself in reacting to that challenge. The tactful interpretation of the distortion in the interpersonal relation in the supervision derived from the activation of such a parallel process may be a very helpful aspect of supervision. It requires, however, not only intuition and tactfulness on the part of the supervisor, but also the capacity to respectfully explore only those aspects of the countertransference that he assumes have been activated by a specific problem of the patient, to help clarifying the transference of the patient in this context.

This process may require the supervisor's sharing with the supervisee his own emotional reaction to the changes in the relationship between them. It is a delicate process that has to be protected from acquiring a therapeutic function, and must respect the supervisee's private life, avoid inquiry into unconscious origins of the supervisee's countertransference reaction, and maintain the sharp focus on the patient's transference. Utilization of parallel process for teaching purposes, however, should also take into consideration the parallel process of the supervisor, who, at times, may be involved in a conflictual relationship with the institute and express it indirectly in a distortion of his relationship with his supervisee. One aspect of the introspective process on the part of the supervisor should involve his reflection on the extent to which he feels under pressure from the psychoanalytic institute in connection with this supervision, in addition to what we expect from a supervisor's honest exploration of his own general motivation and attitude. A consistent concern about the potentially paranoiagenic aspects of all supervisory relations should be part of a genuine knowledge base and educational expertise of the supervisor.

An interesting illustration of the risk of authoritarian contamination of the supervisory process, and its paranoiagenic implications, is reflected in a research project on supervision (Wallerstein, 1981), and particularly Shevrin's (1981) chapter in that book, expressing the conflicts of a candidate in a particular supervision. Shevrin's chapter is a moving contribution to the illustration of authoritarian pressures in psychoanalytic education.

Supervisors must have the willingness and courage to express their critiques or misgivings directly to the supervisee. Supervisory reports should be discussed in such a way that the supervisee feels free to disagree with the supervisor without having to fear any negative consequences evolving from such a disagreement. A similar need for honesty and courage may arise at a different place, namely, in the relationship between the supervisor and the progression committee. The discussion of candidates by the progression committee on the basis of the reports from seminars and supervision obviously would give primary importance to the supervisors' views, and supervisors should be invited to participate in this process, rather than progression committees making decisions about a candidate without the presence of all the supervisors who are involved with him. In very small institutes it may be possible that a joint meeting of all the supervisors and seminar leaders with the progression committee provide a maximum of openness, shared information, and objectivity regarding a candidate's evaluation. An ombudsman or individually assigned mentor acting as the candidate's "advocate" should also be able to participate in such meetings, and, as a facilitator specifically concerned with reducing paranoiagenic effects of the evaluative process, discuss with the candidate his situation in the institution. A perversion of such an ombudsman or adviser's function—not infrequent in some institutes—is the crossover role of the adviser to provide feedback on the candidate's progress to the committee, thus engendering a paranoiagenic climate in which the candidate is inhibited from making full use of the mentor for fear of jeopardizing his progress.

Additionally, supervisors should be thoroughly acquainted with the overall curriculum and where supervisees are within that curriculum, as well as the range of psychopathology they have studied as clinicians. Any potential discrepancies between a particular supervisor's technical approach and that of the general theory of technique the candidate has been learning should be clarified. A non-authoritarian psychoanalytic institute should permit the candidate to freely explore alternative models of technique, to compare the approaches of different supervisors, and to raise these issues at clinical seminars without the fear of reproach.

How can we train good supervisors, given the general lack of knowledge regarding pedagogical principles prevalent in psychoanalytic institutes? Consultation with experts in educational methodology may be helpful. The careful selection of faculty in charge of group supervision of the analysis of control cases may be an important contribution to this issue; training seminars for supervisors based on the criteria referred to in this section may increase the skills of those who are talented in this area.

Part II of this study presents concrete suggestions regarding the curriculum, the selection, progression and graduation of candidates, and the governance of psychoanalytic institutes.

## Note

1 Published in *International Journal of Psychoanalysis*, Vol. 87, No. 6: 1649–1673, 2006.

## References

Amati-Mehler, J. (2000). The Status of Training Analyst. *Int Psychoanal* 9: 16–18.

Arlow, J.A. (1963). The Supervisory Situation. *J Am Psychoanal Assoc* 11: 576–594.

_____. (1969). Myth and Ritual in Psychoanalytic Training. In: Babcock C., eds. *Training Analysis: A Report of the First Three Institute Conference on*

*Psychoanalytic Education*, 104–120. Pittsburgh: Pittsburgh Psychoanalytic Institute.

———— (1972). Some Dilemmas in Psychoanalytic Education. *J Am Psychoanal Assoc.*, 20: 556–566.

Auchincloss E.L. & Michels, R. (2003). A Reassessment of Psychoanalytic Education: Controversies and Changes. *Int J Psychoanal.*, 84: 387–403.

Bálint, M. (1948). On the Psycho-Analytic Training System. *Int J Psychoanal.*, 29: 163–173.

Bartlett, T.A. (2003). My Dream Center for Psychoanalytic Training. Brainstorming List (unpublished manuscript).

Baudry, F.D. (1993). The Personal Dimension and Management of the Supervisory Situation with a Special Note on the Parallel Process. *Psychoanal Q* 62: 588–614.

Beland, H. (1983). Was ist und wozu entsteht psychoanalytische Identität? [What Is and for What Develops Psychoanalytic Identity?] *Jahrb Psychoanal* 15: 36–67.

Bergmann, M. (2004). *Understanding Dissidence and Controversy in the History of Psychoanalysis*. New York: Other Press.

Berman, E. (2000a). Psychoanalytic Supervision: The Intersubjective Development. *Int J Psychoanal.*, 81: 273–290.

———— (2000b). Detoxifying the Toxic Effects of Psychoanalytic Training (unpublished manuscript).

————(2004). *Impossible Training: A Relational View of Psychoanalytic Education*. New York: Analytic Press.

Bernfeld, S. (1962). On Psychoanalytic Training. *Psychoanal Q.*, 31:453–482.

Blomfield, O. (1985). Psychoanalytic Supervision: An Overview. *Int Rev Psychoanal.*, 12: 401–409.

Bruzzone, M., Casaula, E., Jimenez, J.P. & Jordan, J.F. (1985). Regression and Persecution in Analytic Training. Reflections on Experience. *Int Rev Psychoanal.*, 12: 411–415.

Butterfield-Meissl, C. & Grossmann-Garger, B. (1996). Die Frequenz macht einen Unterschied. Zur Bedeutung der hohen Stundenfrequenz für den psychoanalytischen Prozess [Frequency Determines a Difference: The Significance of a High Frequency of Sessions for the Psychoanalytic Process]. *Texte* 16: 7–22.

Cabaniss, D.L., Schein, J.W., Rosen, P. & Roose, S.P. (2003). Candidate Progression in Analytic Institutes: A Multicenter Study. *Int J Psychoanal.*, 84: 77–94

Calef, V. & Weinshel, E. (1973). Reporting, Non-Reporting, and Assessment in the Training Analysis. *J Am Psychoanal Assoc.*, 21: 714–726.

Cooper, A.M. (1990). The Future of Psychoanalysis: Challenges and Opportunities. *Psychoanal Q.*, 59: 177–196.

_____ (1997). Psychoanalytic Education, Past, Present and Future. *Samiksa*, Calcutta, India. 52: 27–37.

Cremerius, J. (1986). Spurensicherung. Die 'Psychoanalytische Bewegung' und das Elend der psychoanalytischen Institution [Tracing Origins: The "Psychoanalytic Movement" and the Misery of the Psychoanalytic Institution]. *Psyche—Z Psychoanal.*, 40: 1063–1091.

_____ (1987). Wenn wir als Psychoanalytiker die psychoanalytische Ausbildungorganisieren, müssen wir sie psychoanalytisch organisieren! [If We Organize Psychoanalytic Education as Psychoanalysts, We Must Organize it Psychoanalytically!]. *Psyche—Z Psychoanal.*, 13: 1067–1096.

Cupa, D., François-Poncet, C.M. & Lussier, M. (2003). Les analystes en formation. Synthèse de l'enquête faite auprès des analystes en formation à la SPP [Analysts in Training: Synthesis of the Inquiry of Analysts in Training at the SPP]. *Bull Soc Psychanal Paris*, 67: 90–105.

da Rocha Barros, E.M. (2001). Final Summary of the Pre-Congress on Training. Presented at Nice International Congress of the IPA.

Davidson, L. (1974). Honesty in Psychoanalytic Training. *Contemp Psychanal.*, 10: 242–247.

Denzler, B. (1995). In Favor of Personal Analysis. *Report from the House of Delegates* (unpublished manuscript).

Dulchin, J. & Segal, A.J. (1982). The Ambiguity of Confidentiality in a Psychoanalytic Institute. *Psychiatry*, 45: 13–25.

Fleming, J. (1961). What Analytic Work Requires of an Analyst: A Job Analysis. *J Am Psychoanal Assoc.*, 9: 719–729.

Fleming, J. & Benedek, T. (1966). *Psychoanalytic Supervision*. New York: Grune & Stratton.

Fonagy, P., ed (2002). *An Open Door Review Outcome Studies in Psychoanalysis.* London: IPA.

François-Poncet, C-M. & Lussier, M. (2001). Les conflits dans la formation du psychoanalyste [The Conflicts in the Training of the Psychoanalysts] (unpublished manuscript).

Garza-Guerrero, C. (2002a). "The Crisis in Psychoanalysis": What Crisis are We Talking About? *Int J Psychoanal.*, 83: 57–83.

_____ (2002b). Organizational and Educational Internal Impediments of Psychoanalysis: Contemporary Challenges. *Int J Psychoanal.*, 83: 1407–1433.

_____ (2004). Reorganizational and Educational Demands of Psychoanalytic Training Today: Our Long and Marasmic Night of One Century (with a rejoinder by Eglé Laufer). *Int J Psychoanal.*, 85: 3–25.

Giovannetti, M. de Freitas (1991). The Couch and the Medusa: Brief Consideration of the Nature of the Boundaries in the Psychoanalytic Institution. Presented at 5th IPA Conference of Training Analysts, Buenos Aires.

Gomberoff, M. (2001). Desafios Actuales de la institucion psicoanalitica [Present Challenges of the Psychoanalytic Institution] (unpublished manuscript).

——— (2002). Crisis y analisis didactico [Crisis and Training Analysis] (unpublished manuscript).

Green, A. (1991). Preliminaries to a Discussion of the Function of Theory in Psychoanalytic Training. Presented at 5th IPA Conference of Training Analysts, Buenos Aires.

Greenacre, P. (1966). Problems of Training Analysis. *Psychoanal Q*, 35: 540–567.

Greenberg, L. (1997). On Transference and Countertransference and the Technique of Supervision. In Martindale, B., Mörner, M., Rodríguez, M. E. C. & Vidit, J-P., eds. *Supervision and Its Vicissitudes*, 1–24. London: Karnac.

Infante, J.A. (1991). The Teaching of Psychoanalysis: Common Ground. Presented at: 5th IPA Conference of Training Analysts, Buenos Aires.

Jacques, E. (1976). *A General Theory of Bureaucracy*. New York: Halsted.

Kairys, D. (1964). The Training Analysis: A Critical Review of the Literature and a Controversial Proposal. *Psychoanal Q*, 33: 485–512.

Kappelle, W. (1996). How Useful Is Selection? *Int J Psychoanal.*, 77: 1213–32.

Keiser, S. (1969). Report of the Outgoing Chairperson of the Committee on Institutes to the Board of Professional Standards. *Bull Am Psychoanal Assoc.*, 25: 1168–1169.

Kernberg, O.F. (1998). *Ideology, Conflict, and Leadership in Groups and Organizations*. New Haven, CT: Yale UP.

——— (2000). A Concerned Critique of Psychoanalytic Education. *Int J Psychoanal.*, 81: 97–120.

——— (2001a). Presidential Address: Given at the 42nd International Psychoanalytic Congress, Nice France. *Int J Psychoanal.*, 83: 197–203.

——— (2001b). Some Thoughts Regarding Innovations in Psychoanalytic Education. *IPA Newsletter* 10: 6–9.

——— (2004) Discussion of the Symposium on "Problems of Power in Psychoanalytic Institutions". *Psychoanal Inq.*, 24: 106–121.

Kerr, J. (2004). "The Goody-Goods Are No Good": Notes on Power and Authority in the Early History of Psychoanalysis with Special Reference to Training. *Psychoanal Inq.*, 24: 7–30.

Kirsner, D. (2003). Psychoanalysis and Its Discontents (unpublished manuscript).

Köpp, W., Korte, B., Neumann, M., Väth-Szusdiziara, R. & Wagner, C. (1990). Die Lehranalyse im Spannungsfeld der Ausbildung [The Training Analysis in the Tensional Field of the Training]. In: Streek, U. & Werthmann, H.V., eds. *Herausforderungen für die Psychoanalyse* [Challenges for Psychoanalysis], 178–195. Munchen: Pfeiffer.

Körner, J. (2002). The Didactics of Psychoanalytic Education. *Int J Psychoanal.*, 83: 1395–1405.

Laufer, E. (2004). Rejoinder: With Reference also to Garza-Guerrero (2002). *Int J Psychoanal.*, 85: 13–18.

Levine, F.J. (2003). The Forbidden Quest and the Slippery Slope: Roots of Authoritarianism in Psychoanalysis. *J Am Psychoanal Assoc.*, 51: 203–245.

Lewin, B.D. & Ross, H. (1960). *Psychoanalytic Education in the United States.* New York: Norton.

Levy, J. & Parnell, Y. (2001). The Benefits and Hazards of Working through the Supervisee's Countertransference in Psychoanalytic Supervision. *J Clin Psychoanal.*, 5: 91–116.

Lifschutz, J.E. (1976). A Critique of Reporting and Assessment in the Training Analysis. *J Am Psychoanal Assoc.*, 24: 43–59.

Lussier, A. (1991). Our Training Ideology. Presented at 5th IPA Conference of Training Analysts, Buenos Aires.

Martindale, B., Mörner, M., Rodríguez, M.E.C. & Vidit, J-P., eds (1997). *Supervision and Its Vicissitudes.* London: Karnac.

Meyer, L. (2003). Subservient Analysis. *Int J Psychoanal.*, 84: 1241–1262.

Michels, R. (1999). Training Analyst Function: Requirements and Philosophy. Presented at IPA Congress, Santiago, Chile.

Orgel, S. (1982). The Selection and Functions of the training Analyst in North American Institutes. *Int Rev Psychoanal.*, 9: 417–434.

Reeder, J. (2004). *Hate and Love in Psychoanalytical Institutions: The Dilemma of a Profession.* New York: Other Press.

Roustang, F. (1982). *Dire Mastery: Discipleship from Freud to Lacan.* Baltimore, MD: Johns Hopkins UP.

Sachs, H. (1947). Observations of a Training Analyst. *Psychoanal Q*, 16: 157–168.

Sandler, A-M. (2001). Neu-Evaluierung der psychoanalytischen Ausbildung: Kontroverse und Wandel [New Evaluation of Psychoanalytic Training: Controversy and Transformation] (unpublished manuscript).

———— (2004). Institutional Responses to Boundary Violations: The Case of Masud Khan. *Int J Psychoanal.*, 85: 27–42.

Shapiro, D. (1974). The Training Setting in Training Analysis: A Retrospective View of the Evaluative and Reporting Role and Other "Hampering" Factors. *Int J Psychoanal.*, 55: 297–306.

Shevrin, H. (1981). On Being the Analyst Supervised: Return to a Troubled Beginning. In: Wallerstein RS, ed. *Becoming a Psychoanalyst: A Study of Psychoanalytic Supervision*, 311–329. New York: International UP.

Szasz, T.S. (1958). Psycho-Analytic Training: A Socio-Psychological Analysis of Its History and Present Status. *Int J Psychoanal.*, 39: 598–613.

Szecsödy, I. (2003). To Become or Be Made a Psychoanalyst. *Scand Psychoanal Rev.*, 26: 141–150.

Target, M. (2001). Some Issues in Psychoanalytic Training: An Overview of the Literature and Some Resulting Observations. Presented at The 2nd Joseph Sandler Research Conference, University College London, March 10.

_____ (2002). Psychoanalytic Models of Supervision: Issues and Ideas. Presented at European Psychoanalytic Federation Training Analysts' Colloquium, Budapest, November.

_____ (2003). Progress Report and Plans for the European Working Party on Psychoanalytic Education (WPE).

Thomä, H. (1993). Training Analysis and Psychoanalytic Education: Proposals for Reform. *Ann Psychoanal.*, 21: 3–75.

_____ (2004). Psychoanalysts without a specific Professional Identity: A Utopian Dream? *Int Forum Psychoanal.*, 13: 213–236.

Thomä, H. & Kächele, H. (1999). Memorandum on a Reform of Psychoanalytic Education. *Int Psychoanal.*, 8: 33–35.

Torras de Beà, E. (1992). Towards a "Good Enough" Training Analysis. *Int Rev Psychoanal.*, 19: 159–167.

Tuckett, D. (2005). Does Anything Go? Towards a Framework for the More Transparent Assessment of Psychoanalytic Competence. *Int J Psychoanal.*, 86: 31–49.

Virsida, A.R. (2004). The Training Analysis: An Analysis (unpublished manuscript).

Wallerstein, R.S., ed. (1981). *Becoming a Psychoanalyst: A Study of Psychoanalytic Supervision.* New York: International UP.

Wallerstein, R.S. (1993). Between Chaos and Petrification: A Summary of the Fifth IPA Conference of Training Analysts. *Int J Psychoanal.*, 74: 165–178.

Weinshel, E. (1982). The Functions of the Training Analysis and the Selection of the Training Analyst. *Int Rev Psychoanal.*, 9: 434–444.

# 10

# THE COMING CHANGES IN PSYCHOANALYTIC EDUCATION

## Part II[1]

What follows is the continuation of concrete recommendations to deal with the current problems in psychoanalytic education. Part I of this study (Chapter 9) explored the challenges that psychoanalytic institutes face at this time, and proposed significant changes in the training analysis system and in the supervisory process. The present Part II presents concrete recommendations regarding institute governance, the curriculum, the admission, progression and graduation of candidates, and the process of certification and accreditation of institutes.

### Seminars and classroom teaching

Clinical and theoretical seminars, obviously, should be taught by teachers who are competent, enthusiastic, and able to communicate their knowledge and enthusiasm regarding a particular subject to the candidate. Selection of seminar leaders may be made on the basis of experiences in group seminars, supervision, and post-graduate activities of the society. For psychoanalytic institutes connected with or located within a university setting (e.g. a department of psychiatry or clinical psychology), faculty from related disciplines should be maximally utilized for teaching. In general, the artificial dissociation between institute activities and the psychoanalytic society's life is clearly detrimental to the selection of institute faculty, by constricting the pool of talent from which seminar leaders may be recruited.

Teaching assignments should be for a limited period of time, rather than becoming a permanent right or monopoly of some faculty for certain subject matters. Joint clinical or theoretical seminars of candidates and society members may further break down the isolation of the psychoanalytic institute.

Bartlett (2003) proposes abandoning the practice of closed cohorts from year to year, suggesting that seminars should start out with the same cohort in order to facilitate bonding of the candidates' group and to provide a minimum common basis of knowledge, after which candidates should feel free to take seminars in any order they prefer, as long as they fulfill a certain quota of each of the major fields of theory, development, psychopathology, and technique.

In line with my proposal (Kernberg, 2001a, 2001b) regarding joint seminars of the psychoanalytic society and the institute, Bartlett proposes open seminars, in which not only candidates with different levels of experience would come together with members of the faculty, but potentially also invited scholars from related fields and, of course, interested society members. Such seminars represent an opportunity for the development of new knowledge, and may become an exciting expansion of the ordinarily content restricted seminars that usually only permit a limited dialogue and discussion. Only technical seminars should be restricted to faculty and candidates proper.

This description of proposed changes in the methodology of the seminar structure of psychoanalytic institutes does not, of course, cover the broad potential for new teaching instruments that has evolved in recent years. The re-introduction of selected lectures within the seminar series, frowned upon years ago, also has proven to be an important contribution to the intellectual quality of seminars. The use of audio–visual equipment provides interesting technical possibilities. Video or audio recording offers students the opportunity to follow the course of treatment with severely disturbed patients, to observe primitive transference developments, acting out, and the appropriate use of interpretative technique in dealing with these dynamics. The use of group analytic methods as part of the teaching methods for continuous case seminars is another important contemporary tool, derived from the developments of psychoanalytic understanding of small group processes. Teachers skilled in the utilization of such group processes may add enormously to continuous case seminars; and seminar leaders for continuous case seminars should be expected to learn methods of analysis of group processes as part of their task in clarifying the dynamics of the patient–analyst relationship examined and its impact on the group process of the seminar.

In this connection, continuous case seminars provide a potentially crucial contribution to the overall learning of technical skills and the acquisition of a psychoanalytic attitude. The tendency to break up such seminars into small segments may dilute the learning experience with regard to a teacher's systematic technical approach, and represent a loss of richness in the teaching of technique. On the other hand, the monopoly of such continuous case seminars by a few teachers may perpetuate a monolithic approach to psychoanalytic technique. It is impressive how little attention has been paid to innovating teaching methodology and systematic presentation of an integrated theory of technique to this entire area of seminar teaching. I believe that, together with the personal supervision, continuous case seminars are the most important tool for the development of the professional competence of the future psychoanalyst.

All of this points to the extreme importance of selecting seminar leaders who fulfill the requirements for these tasks, whose talents may be different from those required for supervisors, although, of course, they may overlap. The need to provide teaching opportunities for creative members of the faculty, to consider the changing interests and background of psychoanalytic candidates, to be alert to important advances in the field, all require flexible structuring and changes of seminars. A significant majority of seminars should be optional while some basic, obligatory ones should be available at different points of time, following the preferences of individual candidates. Ongoing review of the effectiveness of teachers should be carried out in parallel to the ongoing review of the participation of candidates. Regarding this latter point, much of what has been criticized as the prevailing "passivity" of psychoanalytic candidates may be a response to the lack of excitement and inadequacy of the current seminar structure. Sadly, such passivity may also reflect, in some instances, the selection process of the institute privileging passive and compliant applicants.

## Institute governance

Although the selection of supervisors typically is a permanent appointment it, too, should be subjected to periodic review by the central administrative structure—the Executive Committee or Education Committee—of the psychoanalytic institute. This executive body

201

should be constituted by representation from the various types of professionals engaged in psychoanalytic education, that is, supervisors, seminar leaders, candidates and researchers. The neglect of the research function of psychoanalytic institutes is one of the major scandals of contemporary psychoanalytic education. The development of a department of research within each psychoanalytic institute, with faculty dedicated to teaching research methodology and facilitating interested candidates' participation in specific research projects constitutes a desperately urgent necessity for the scientific development of psychoanalysis. The utilization of the patient material and of the human resources of psychoanalytic institutes is valuable capital to be invested in the pursuit of this goal.

Representatives of the supervisors' department, the seminar leaders' department, the research department, and the candidates' organization, I repeat, should constitute the Executive Committee or Education Committee of the psychoanalytic institute. I see no reason why representation from the candidates' organization should not participate in the overall administrative leadership of the psychoanalytic institute. If and when personal issues affecting individual candidates come up for discussion at Executive Committee meetings, candidates could be excused, but generally, issues involving development of curriculum, candidate responsibilities, innovations in methodology, and organization of particular programs should be discussed with the participation of the candidates' representatives. The leadership of the psychoanalytic institute also should include a representative of the psychoanalytic society. In small psychoanalytic institutions, the easiest way to achieve a harmonious integration between the society and the institute's activities would be for the president of the society to become part of the Executive Committee of the psychoanalytic institute, while the director of the institute serves on the Executive Committee of the psychoanalytic society.

The director of the institute should be elected by a process that gives a voice to both the faculty of the institute and the society at large, signalling the psychoanalytic society as the overall organization that authorizes and monitors the functions of the psychoanalytic institute, and carries out a trusteeship for the assurance of the functional nature of the administrative structure of the psychoanalytic institute. Obviously, the situation is different for a psychoanalytic institute that has been developed within a department of psychiatry or psychology of a university setting, and in this case it should be the academic department that constitutes the controlling body of the psychoanalytic institute. There may be alternative models, in which psychoanalytic education may be both integrated within the psychoanalytic society and yet have an independent controlling body that assures the quality control of psychoanalytic education. Or else, in the case of a joint venture of a psychoanalytic society and a university department, a shared monitoring and control system may constitute an optional administrative arrangement. One psychoanalytic society and institute in Buenos Aires (APDEBA) has been successful in obtaining an independent university college status within the official Argentinean educational system. This and related initiatives to incorporate psychoanalytic education within universities are to be encouraged, as part of an effort to reduce the isolation of psychoanalytic institutions.

My main point is the need to develop an administrative structure that is functional, democratic where appropriate, and in which there exists no particular body of a self-perpetuating elite that distorts this administrative structure. In fact, regardless of how the director of the psychoanalytic institute is elected, he or she should be responsible to the faculty of the psychoanalytic institute at large. The faculty should be able to monitor the extent to which its executive committee is carrying out the educational tasks of the institute. The duration of the tenure of the director of the institute should depend on the extent to which a relative stability of the educational system justifies a duration of two to three years for such a directorship, in contrast to educational systems where the need for educational innovation and change would warrant a longer directorship in order to bring about fundamental organizational change, say, in the course of five years. The Executive Committee should include faculty representation from all the other committees within the institute, and except for the progression committee, should include candidate representation as well. A well-functioning candidates' organization, in ongoing contact with the institute leadership, would complement such a functional organization, the replacement of the present training analyst system.

## Functional integration of psychoanalytic institutes within their corresponding society or university department

As mentioned above, the effective control and monitoring of the psychoanalytic institute by its corresponding society (or university department) is a guarantee for the functional nature of its administration. It provides an ultimate instance for redress of grievances that may evolve within the institute. From this viewpoint, an ideal model for the selection of institute leadership might involve the institute faculty nominating candidates for directorship of the psychoanalytic institute, and the society at large electing the institute director. This provides the responsibility for the institute faculty to propose respected candidates, and signals the final authority of the psychoanalytic society in the election of the director. As an alternative, the appointment of a selection committee for the directorship of the institute composed of institute faculty as well as of the society leadership (or the university department) may provide the same assurance.

In any case, consideration in the usual case of the institute as one component of the psychoanalytic society, with the institute director as part of the executive committee of the psychoanalytic society, provides an overall integrative link that should permit an optimal integration of educational activities of the institute and the post-graduate educational activities of the society. The participation of the president of the society as a member of the executive committee of the psychoanalytic institute, or of a delegate of the president for that purpose, would complement such a process. Joint activities in post-graduate education involving society and institute, and joint research projects involving both, as well as the organization of particular conferences and seminars in collaboration between society and institute may be facilitated by such arrangements.

This administrative structure, corresponding to the concept of psychoanalytic education as a central responsibility of a psychoanalytic society, has always been the model theoretically pursued by the International Psychoanalytic Association in its development of new societies. Historically, however, this intended structure has been subtly subverted, as institutes consolidated the training analysis system into a stable power elite that evolved along the lines mentioned before. The evolution of the Board of Professional Standards of the American Psychoanalytic Association (APsaA), as a practically parallel body of authority to the Association's Executive Council illustrates the same process, and is related to significant conflicts within the American Psychoanalytic Association (APsaA) around certification, and the political aspects of membership's rights. The power struggles between Executive Council and the Board of Professional Standards of the APsaA detracts from the urgent shared need to explore innovation in psychoanalytic education in the light of the challenges to psychoanalysis in its surrounding academic, social and cultural environment in the United States. Some affiliate societies of the American Psychoanalytic Association have undertaken initiatives to change the structural arrangements between their psychoanalytic institute and the society to integrate the institute's and society's efforts to assure and strengthen the local position of psychoanalysis.

Related questions are, of who should be considered members of the institute faculty and what are their functions, responsibilities and privileges in comparison with non-faculty members of the psychoanalytic society? Obviously, all supervisors and seminar leaders, as well as the members of the research department and special lecturers and professors should be considered faculty members and involved in the nomination and monitoring of the institute's leadership in the course of regular faculty meetings. Faculty members should be eligible for participation in all institute committees. The appointment to "training analyst" should not be a requirement for faculty status, nor imply an automatic appointment as a member of the faculty. In this regard, strict separation of the personal analysis of candidates and all other educational functions should be assumed. Obviously, there will be analysts with authorization to analyze candidates who, at the same time, have been selected as supervisors, seminar leaders, or research faculty. The decision regarding the selection of faculty should rest in the hands of the leadership of the psychoanalytic institute. The faculty of each institute department—seminar leaders, supervisors, and researchers, should be involved in this selection process.

Should psychoanalytic institutes be developed within university settings or contribute to setting up psychoanalytic training programs within university settings? To begin, it needs to be reiterated that, obviously, university settings are not free from dysfunctional administrative structures, bureaucratic rigidities, and authoritarian power elites. Universities, however, usually have well-established mechanisms of quality control, protection against arbitrary decisions, and for redress of grievances, together with public processes of selection of leadership, that may be temporarily perverted, but, in the long run, are exposed to corrective scrutiny. And universities' commitment to their task, high level education and generation of new knowledge, is a genuine, ongoing effort in a competitive world. For that reason we may take a leaf out of the university model. The initiative to develop a Master's degree program of psychoanalysis under the aegis of the Humanities and Social Science departments is being explored, and is in different stages of development and implementation, in different countries at this time. Such a Master's program, in turn, might be the first step toward a doctorate in psychoanalysis, with full clinical training within a department of clinical psychology or psychiatry, and thus constitute a joint program of a psychoanalytic institute with a university setting proper. Obviously, the integration of a psycho-analytic institute within a department of psychiatry would raise some different educational and administrative questions than those emerg-ing within a department of psychology. However, the advantages of such arrangements for the enrichment of the institute's seminar programs, the development of research, the very attractiveness of psychoanalytic education, are enormous and such arrangements should be vigorously explored.

The downside to psychoanalytic programs leading to a Master's degree is the risk that graduates, with insufficient clinical training, would declare themselves psychoanalysts, and further, that institutes that subsume their training programs within a university may lose control of the educational program. I believe that, while these are reasonable concerns, safeguards against them can be implemented. The concern about loss of control reflects to quite an extent the ubiquitous fear of present day power elites in psychoanalytic insti-tutes: the shared responsibility and overall authority over an institute by the psychoanalytic society or a university setting may be a healthy counterpart to the authoritarian problems of present day psychoana-lytic education. The experience of the Columbia University Center for Psychoanalytic Training and Research, a psychoanalytic insti-tute functioning within the prestigious Department of Psychiatry of Columbia University, has proven this point over many years.

## Scientific development and research

I have pointed out that psychoanalytic education has been stagnant, become less attractive to leading members of the psychiatric and medical profession, not able to respond creatively to the challenge of competing psychological theories, psychotherapeutic approaches, and neurobiological—including psychopharmacological—developments. I also have suggested that the decrease in the respect and consideration for psychoanalysis is not simply a consequence of social and cultural

206

bias but, to a significant degree, a consequence of elitism and even arrogance of psychoanalytic institutions. If all of this is true, then a major effort to increase the excitement of intellectual life in psychoanalytic institutes and societies is warranted. I believe that psychoanalytic institutes have the human resources and patient material to achieve these goals.

Such a major intellectual thrust requires, first of all, a creative review of the curriculum, combining basic courses in normal and abnormal psychic development, psychopathology, and psychoanalytic treatment with an exploration of the boundaries of psychoanalysis with related sciences, in an authentic effort to explore the mutual impact of new developments in psychoanalysis and its surrounding scientific disciplines. Cross-fertilization with other fields of endeavor would greatly enliven the overall curriculum and, ideally, stimulate innovative educational methods that include an active participation of candidates in exploring areas of controversy and new knowledge. Combining basic, obligatory courses with elective seminars that reflect particular interests of faculty members and invited scholars in other fields would promote a challenging approach to the limits of present day knowledge, while lending support to ongoing research.

It may be argued that, given the paranoiagenic atmosphere that permeates psychoanalytic institutes, no change in curriculum or methodology of teaching may be effective in changing the nature of the learning on the part of candidates, namely, "strategic" learning, in the sense of learning for winning approval or passing examinations. In contrast, "deep" learning, in the sense of accentuating critical thinking and confrontation with what is known and still unknown, demands an openness to new ideas, and confidence in the student's capacity to evaluate freely and independently given knowledge and its limits; and absence of dogmatic indoctrination. This kind of learning fosters scientific development and generation of new knowledge. In agreement with this argument, I am proposing in this chapter the simultaneous work on the content of the intellectual learning, the educational methodology, and the administrative structure of the educational institution.

The profession's longstanding distrust and avoidance of systematic research into psychoanalytic process and treatment outcome tends to be couched in philosophical questions about whether psychoanalysis can be studied empirically, and in the politically motivated separation of research into "empirical" and "conceptual" research, while it is evident that conceptual research requires systematic and critical review of ideas while no empirical research can operate meaningfully without conceptual clarity. My point is that a broad spectrum of research, from the hermeneutic to the empirical, from small projects limited to an individual candidate's scholarly investigation to large inter-institutional projects carried out among various institutes or between a psychoanalytic institute and a university setting all need to be developed.

It is important to reestablish the links of psychoanalysis to academia, particularly with the university departments of psychiatry and clinical psychology, where interdisciplinary interests may facilitate creative interchange, and with the humanities and social sciences at large. It may well be that the initial steps in such joint approaches require the incorporation, as part of the institute faculty, of scientists from other fields, not necessarily psychoanalysts, but open to and interested in collaboration with psychoanalytic researchers. Small institutes may have to invite a leading methodologist in empirical research from another field as the first step to develop an autochtonous research expertise. To foster and reward scientific work by candidates, institutes and societies should provide recognition and prestige for scientific contributions, as well as for competence in clinical work. Prestige, for sure, should not derive from the unique ladder that leads to training analyst status within the present system.

The question has been raised, to what extent the building up of a research department as an essential section of any psychoanalytic institute may reflect a utopian aspiration. To begin, the financial limitations to the possibility of establishing a viable research enterprise are staggering; and would require a major reorientation of the nature of fund raising at the local, national, and international level. Collaborative research with major academic institutions may be one helpful feature, together with the optimal utilization of the enormous human resources and patient material of psychoanalytic institutes. There is no doubt that, while the development of psychoanalytic institutes at departments of psychiatry or clinical psychology may constitute an excellent medium for a harmonious integration of research within the psychoanalytic institute, that option is not available to free standing institutes, that is, to the immense majority of psychoanalytic institutes throughout the three regions. The possibility, however, of attracting a leading research methodologist, who may help to transform questions raised throughout the seminar structure into workable research designs, including not only empirical research proper, but also clinical/ naturalistic, historical, and hermeneutic research is eminently viable. The stimulation of candidates to explore and write about controversial issues may have an energizing effect for the institute at large. The availability of successful empirical research sponsored by or carried out in collaboration with psychoanalytic institutions in Germany, Sweden, and the United States illustrate this enormous untapped potential.

This brings me to the issue of research on psychodynamic psychotherapy, which is much more advanced presently than research on psychoanalysis proper (Fonagy, 2002). This research into psychodynamic methodology and treatment techniques, in response to the present concern with evidence, based treatments (Kernberg, 1999), potentially strengthens psychoanalysis. The integration of systematic teaching of psychoanalytic psychotherapy at the highest level, its indications and contraindications, its common features and differences with psychoanalytic technique proper may have important functions in the facilitation of development of research in this domain, and importantly, in providing candidates with a broad spectrum of techniques derived from psychoanalytic theory that will be eminently helpful to them in their daily practice.

At this time, I do not think that it is exaggerated to state that the old fashioned policy of banning the teaching of psychoanalytic psychotherapy from psychoanalytic institutes, or reserving it only for therapists who are not in psychoanalytic training proper, is practically suicidal for psychoanalysis as a profession. This self-destructive practice has fostered and continues to foster the development of independent societies of psychoanalytic psychotherapy, that often enter into competition with psychoanalytic institutes and societies, and evolve at times into independent institutions that call their graduates psychoanalysts, contributing to the present day confusion in this field. And, at the same time, institutes may give candidates the impression that they are getting the highest level of training in standard psychoanalytic technique for a small segment of the patients they are going to see in their daily practice, and none whatsoever for the large majority of patients whom they will see in psychotherapy, and for whom applied psychoanalytic techniques may be the treatment of choice. In addition, the profession of psychoanalysis has to struggle with its abuse by those analysts who believe, or even proclaim, that psychoanalytic training, by itself, permits carrying out high quality psychoanalytic psychotherapy. This destructive, potentially danger-ous illusion is one more problem psychoanalytic institute face as a consequence of their lack of training in contemporary psychoanalytic psychotherapy.

## The admission, progression, and graduation processes; certification and accreditation

In contrast to the present French system of admission to candidate status after years of a personal psychoanalysis and the demonstra-tion of a psychoanalytic attitude on the part of the future candidate that tends to excessively prolong psychoanalytic training, I believe that broad criteria for suitability of candidates before the start of a personal analysis are warranted. This aspect of the Eitingon system, that predominates in psychoanalytic education internationally, seems preferable over the French system. It means, in practice, that can-didates are eligible for starting clinical and theoretical seminars after one year of personal analysis, or even sooner, sometimes immedi-ately, and should be encouraged to take their control cases relatively early in their training, and, whenever possible, as I have proposed, several cases at the same time.

The literature on the selection of psychoanalytic candidates, referred to above in the overview by Kappelle, confirms the clin-ical experience in all three regions, that we do not have reliable, objective criteria for selection, beyond the almost provocative (or amusing?) general conclusion by the CEA (Committee on Evaluation of Applicants, quoted in the bibliography review in Part I of this study) (Heimann, 1968; Klein, 1965; Kappelle, 1996; Beland *et al.*, 2000). Sadly, there is a strongly prevalent temptation to admit "safe" applicants, who, it is expected, won't challenge the status quo, while the unusual restless, creatively different ones have a difficult time with admission committees. I personally know of too many outra-geous examples of rejection of very creative applicants on the basis of narrow-minded biases. For example, one applicant was rejected by one institute because "she was too eager to start training" (she was accepted by another institute and is now a respected member of the psychoanalytic community). Another applicant was rejected in an other institute because "she was too interested in biological research" (!!!), again, to be later accepted by three other institutes. A leading professor of psychiatry was rejected because he made it very clear that he sought psychoanalytic training in order to acquire a broader view of psychology and psychopathology, but that he was not interested in psychoanalysis as his predominant professional activity. He became an enemy of psychoanalysis.

I strongly believe, as pointed out in earlier work (2001a, 2001b), that the admissions criteria should be very broad and flexible, and that, once accepted, evaluation of candidates should be carried out on a "step by step" basis, in honest and open evaluative interchanges with them as part of their supervisory and seminar experience. Obviously, I am not proposing a policy of "Big Brother is watching you," but a collegial, supportive and stimulating professional relationship reflecting the best traditions of a university college model.

A dearth of control cases has been a major problem in many countries in which competing psychotherapeutic institutions have decreased the number of applicants seeking psychoanalytic treatment. This problem translates into the economic reality that institutes receive requests for psychoanalysis largely from patients with very limited financial resources, forcing candidates to see analytic patients at very low fees, and, consequently, reluctant to take on several such treatments at the same time. One offset to this trend would be to improve and increase involvement within the local community to provide information regarding the value and availability of a broad spectrum of psychoanalytically derived treatments.

By the same token, I believe that psychoanalytic psychotherapy with some cases should be one modality of treatment carried out simultaneously with standard psychoanalysis of other cases by psychoanalytic candidates. Such an experience would increase the immersion in psychoanalytic practice and facilitate a sharper understanding of differential indications for treatment, of commonalities and differences in technique in the expected psychoanalytic and psychotherapeutic process. In this connection, the concept of "psychoanalytic process" has been mythologized, to the extent there is little agreement of what this originally relative simple concept now means. It originally referred to the product of the interaction between a clearly designed and carried out psychoanalytic technique, on the one hand, and a patient's capacity to respond to such a technique with a development of understanding of his unconscious by means of the resolution of unconscious resistances and the clarification of unconscious material in the context of transference interpretation and countertransference analysis.

211

The possibility of simultaneously carrying out the treatment of psychoanalytic cases and psychoanalytic psychotherapy cases would also reduce the financial burden on candidates. In some countries, the financial survival of the candidate is seriously threatened due to excessively low fees which do not offset the considerable expenses incurred in analytic training. Obviously, the policy I recommend signifies the need to teach psychoanalytic technique in great detail, to differentiate it from psychoanalytic psychotherapy technique, and to teach psychoanalytic psychotherapy technique in specialized seminars for psychoanalytic candidates. Such a process is beginning to appear in some psychoanalytic institutes in the three regions.

Psychoanalytic psychotherapy has evolved significantly from its origin in (mostly) American ego psychology and the depth psychological approach in Germany into a specific modality of a psychoanalytically derived therapeutic methods indicated in the treatment of severely disturbed patients for whom standard psychoanalysis would be contraindicated or not tolerated, as well or for application to still further modified treatment settings, such as couple and group psychotherapy. All these modalities of treatments are being widely applied presently, in a questionable, diluted form, while the basic theory and technique of psychoanalytic psychotherapy proper has advanced and has been supported by empirical evidence (Fonagy, 2002; Clarkin *et al.*, 2006; Mullen & Rieder, 2002).

The specificity of these approaches, such as v.gr., the transference focussed psychotherapy (TFP) (Clarkin *et al.*, 2006) that focuses on transference, unconscious intrapsychic conflicts, and interpretation, potentially stimulates and facilitates a comparison with standard psychoanalysis that may sharpen the awareness of what is specific to psychoanalytic technique as well. There have been fears expressed in the past that a focus on psychoanalytic psychotherapy "dilutes" the interest in psychoanalysis proper; that many seasoned psychotherapists have difficulty in shifting into a strictly psychoanalytic technique in their experience as candidates, and that candidates may get lured away from psychoanalysis in such a combined training experience.

I believe these fears can be put to rest when both standard analytic technique and psychoanalytic psychotherapy are taught at a contemporary, sophisticated level: and the pressure that such teaching may exert in the direction of a sharper focus on the specificity of psychoanalytic, theory and technique, is a healthy one. Psychoanalytic institutes have the potential for training professionals to become highly competent in a broad modality of psychoanalytically based treatments, appropriate for a broad spectrum of patients, geared to increase their professional competence in the contemporary field of delivery of mental health services, centered in the knowledge of psychoanalytic theory and technique.

One additional advantage of treating several patients from the beginning of training would be a reduction of the fear of "losing" a case, thus not obtaining "credit" for it. In this connection, the reluctance to analyze the negative transference out of the fear of the beginning candidate that this may risk the patient's interrupting the treatment is one of the troubling consequences of the prevailing tendency to evaluate a candidate's immersion in analytic work by the number of hours or the duration of the analysis of control cases. The candidate's evaluation should not be based on "bean counting," but on the assessment of the total quality of his work.

The immersion in treatment of control cases from early on should provide ample information to supervisors regarding the functioning of candidates. Supervisors' evaluation of candidates on a "step by step" basis should constitute the main criterion for progression and, together with satisfactory completion of the intellectual learning derived from seminars, for evaluation of the possibility of candidates' graduation as well. Intense immersion in treatment facilitates the selective process evolving gradually throughout the training, in contrast to a strict "pre-selection" of candidates, or, to the contrary, at a final step, a "post-selection," after candidates have remained relatively free from ongoing evaluation over several years. Obviously, I repeat, such an ongoing evaluation should not be a "persecutory process," that would induce fearfulness and excessive caution in the behavior of the supervisee, but a collegial, ongoing dialogue regarding the tasks and professional requirements of the supervisor.

Graduation from the psychoanalytic institute based on the assessment of the candidate's skill, knowledge, and attitude should be a sufficient guarantee for acceptance as a member of the local psychoanalytic society. In this regard, the traditional "membership paper," which may be a welcome gesture for the new member of the society to become known by the membership, should not be utilized as an additional ritual, the first one of a series that traditionally leads from associate member to full member to training analyst. If an honest interest in psychoanalytic science and development of new knowledge exists at a society and its institute, and candidates interested in developing research are rewarded for their writings, such papers will have an authentic value to foster science and motivate research efforts, in contrast to the ritual presentation of papers supposedly assuring the quality of an applicant to an institution that implicitly may mistrust any truly challenging scientific development in theory and technique.

Graduation from a psychoanalytic institute should be a process involving a minimum of bureaucratic complications. The candidate should be sufficiently well known by the faculty to be assessed as ready for graduation, regardless of what mechanism is established that brings together the information from supervisors, seminar leaders, research consultants, and the progression committee. Mechanisms for redress of grievances involving the candidates' organization as well as a corresponding faculty committee may assess and correct injustices.

Graduation and membership in the local psychoanalytic society should, practically, coincide. In contrast, certification, a higher level of acknowledgement of expertise, corresponding also to the right to analyze candidates, should correspond to a nationally and internationally recognized competence guaranteed by an independent evaluation of the graduates. Here there emerge two major problems: (1) the issue of professional standards, and (2) the risk of excessive bureaucratization and politicization of this process.

Certification implies an independent, objective evaluation of the quality of a graduate's work in fulfillment of professional standards. I believe it is one of the major scandals of psychoanalytic education and of the profession in toto, that so little concern and efforts have been dedicated to the establishment of true *standards of professional competence*, in contrast to our obsessive concern with the *criteria for training*, particularly with "quantifiable" criteria, such as the number of sessions of training analysis per week, the total number of training analytic sessions, the corresponding numbers regarding control cases, the number of supervisory hours, and of seminar attendance. It is an ironic twist that, not infrequently, the same colleagues who seem totally focused on these numbers are also strongly opposed to "quantitative" methods of empirical research. This is another area of major controversy, in which the temptation to mystify psychoanalytic technique, process, and outcome is utilized to question any truly objective standards of competence other than the subjective criteria of experienced clinicians.

Now, of course, the subjective criteria for psychoanalytic competence on the part of experienced clinicians constitute a highly

214

sensitive instrument, and must represent the basis on which the state of the art of the profession may be clarified and utilized as a comparison with the work of a particular graduate. But this subjective evaluation is a far cry from a certification process that would be objective, cross-validated and reliable, applicable to graduates from psychoanalytic institutes in different countries and regions, a certification process that would guarantee a truly valid standard for the knowledge of psychoanalysis, its application to treatment, and to its derived therapeutic methods.

Certification committees, regardless of how they are designed and appointed, run the risk of bureaucratization, of latent sadistic acting out and political infighting. There is no ideal solution to this, but a maximum of openness regarding standards and their corresponding expected criteria, rotation of committee membership under the control of national or regional psychoanalytic associations through their education committees, and mechanisms for the redress of grievances independently staffed and authorized by the same organizations should significantly reduce those problems. This is, obviously, not the present state of affairs.

There are unavoidable psychological problems in evaluating candidates for certification: there are significant differences in individual capacities, talents, interests and dedication, and the risk is to gradually veer the criteria originally applied to evaluating the accomplishment of standard performance into criteria derived from the achievement of superior applicants. This development, in turn, may move the field into a gradual restriction of the certification process, and the fantasy of the "ideal psychoanalyst"—that is, the defensive idealization of our profession, may reemerge in spite of generally acknowledged and accepted criteria of adequate competence. The consciousness of this process within the corresponding educational faculty may contribute to limit this problem.

In some psychoanalytic societies, the presentation of a membership paper and its acceptance by a secret vote of a majority constitutes, at the same time, acceptance to the society and, indirectly, to the International Psychoanalytic Association, totally replacing any process of certification except the graduation approved by the local institute. The lack of objective standards of competence for certification also practically blocks comparative studies of the educational proficiency of particular institutes, and, therefore, weakens the possibility of objective evaluation for the purpose of accreditation of psychoanalytic institutes. The usual rationale in opposing research toward objectification of standards of competence is that it is impossible to establish objective criteria for a professional approach to the dynamic unconscious, to conscious and unconscious subjectivity and intersubjectivity, to their understanding and modification. This rationale runs counter to the evidence that is accumulating from related fields, particularly ongoing research on psychoanalytic and psychodynamic therapy process and outcome. This research indicates the possibility of objectifying criteria for psychoanalytic process as well as outcome, and, particularly, for therapists' skills.

Körner (2002) has convincingly proposed that psychoanalytic expertise can be defined in terms of knowledge, technical skills, and attitude. There is no doubt that knowledge may be objectively evaluated: here emerges the problem of the lack of a focused, sophisticated reflection about what is the knowledge base that should be required from all graduates of psychoanalytic programs, and what are the implications of these requirements for the curriculum of the corresponding institute seminars. There is no question that, regarding objectifying a candidate's capability in the area of technique, much work needs to be done. Probably the most difficult area to objectify is that of the "psychoanalytic attitude." It may well be that the first step in the direction of objectivation of technique and attitude may be the development of standardized psychoanalytic "text" sessions to be evaluated by candidates. Regarding the concepts of a "psychoanalytic attitude," as well as a "psychoanalytic identity," mystification of what is being meant by these terms has contributed to blur the objectivation of the issue. In practice, a psychoanalytic attitude involves the capacity for reflectiveness and intuition about others and self, the capacity for absorption and containment of powerful affects, while reflecting upon, rather than acting upon them, in order to access levels of depth in conscious and unconscious mental processes in self and others that translate, eventually, in the analyst's exploration of transference and countertransference.

But even given objective criteria of standards of competence for certification, from an organizational standpoint, there is no doubt that certification should be carried out by an institution independent from any particular training center and from the political currents of the professional organization. One can envision such a certifying institution to be jointly organized by the entire psychoanalytic field, staffed with recognized professional and scientific leaders, functionally exposed to monitoring by all component institutions whose graduates would undergo the certification process.

The development of an objective system of certification based upon the scientific definition of competence in carrying out psychoanalytic treatment, reflecting the integration of criteria regarding knowledge, clinical skills, and attitude will have to wait until such knowledge has been consolidated and objectified. For the time being, the combined clinical criteria of supervisors and seminar leaders will have to do the job. Eventually, the objective criteria of competence may lead to true standards of quality of care. Such true standards, objectified and in the hands of a responsible entity, widely respected for its objectivity, may then make it possible to certify psychoanalysts across training institutions, and be appropriate to be proposed within a broader social setting as standards to be authorized by a country as part of its legalization of professions in the mental health system. Prematurely establishing processes of certification without such an authentic achievement of definition of psychoanalytic quality of care risks ideological and political pressures, and increases the paranoiagenic problems of the present system. In contrast, an objective certification process may complement an objective accreditation process for psychoanalytic institutes and facilitate the comparison of the effectiveness of educational methods across psychoanalytic institutions.

Local psychoanalytic societies are as concerned with their education departments, that is, their psychoanalytic institutes, as any institute may be realistically concerned about its own future: the accreditation system for institutes should probably be left to an umbrella organization of psychoanalytic societies, be it regional or international, that will consider the extent to which the desirable and agreed upon educational principles and goals are being developed and carried out. The International Psychoanalytic Association should be actively involved in fostering innovation in psychoanalytic education and promulgating internationally agreed upon standards, thus assuring the high quality of IPA certified psychoanalysts internationally, but definitely should not be an international "policeman" controlling education. Internationally agreed upon standards probably should be maintained by regional organizations or national ones (in the case of countries with several psychoanalytic societies).

The certification of members authorized to train psychoanalytic candidates while, at the same time, they thus are practically acknowledged as highly specialized psychoanalysts, would be similar to that of graduates from psychiatric training programs, who then may become board eligible and certified by a specialty board of psychiatry. Non-board certified psychiatrists may equally practice their profession, in the same way as non-certified psychoanalysts actually practice theirs. Nowadays, while in some psychoanalytic societies all the graduates of their corresponding institute are accepted as members, other societies, as mentioned before, maintain the practice of requiring a membership paper presentation, on which the membership then votes secretly to accept a graduate as associate member of the society, and later again, whether to accept that associate member as a full member by the presentation of an additional paper. The status of full membership of the society, in turn, may be an essential requirement for eligibility to the ultimate appointment as training analyst.

It is not surprising that societies that still adhere to this bureaucratization of the promotional process are most affected by political cross currents, possibly subverting the promotion of potential opponents of the presently dominant political establishment at the society and/or institute. While the destructive effects of these procedures on the morale of psychoanalytic societies, on their level of professional functioning, and on scientific creativity have by now been at least partially reduced by corrective measures, there is still enough of this tradition, unquestioned in many places, to negatively affect the entrance of graduates into their local society. Institutionally, this may be considered as an unconscious protest of the psychoanalytic society against the authoritarian elitism of its corresponding institute. From a functional viewpoint, it would seem obvious that all graduates from a local institute be accepted as members of the corresponding society, and that only in very special cases, for reasons of late emerging information regarding professional incompetence, malpractice, or ethical issues a particular graduate should be rejected. It would also seem reasonable that the same privilege of acceptance be granted to graduates of all other IPA psychoanalytic institutes nationally and internationally, with due information from the corresponding institute about the graduate's training record. This process, however, cannot be confused with authentic, nationally and internationally recognized certification, the achievement of objectively defined professional standards, the universal recognition of which should strengthen psychoanalysis significantly throughout all three regions.

Certification is intimately linked with the issue of accreditation of psychoanalytic institutes. The present process of accreditation by site visiting committees from the International Psychoanalytic Association, which accredits the psychoanalytic educational structure of newly developing study groups and psychoanalytic societies, has worked remarkably well, particularly in setting up an overall homogenous educational system as a common base for all psychoanalytic societies, and in providing an administrative educational structure that assures the transmission of psychoanalytic knowledge to the next generation of psychoanalysts. Once in place, the institutes continue functioning autonomously within their corresponding society, without any further evaluation or monitoring from the International Psychoanalytic Association, with the assumption that such a monitoring process and assurance of quality control would be carried out by the corresponding local society itself.

What should be done? It would seem to be highly desirable that an effective monitoring process be established to assure not only the functional effectiveness of psychoanalytic education, but contribute to processes of innovation and experimentation that would assure the development of psychoanalytic institutes as an exciting focus of intellectual, scientific, and professional activities, and attract the best professionals in psychiatry and clinical psychology, in addition to other specialists in the humanities, the social sciences, and neurobiology. These professionals would acquire the psychoanalytic instrument as one of two basic approaches—together with neurobiology—to explore the mind/body relations, psychological functioning in normality and abnormality, the mutual influences of the dynamic unconscious and biological systems, on the one hand, and of unconscious dynamics on psychosocial and cultural processes, on the other. This should be a central mission of the component societies of the International Psychoanalytic Association, and an ongoing mission of the International Psychoanalytic Association itself.

I strongly believe that the monitoring function by psychoanalytic societies of their corresponding institute has to be assured clearly, not only in their constitution and bylaws, but in actual administrative arrangements by which the society has a strong and stable representation at the psychoanalytic institute, and constitutes the last resort for redress of grievances derived from failure, authoritarian mismanagement, or ethical breaches occurring in the context of institute functioning. For psychoanalytic institutes functioning within a Department of Psychiatry or Clinical Psychology of a university structure, this monitoring function may be carried out optimally by the university administrative structure, operating through the corresponding Department or School.

In the case of the American Psychoanalytic Association, it would seem reasonable to integrate the leadership of psychoanalytic institutes—the institute directors—into an organizational structure that directly exchanges information and actively engages in educational improvement and experimentation. This requires, of course, that the elected leadership of psychoanalytic institutes be identified with these goals, which, in turn, implies changes in the executive structures of institutes, such as those proposed elsewhere in my present proposals. At the same time, the overall functioning of the body constituted by psychoanalytic institutes should be supported and monitored by the American Psychoanalytic Association at large, through a high level Education Committee of the Executive Council of the Association that, in turn, as one of its functions, should monitor problems in psychoanalytic education by setting up a sub-committee for the redress of grievances that would permit local societies to raise issues related to their corresponding institute, and ad hoc site visiting Committees that may monitor these developments. This committee should also take over the function of monitoring and re-accrediting APsaA institutes every five to ten years, and develop the instruments and methods for objective evaluation of professional standards. Its main task would be the integration of the functions of research in innovative educational methodology and liaison between the American Association executive structures, on the one hand, and the organization of institutes' leadership, on the other.

The Board of Professional Standards would be replaced by these structural arrangements, with the saving of human and capital resources, that now may be employed in the task of developing objective standards of professional competence, the corresponding objective criteria for certification, and also the standards for accreditation, our next point.

The development of objective standards of certification, implying an agreed upon and objectified minimum knowledge base, an agreed upon and objectified minimum base regarding technical skills, and an agreed upon and objectified set of criteria for a psychoanalytic attitude would clearly energize the kind of training and educational processes expected from psychoanalytic institutes. Objective criteria for accreditation would naturally flow from agreed upon professional standards, and could be developed on the basis of the work done regarding certification. Once it is clearer what we really do expect from a competent psychoanalyst, the question, what does a candidate need to learn, in what way does such a candidate's previous knowledge and experience need to be enriched and modified, becomes clearer. A committee working on universally acceptable standards of certification may provide the background for universally accepted minimal criteria for training and related educational programs.

Once again, it could be argued that, while a psychoanalytic knowledge base would not be too difficult to develop, and even be operationalized in the form of instruments that could objectify the acquisition of this knowledge, this would be much more difficult for technical skills, and perhaps impossible at this time for a psychoanalytic attitude. There is evidence, however (Mullen & Rieder, 2002), of valid and reliable evaluation of technical skills in psychoanalytic psychotherapy by means of presenting specific case material that might stimulate alternative technical interventions against which the skills of an applicant can be tested. This is a promising beginning for a potential methodology to evaluate psychoanalytic expertise and technical skill. Regarding psychoanalytic attitude, efforts to clarify and define criteria of what it really implies may contribute significantly to demystify this concept and to permit developing objective instruments for it as well. However, this may be an area that might still require an individualized, subjective assessment, limiting to some extent, at least for a significant time, the objectivation of this aspect of the psychoanalyst's competence.

The expected knowledge base and experiential learning opportunities provided by the psychoanalytic institute may be specified in the curriculum, the content of theoretical and clinical teaching and the adequacy of the supervisory process spelled out above. Such objective criteria for accreditation of institutes may still be complemented by periodic site visits organized by an independent accrediting organization—if and when such exists—and, in the case of the American Regional Association, by ad hoc site visiting committees of the American Psychoanalytic Association. Such site visits would have to be constituted both by representation from the faculty of other psychoanalytic institutes and members of the Association's Education Committee. In receiving the corresponding reports, the Education Committee would acquire valuable material for further considerations regarding improvement and experimentation in psychoanalytic education.

Objective standards of accreditation, legalized and promoted by the International Psychoanalytic Association, would also facilitate the incorporation within the IPA (and within the American Psychoanalytic Association) of other psychoanalytic societies and societies of psychoanalytic psychotherapy, interested and willing to upgrade their education programs. Once we are concerned about the overall spectrum, depth, and quality of educational processes and content at large, the present obsession with counting numbers of sessions and meetings may be replaced by a broader concern with psychoanalytic education in a deeper sense. Once we have objective standards of psychoanalytic competence, tested and routinely applied, and corresponding standards of accreditation of psychoanalytic institutes, the accreditation of a psychoanalytic institution by the International Psychoanalytic Association may contribute to that institution's prestige locally, and to strengthen its position regarding its local legal, academic, and health delivery systems at large. Certification by an International Psychoanalytic Association backed degree in psychoanalysis, in turn, may provide a guarantee of professional competence that effectively may contribute to the prestige of its holder, and signify more than whatever nationally or federally approved minimum standards for the exercise of the profession of psychoanalysis might become. The IPA could perform a valuable assessment function for those training organizations that wish to assess themselves of a visiting consulting team who would spend their time learning about the history and current functioning of the institution, provide advice, and, if mutually agreed upon, could certify or re-certify the institute as meeting the criteria for IPA accreditation for a five- to ten-year period.

In the last resort, the concern for the future of psychoanalysis and the role of psychoanalytic education in this regard, lies within the psychoanalytic societies, who are directly engaged in the professional, scientific and political interaction with their environment. The clear exception to this rule is the case of psychoanalytic institutes developed within departments of psychiatry or clinical psychology in university settings. Here the institute leadership and faculty are responsible to the chairperson of the Department and the University College, who must make available to themselves the expertise required for such an overview. The experience of the Columbia University Center for Training and Research has been highly satisfactory, and this is a model that should be encouraged strongly as an alternative to free-standing psychoanalytic institutes. In general, however, at this time, the role of psychoanalytic societies in protecting, stimulating, and controlling their psychoanalytic institutes is essential, and will protect the functional nature of psychoanalytic education and with it, the most important potential contributions to the future of psychoanalysis as a science and a profession.

Naturally, such an integration between psychoanalytic institutes and their corresponding psychoanalytic societies should also invigorate the post-graduate education within the psychoanalytic society. In contrast to the present implicit and subtle downgrading of post-graduate education carried out by the society as opposed to the educational activities of the psychoanalytic institute, intimate collaboration between society and institute in post-graduate education, together with the before mentioned joint seminars of candidates and society members should increase the enthusiasm for educational, research, and outreach activities of the psychoanalytic society. The pernicious psychology of the idealization of the training analysis system has tended to systematically downgrade the intellectual pursuit of post-graduate education of psychoanalytic societies, often treated as a "consolation prize" for those society members who have not been appointed as training analysts. The end of that institutional psychology will be a most welcome indication of the vitality of both psychoanalytic education and psychoanalytic societies.

## Note

1 Originally published in: *International Journal of Psychoanalysis*, Vol. 88, 183–202, 2007.

## References

Bartlett, T.A. (2003). My Dream Center for Psychoanalytic Training. *Brainstorming List* (unpublished manuscript).

Beland, H., Brodbeck, H., Legueltel, C. & Rupprecht-Schampera, U. (2000). DPV-Transparenzkommission. Befragung zum Bewerbungsverfahren *Deutsche Psychoanalytische Vereinigung. DPV-Informationen* Nr. 28: 14–23.

Clarkin, J.F., Yeomans, F.E. & Kernberg, O.F. (2006). *Psychotherapy for Borderline Personality: Focusing on Object Relations.* Washington, DC: American Psychiatric Publishing, Inc.

Fonagy, P. ed. (2002). *An Open Door Review of Outcome Studies in Psychoanalysis*. London: International Psychoanalytic Association.

Heimann, P. (1968). The Evaluation of Applicants for Psychoanalytic Training: The Goals of Psychoanalytic Education and the Criteria for the Evaluation of Applicants. *International Journal of Psychoanalysis*, 49: 527–539.

Kappelle, W. (1996). How Useful Is Selection? *International Journal of Psycho-Analysis*, 77: 1213–1232.

Kernberg, O.F. (1999). Psychoanalysis, Psychoanalytic Psychotherapy and Supportive Psychotherapy: Contemporary Controversies. *International Journal of Psychoanalysis* 80: 1075–1091.

_____ (2001a). Presidential Address: Given at the 42nd Intl. Psychoanalytic Congress, Nice France. *International Journal of Psychoanalysis*, 83: 197–203.

_____ (2001b). Some Thoughts Regarding Innovations in Psychoanalytic Education. *Newsletter of the International Psychoanalytic Association*, 10: 6–9.

Klein, H.R. (1965). Selection Techniques. In *Psychoanalysts in Training*. New York: Columbia University Press, pp. 89–128.

Körner, J. (2002). The Didactics of Psychoanalytic Education. *International Journal of Psychoanalysis*, 83: 1395–1405.

Mosher, P.W. & Richards, A. (2004). The History of Membership/ Certification in the APsaA: Old Demons, New Debates (draft 6a, unpublished manuscript).

Mullen, L.S. & Rieder, R.O. (2002). The Psychodynamic Psychotherapy Competency Test (unpublished manuscript).

# 11

# PSYCHOANALYSIS AND THE UNIVERSITY

## A difficult relationship[1]

### The problem: i. external reality

The pressing need for psychoanalysis to establish or re-establish a strong relationship with universities and academic centers of higher learning has become broadly acknowledged and accepted by the psychoanalytic community in recent years—at least, in principle. Statements by leading educators and scholars of the International Psychoanalytic Association have underlined this need, and called for action in this regard (Auchincloss & Michels, 2003; Cooper, 1987; Ferrari, 2009; Garza Guerrero, 2006, 2010; Glick, 2007; Holzman, 1976, 1985; Levy, 2009; Michels, 2007; Paul, 2007; Wallerstein, 1972, 1980, 2007, 2009). The reasons for these alliances are quite obvious: psychoanalysis has been accepted as a major contribution to the culture of the twentieth century, but its future role as a science and a profession is uncertain and being challenged.

Attacks from academic and cultural centers, challenging the scientific status of psychoanalysis and its effectiveness as a treatment, have become fashionable as psychopharmacology and cognitive behavioral treatments have gained ascendancy, offering as they do, short term, less costly alternatives to all manner of psychopathology once the exclusive province of psychoanalysis. From a simple economic viewpoint, the restriction of payment for extended psychotherapies on the part of insurance companies and National Health Service systems have particularly affected psychoanalysis, reinforcing its negative image within the professions of clinical psychology and psychiatry. Psychoanalytic institutes, in regions where they have long been established, have experienced significant reduction in candidates seeking psychoanalytic training, and in patients seeking analysis (Thomä, 2010).

The fundamental contributions that psychoanalysis has made to the related fields of psychology and psychiatry have been absorbed and integrated by those disciplines, but are less and less cited as scientific and professional contributions of psychoanalysis. The most recent example, perhaps, is the important development of attachment theory. Bowlby, steeped in the psychoanalytic tradition, saw attachment paradigms as intrapsychically central to development across the lifespan. Attachment theory is increasingly being explored from a predominantly behavioral perspective, ignoring the development of intrapsychic structures and unconscious fantasy. The description of major personality disorders, such as the narcissistic, masochistic and borderline personality disorders, that stem from psychoanalytic research, are acknowledged, but tend to get incorporated into classificatory systems and theories of etiology that, again, bypass the developmental history of unconscious intrapsychic structures. Psychoanalytic contributions to the understanding of early sexuality, gender determined differentiation of psychological development, and disturbances in sexual functions equally have been absorbed and reformulated in a combination of neurobiological and cognitive behavioral perspectives. The psychoanalytic basis of psychodynamic psychotherapies has expanded this field into a broad spectrum of autonomous psychotherapeutic institutions and applications that have become disconnected from their original psychoanalytic sources.

Also, important psychoanalytic contributions to the field of early childhood development, as well as personality studies, psychopathology, and psychotherapy, have been carried out by psychoanalysts embedded in university settings as professors of social work, psychiatry, and psychology. Many such academic positions have disappeared over the years, particularly in countries where psychoanalysis had managed to have a firm basis in the university, such as in Germany and the United States. In recent generations of psychoanalysts we see a decreasing number of academically active, scientifically engaged professionals. In fact, a major problem posed in the development of new academic leadership in psychology and psychiatry is that it has become more and more estranged from psychoanalysis, as few psychoanalytic scholars are able to compete academically for such positions. To some extent, this process has not been as pervasive in the humanities, where interest in psychoanalysis persists in areas such as linguistics, literary analysis, and the arts, but it is painfully clear in the mental health sciences. All of this reflects the social and cultural environment that psychoanalysis is facing at this time. These challenges are compounded, unfortunately, by important internal realities affecting the psychoanalytic community.

## The problem: ii. internal reality

A major problem is the discrepancy between the general recognition, on the part of the psychoanalytic community, that a move to approach the university and establish a closer link with it would be highly desirable, while, in practice, very little, if any, move in that direction has taken place, because the main center of educational activity and potential research interests naturally would be linked to the tasks of psychoanalytic institutes, the educational enterprise of psychoanalysis, rather than to psychoanalytic societies, the professional side of the field. Universities, of course, have as their major mission to transmit knowledge and to create new knowledge, education and research being their major, intimately linked functions.

Psychoanalytic institutes, to the contrary, are strongly focused on transmitting knowledge, but reluctant to carry out research to develop new knowledge. In so far as all research implies questioning what is known to this point, as part of the process to advance further knowledge, this challenge actually has been reacted to as a threat by the general culture of psychoanalytic institutes (Cooper, 1995; Chapter 6 of this volume).

The scientific isolation of institutes from the development in science at the boundaries of psychoanalysis generates a further, threatening, implicit insecurity regarding new knowledge, and distrust of external sources of knowledge that might influence or even threaten psychoanalytic thinking. A fearful attitude regarding any challenges to traditional psychoanalytic thinking reflects the sense of isolation and implicit frailty of psychoanalytic institutes, stimulates the phobic attitude toward empirical research that still dominates large segments of the psychoanalytic educational enterprise, rationalized most frequently on the basis of the "uniqueness of each long-term psychoanalytic encounter" that defies generalizations and efforts at quantitative assessment.

The regressive effect of a personal analysis does not only operate upon the student body in inducing anxiety, excessive idealizations and paranoiagenic reactions, but also affects the training analysts. Immersed in a social atmosphere of candidates whose personal intimacy they know, and over whom they wield unchallenged decision-making authority as to selection, supervision, progression, graduation, and, above all, evaluation of analytic competency, creates gratifying power for the training analysts' body, on the one hand, and distrust of an external world that may challenge this power and this entire structure, on the other. A permanent ambience of transference and countertransference reactions is reflected in the establishment of guru like figures, on the one hand, and vehement critique of alternative theories to those that dominate within a particular institute, on the other. Add to this a basic anxiety about the firmness and stability of cherished convictions and approaches and you have a breeding ground for conservatism, ideological monopolies, and a petrified intellectual atmosphere that runs counter to the generally growing conviction within the psychoanalytic community at large that a major rapprochement with the university is essential for the future of psychoanalysis.

In short, the basis of the major potential of transmission of knowledge and development of knowledge, of potential research on psychoanalytic theory and technique and on its application to a broad spectrum of related disciplines in the humanities and in neurobiology and medicine, as well as to psychotherapeutic approaches in general as major contribution to the mental health professions, resides precisely in the same institutions where opposition to change, and, at best, a defensive indifference to it are maximal. Thirty years ago psychoanalytic candidates in many countries were implicitly or explicitly dissuaded within psychoanalytic institutes from following parallel careers in psychiatry and psychology and other fields. Only after the more recent decrease of candidates interested in psychoanalytic training, and the aging of the profession throughout established psychoanalytic societies made it clear that we are at risk of becoming irrelevant to a younger generation, has this negative attitude slowly began to change.

It would be unfair, however, to describe psychoanalytic institutes as places where no new knowledge and experimentation occurs. After all, important new psychoanalytic theories and techniques have evolved, and the exploration of the psychoanalytic situation has led to significant advances in knowledge regarding early development, psychopathology, diagnosis and treatment, as well as creative ideas regarding the application of psychoanalysis to other fields.

In all fairness, in spite of the organizational and cultural restrictions operating in the realm of psychoanalytic education, psychoanalytic institutes and societies witnessed the development of important new knowledge, innovative new theories and their applications to psycho-analytic technique and derivative psychotherapeutic procedures. The second half of the last century witnessed the development of Kleinian and neo–Kleinian, particularly Bionian theory and technical innova-tion in psychoanalysis in Great Britain, the emergence of relational psychoanalysis in the United States, the influence of Lacanian con-cepts on French psychoanalysis, new applications of ego psychology to a vast field of psychoanalytic psychotherapy, and new knowledge regarding the psychopathology of severe personality disorders, sexual pathology, the application of psychoanalytic psychotherapy to group, couple, and family therapy, advances in the application of psychoana-lytic understanding of group processes to the study of ideology and political processes, and, more recently, progress in the understanding of the relationship between neurobiology and psychodynamics of affects, with particular reference to depression. In the humanities, psychoanalytic concepts were applied to the study of linguistics and literary criticism, and to the analysis of the social pathology related to totalitarian regimes.

However, the conservative and restrictive atmosphere within psy-choanalytic institutes precluded research into the implications of these new developments within the institutes themselves, nor to develop comparative studies on the differential effects of alternative new psy-choanalytic formulations, indications and limitations of the expanding modalities of psychoanalytically oriented psychotherapies. Within psychoanalytic institutes, alternative theories to the locally dominant one were initially ignored, and subsequently attacked, such as the "wars" between Kleinian and ego psychological institutes and authors during the 1950s through the 1970s. More recently, in an ecumenical spirit that reflected the gradual intellectual opening of psychoanalytic institutes, alternative theories were taught and comparative discus-sions regarding them tolerated within many institutes themselves. But the resistance against formalized research has led to a passive accept-ance of multiple, in many ways contradictory approaches, with an implicit devaluation of the scientific importance to advance in the knowledge of their true value. At times, theories have been treated as metaphors, contrasting them with the practicality of psychoanalytic technique itself. At the same time, however, systematizing psychoanalytic technique to a degree that would permit empirical study of the relation between alternative technical approaches and outcome has been lacking. Empirical research regarding psychoanalytic psychotherapies has been carried out within college and university settings by psychoanalytically trained researchers, but not within psychoanalytic institutes proper. The theoretical work of applying psychoanalysis to the study of group and social processes, religion and philosophy, the understanding of artistic language, for the most part have all occurred in university settings unrelated to psychoanalytic institutes. As mentioned before, psychoanalytically based new knowledge and derived research was incorporated by other disciplines and became disconnected from the mainstream of psychoanalytic endeavors. Within the clinical realm, the development of independent institutes centered on psychoanalytic psychotherapy, competing with psychoanalytic institutes proper, has represented the clinical side of this paradoxical growth and alienation of psychoanalytically derived knowledge.

## The transformation of psychoanalytic institutes: some general preconditions

If the preceding overview of the challenges that psychoanalysis faces at this time, the internal dynamics of the training analyst system within psychoanalytic institutes, the paradoxical development of psychoanalytic knowledge, on the one hand, and a stultifying absence of scientific spirit, and educational stagnation of institutes, on the other, represent an adequate overview of the present situation, some interrelated strategies for overcoming the present crisis of the psychoanalytic profession and science seem promising. Several major contributions to a potential response required at this time have signaled the components of such an approach.

1. Psychoanalytic education has to be radically innovated. The hierarchical rigidity and its derivative deadening of intellectual curiosity needs to be overcome. This requires an embrace of the knowledge explosion in boundary sciences by inviting leading faculty of related fields to become part of the teaching faculty of institutes. Structurally,

the functions of seminar leaders and supervisors should be separated to recognize those who have demonstrated specific capacity for supervising clinical work on the one hand, and those who have original contributions to make to the understanding and development of the cognitive body of contemporary psychoanalysis, on the other. The personal psychoanalysis should be completely separated from the educational functions of the institute, and politically loaded appointment of training analysts should be replaced with a generally accepted method of certification in proficiency as psychoanalytic practitioner, equivalent to the specialty boards in medicine, with free selection by psychoanalytic candidates of their personal analyst within all those certified by such a generally recognized, supra-institutional specialty board. I have described in Chapters 9 and 10 the advantages, preconditions and methods of implementation proposed to abolish the training analysis system and to replace it with a functional arrangement for a high quality personal analysis for psychoanalytic candidates.

2. Formalized research, as an essential aspect of psychoanalytic education, not with the intention of making every psychoanalyst a researcher, but fostering and rewarding research oriented candidates and faculty, particularly those with academic aspirations, and providing them with appropriate institutional mentoring and support, drawing on the vast clinical material available to psychoanalytic institutes, would lead to the development of new psychoanalytic knowledge. This means, at the very least, the establishment of a department of research in psychoanalytic institutes with the freedom to extend inquiry into every aspect of theory, technique, and applications that is part of the curriculum, and reflecting, at all levels, a concern for critical evaluation of what is taught. Experts in research methodology should become an essential part of the leadership of the psychoanalytic institution. The academic credentials of research methodologists within the psychoanalytic institute would facilitate an alliance with the corresponding academic centers, within which collaborative research with the institute could be carried out. university faculty working within the institute would have access to its human resources as well as clinical material, while collaborative research with the university might provide the funding support that would facilitate candidates and faculty to pursue an academic career, in parallel to their analytic one. Again, such a career probably would

hold true only for a small proportion of psychoanalytic candidates, but the benefit of the critical input from related disciplines within the educational atmosphere of the institute would be powerfully strengthened. This development, of course, would imply overcoming the past prejudice against candidates and analysts not dedicated exclusively to their analytic career.

3. The development of a cadre of scholars within psychoanalytic institutes has been the potentially strongest element in fostering new knowledge in the context of psychoanalytic education. Radical innovators have come from the intense involvement with psychoanalytic work, and often have been able to imprint an atmosphere of exciting new developments in psychoanalytic theory and technique. Total immersion in psychoanalytic treatment of patients should be fostered and facilitated for those candidates and faculty evincing particular interests and creativity in their clinical work, and related scholarly writing. But this should not be the only path to the development of new knowledge, nor a rationalization for discouraging all other roads to progress.

In the past, original scholars whose thinking strongly diverged from the dominant ideology of a particular institution were driven into the periphery of the educational process, leading to contentious splits within the psychoanalytic institution. Rather than merely tolerate originality it should be actively fostered as a stimulus for intellectual productivity by inviting distinguished scholars from fields related to psychoanalysis to join the faculty, with the purpose of stimulating a mutually enriching dialogue. The participation of such distinguished scholars from other fields, as well as from the particular institution itself, requires, naturally, an adequate forum to provide a real opportunity for intellectual interchange rather than an implicit isolation of such scholars from the daily educational enterprise. All of this implies open, systematic discussion of new developments and controversial subjects, while strengthening clarity and the realistic potential for theoretical integration, as well as a scientific approach to incompatible hypotheses.

4. Last but not least, the teaching faculty of the institute should include psychoanalytic practitioners whose clinical practice has been expanded to analytically derived areas, the various forms of psychoanalytic psychotherapy, a broader psychiatric practice oriented within a psychoanalytic viewpoint, institutional work, forensic

232

work, organizational consultation, and the Arts. This development would end the wide-spread, painful alienation of many psychoanalytic graduates who have chosen to pursue other clinical specialties rather than focusing on specific psychoanalytic treatment, and in general, the disappointed alienation presently prevalent among graduate analysts who were interested in participating in the work of psychoanalytic institutes, and who, not having been appointed as training analysts, constitute an implicitly devaluated group within the present ambience of the institute.

Here, naturally, the question may be raised whether this is not the task of psychoanalytic societies rather than psychoanalytic institutes proper. The reality, at the present, is that educational activities within the society are generally treated as a secondary type of educational activity, mostly the communication of psychoanalytic knowledge "to the uninformed," or training in psychoanalytic psychotherapy of other mental health professionals, often given to teachers as a "consolation prize" for those who have not become training analysts. Distrust and fear of the introduction of teaching psychoanalytic psychotherapies within the setting of the institute proper plays an important role, and with it, the striking paradox that analytic candidates are being trained to carry out a treatment geared to only a minority of the patients they will see, while their main practice of psychoanalytic psychotherapy remains largely unaddressed and is being taught at competing institutions.

## Practical solutions under way

If we examine jointly the required preconditions proposed as the basis for the urgently needed change within our training institutes, the relationship of psychoanalysis to academia emerges as the central pillar of the establishment of a new system of psychoanalytic education. Psychoanalysis needs the university, although it is not clearly aware of it at this time, and, I believe, in the long run failure to establish these alliances will constitute a severe threat to the future of the psychoanalytic profession and science (Cooper, 1987; Garza Guerrero, 2006, 2010; Thomä, 2010). By the same token, a case can be made for the benefit to academia of psychoanalyses as a science that illuminates the impact of unconscious determinants on psychic life, in the world of the humanistic disciplines as well as in the psychosocial and the naturalistic sciences, particularly in the interface between neurobiology and the functions of the mind. But academia, of course, can very well survive without psychoanalysis, while it is questionable whether, in the long run, psychoanalysis can survive without this link (Auchincloss & Michels, 2003; Michels, 2007). I believe that this fact is gradually being recognized throughout the psychoanalytic community, and has led to a number of attempted solutions.

First of all, an "internal" solution, totally in the hands of the psychoanalytic community itself, is a new relation between the training institute and the psychoanalytic society. There has tended to be a destructive ideological barrier between the psychoanalytic institute as the "elite" of psychoanalysis, and the psychoanalytic society as a second range body, that threatens the preservation and development of psychoanalysis. Within the United States, the concept of the development of a "psychoanalytic center," that is, an integration of the educational, professional, application, and outreach functions that jointly constitute the psychoanalytic enterprise has fostered a new organizational model on the basis of a shared and integrated direction of all of the activities of such a center (Wallerstein, 2007; 2009). It facilitates the teaching of psychoanalytic psychotherapy as part of the regular educational program of the institute, using the clinical expertise as well as theoretical developments of the society members mostly engaged in some form of individual, group, or couples psychotherapy, and the application of psychoanalytic approaches to psychotherapeutic as well as psychiatric consultation.

The center fosters the participation of senior faculty in outreach involvements organized by the society in the form of symposia and conferences that relate psychoanalysis to its local community. It facilitates the development of specialized seminars of interests to both candidates and members of the society, involving candidates early in their training in society activities, as well as their participation in important clinical or theoretical new interests or controversies within the society life. It also facilitates the dismantling of the traditional assumption that anointed training analysts are the best seminar leaders and supervisors. If the leadership of such an integrated psychoanalytic center is constituted, at least, by the director of the institute, a representative of the faculty at large, the President of the Society, a representative of the Outreach Division, the chairperson of the society's program committee, and a representative of the research enterprise (if and when such a specialized department has been developed), in addition to a representative of the candidates' organization, a workable cooperative and functional structure may evolve.

This model does not resolve the isolation of the center from the university, but may be an important step toward greater awareness of the reality faced by the psychoanalytic practitioner in the external world in the current socio-cultural environment. Exciting conferences and scientific activities carried out jointly by society members and students, clinical conferences of candidates and members, joint study groups and supervisory experiences foster a stimulating atmosphere for the educational enterprise. Psychoanalytic institutes and societies in Philadelphia and in San Francisco have reorganized their structure to implement a center model, with various features among those outlined here.

However, as mentioned before, the model of the psychoanalytic center does not resolve the basic problem of the isolation of the psychoanalytic institution from the world of science and academia. A more direct and organizational relationship with university settings may offer many more opportunities, and the possibility of a qualitative transformation of psychoanalytic education, and with it, of the science and the profession as well. A close relation with university settings facilitates creation of departments of research within the psychoanalytic institute, the availability of experts on research methodology from the university, and the linkage with technical and financial resources from the university in a mutually beneficial interaction between the faculties of both institutions. The fact that models involving this rapprochement with universities have already been developed and are flourishing is an extremely encouraging and promising development of psychoanalysis (Levy, 2009; Michels, 2007, Wallerstein, 2007, 2009).

One obvious model is that of a psychoanalytic institute which is part of a university department of psychiatry or psychology. The Columbia University Center for Psychoanalytic Training and Research is such an institution that, for many years, has been part of the Department of Psychiatry of Columbia University, with financial and space support from the Department of Psychiatry, and a corresponding commitment to participate actively in the education of psychiatric residents and trainees, and participation in the research enterprise of the Department of Psychiatry. The director of the psychoanalytic institute is appointed by the Chairman of the Department of Psychiatry, on the basis of the proposal by a committee constituted of representatives from the Department of Psychiatry, the medical school, and the institute faculty. The faculty of the institute is eligible for university appointments, following the general rules and regulations for academic promotion, with heavy emphasis on the research and educational background of candidates for academic promotion. A department of research within this psychoanalytic institute stimulates and coordinates research activities including faculty and psychoanalytic candidates, as well as selected trainees within the department of psychiatry. Important publications in the area of research on education have been achieved, and the intellectual atmosphere of the institute is remarkably open to absorbing new theoretical formulations and technical developments within the psychoanalytic realm. The Association for Psychoanalytic Medicine, the psychoanalytic society of the Columbia Psychoanalytic Community, is an independent institution that has been involved, jointly with the Columbia Psychoanalytic Institute, in outreach activities including the provision of teachers within various colleges of Columbia University, interdisciplinary activities in the form of public conferences involving faculty from the psychoanalytic community as well as other university colleges.

Another variation of this model is offered by the Psychoanalytic Center of Emory University in Atlanta, Georgia, in the United States (Levy, 2009). This is a complex structure, that includes a psychoanalytic institute within the Department of Psychiatry of the medical school, and an autonomous center dedicated to facilitate psychoanalytically oriented education and research throughout the entire university, offering consultation and teaching to various university departments, and arranging for the participation of interested students throughout the university to participate in classes of the psychoanalytic institute. All institute seminars, with the exception of the supervision of clinical cases and seminars on psychoanalytic technique, are open to all Emory students, and the Center organizes specific educational activities and conferences for the university at large. This original program seems an ideal solution to the problem and challenges outlined above.

A major problem with this model is that it is difficult to replicate at this time. A psychoanalytic institute, in order to become eligible to function within or in relation to a Department of Psychiatry or Clinical Psychology of a major university would require the availability of senior, academically productive and recognized members of the psychoanalytic community whose curriculum vitae would permit them to compete successfully for faculty positions—or even chairmanships of university departments in those disciplines. The lack of a strong body of psychoanalytic academicians within a younger generation of psychoanalysts makes this a major constraint: hopefully, it might become a more generalized model in the long run, if and when academically active and recognized psychoanalytic candidates for senior faculty positions and for chairmanships become again available, as was the case for an earlier generation of psychoanalysts in countries such as Germany and the United States. A more viable variation of this model, however, is the possibility of a more loose and flexible association of an independent psychoanalytic institute with a university Department of Psychiatry or Psychology, with teaching commitments of the psychoanalytic faculty in return for voluntary faculty positions affiliated with the university. The cooperative arrangement between the New York University Psychoanalytic Institute and the Department of Psychiatry of the New York University Medical School represents this type of the university-linked model.

An alternative model is the development of an autonomous university institute within or related to a major university setting, the psychoanalytic institute taking on the responsibility of developing a fully fledged program—say, in clinical psychology, acceptable as part of the educational and professional standards of the university, within the rules, regulations, and overall control of the university of such a program. Large psychoanalytic societies may have sufficient intellectual resources to be able to carry out such a program, and this is the model adopted by the Psychoanalytic Association of Buenos Aires (APDEBA), who have developed an Institute of Psychology granting a Master's Degree in Clinical Psychology, under the sponsorship and control of ABDEBA, following the general Argentinean rules and regulations governing private universities, and in close professional interchange with the Association of Private University Institutes (Ferrari, 2009). The psychoanalytic institute provides the faculty that is committed to teach all the requirements for a Master's Degree in Psychology of the university, with a particular accent on psychoanalytic theory and its applications. The students acquire knowledge of psychoanalytic theory and its development, the epistemological questions raised by the study of the dynamic unconscious, the evidence supporting psychoanalytic theory, as well as controversial aspects of it, and a theoretical knowledge about the application of psychoanalytic theory to diagnosis and treatment of the major types of psychopathology within the realm of a psychoanalytic approach.

They do not receive clinical training in psychoanalysis proper, but are encouraged, if they are so interested, to undergo a personal psychoanalysis or psychoanalytic psychotherapy. The success of this program is reflected in the increasing awareness of and attention to psychoanalysis within the overall university ambiance, an increase in interdisciplinary activities, and, last but not least, many students seeking their own analysis, regardless of their eventual career choices.

A somewhat similar program has been initiated in Berlin, with the creation of the International Psychoanalytic University, an independent University Institute that offers a Bachelor's Degree in Psychology and a Master's Degree in Psychology, fulfilling all the requirements for granting these degrees by the German Law governing university mandates and requirements, including the teaching of a comprehensive spectrum of psychological theories and approaches and the development of a research program and corresponding research training that satisfies the general criteria of standards of research training in German University settings (Körner, 2009).

This program does not include clinical teaching of psychoanalytic techniques nor psychoanalytic psychotherapy, but its graduates, hopefully, will be able to apply psychoanalytic theory to the diverse specialties they will be involved in later, and provides an important gateway to psychoanalytic training proper for some of them. The impressive initiative of the International Psychoanalytic University in Berlin was funded by a private donor, a senior, highly respected training analyst who had for many years held the chairmanship of a department of psychology of another university in Germany.

Financial constraints remain, in general, a major factor that limits innovative programs in university settings. At the same time, however, collaborative efforts between university departments interested in research development and with access to particular sources of funding, on the one hand, and the willingness of psychoanalytic institutes to provide both faculty time, patient material, and even space for joint research and educational programs on the other, should offer realistic possibilities.

Another significant constraint may be the hostile reception of psychoanalysis in many departments of psychiatry and psychology, particularly under conditions when long-term competitive struggle between psychodynamic approaches and cognitive behavioral approaches have characterized the mental health field. I believe it is the task of psychoanalytic institutes and societies to try to reverse the

238

bias against psychoanalysis derived from such an intellectual background. Particularly in the United States, the historical dominance of psychoanalysis in many leading university departments of psychiatry in the 1950s and 1960s—characterized in some cases by gross neglect (if not outright opposition to) of the parallel development of biological psychiatry—led to a corresponding "revenge" once biologically oriented psychiatry gained ascendancy, while a parallel process shifted departments of clinical psychology from a psychodynamic into a cognitive behavioral direction. Here patience and political action are required, opening up the psychoanalytic institute to influences from the university, and the institute offering faculty and space, and patient material resources for joint projects with university based disciplines.

The programs referred to in this presentation are major illustrations of viable models of integration or reintegration of contemporary psychoanalysis into university settings and academic life. The enormous resistances of psychoanalytic institutions against change, and the slowness of the process throughout the international psychoanalytic community should not deter us from working in pursuit of this objective. As mentioned before, I believe the future of psychoanalysis as a science and a profession depends on it, even while the contribution of psychoanalysis as a body of knowledge to the cultural development of humanity may already be assured.

## First steps

What follows are some early developments in the creation of new relationships of psychoanalytic institutes with university settings, that, I believe, are open to institutes now, and are realistic possibilities in many countries. To begin, it would be helpful, in the acceptance of candidates for psychoanalytic training, to foster the selection of academically interested and active applicants, such as psychiatrists and psychologists interested in academic careers in research in specialized fields at the boundary sciences of psychoanalysis, as well as distinguished scholars in the humanities and the social and natural sciences. It would be desirable to combine a selection process for candidates that includes students interested exclusively in psychoanalysis as well as students with other creative professional interests who may wish to apply psychoanalysis to their specialty field. Naturally, the latter group of candidates needs to be supported in their efforts to apply psychoanalysis to other specialty fields.

Institute leadership should attempt to approach chairpersons of departments of psychiatry and clinical psychology of universities to explore the possibility of collaborative projects. Inviting leading scientists and scholars to teach relevant subjects at the institute, while offering institute faculty for teaching and supervision at those university departments, and holding jointly sponsored public conferences, may be confidence generating, mutually helpful initiatives. Particularly experts in sciences at the boundary of psychoanalytic theory and developments may enrich psychoanalytic education and create an atmosphere favorable to possible collaborative studies and research.

Sometimes the ideal area for a productive collaboration resides in the humanities: literature, cultural anthropology, linguistics, and philosophy. Interdisciplinary approaches, of course, have to be based on an honest desire for mutual learning: it cannot be a one-way street. The area of psychosomatic medicine offers an opportunity for collaboration, as both psychiatry and psychoanalysis can benefit from one another's contribution to the understanding of this issue.

Opening up courses at the psychoanalytic institute to students and faculty of a university with which the institute is engaged in some collaborative effort may be an optimal channel for interesting young academicians in a psychoanalytic career: such interest has already been actualized in some of the initiatives mentioned such as the Emory Center and the German International Psychoanalytic University (Levy, 2009).

In short, opening the psychoanalytic institute to a genuine attempt at rapprochement with the university may be a viable beginning for creative and really essential new avenues for the future development of psychoanalysis as a science and a profession.

## Note

1 Originally published in: *International Journal of Psychoanalysis*, Vol. 92: 609–622, 2011.

## References

Auchincloss, E.L. & Michels, R. (2003). A Reassessment of Psychoanalytic Education: Controversies and Changes. *International Journal of Psychoanalysis*, 84: 387–403.
Cooper, A. (1987). Changes in Psychoanalytic Ideas. *Journal of the American Psychoanalytic Association*, 35: 77–98.

_____ (1995). Discussion: On Empirical Research. In: T. Shapiro & R.N. Emde (eds). *Research in Psychoanalysis-Process, Development, Outcome.* Madison, CT: International Universities Press, pp. 381–391.

Ferrari, H. (2009). IUSAM-APdeBA: A Higher Education Institute for Psychoanalytic Training. *International Journal of Psychoanalysis*, 90: 1139–1154.

Garza Guerrero, C. (2006). *Crisis del psicoanálisis. Desafíos organizativos y educativos contemporaneous [Crisis of Psychoanalysis: Contemporary Organizational and Educational Challenges]*. Mexico: Editores de Textos Mexicanos.

_____ (2010). Psychoanalysis-Requiescat in Pace? (A Critique from within and a Radical Proposal (unpublished manuscript).

Glick, R.A. (2007). Psychoanalytic Education Needs to Change: What's Feasible? Introduction to Wallerstein. *Journal of the American Psychoanalytic Association*, 55(3): 949–952.

Holzman, P.S. (1976). The Future of Psychoanalysis and Its Institutes. *Psychoanalytic Quarterly*, 45: 250–273.

_____ (1985). Psychoanalysis: Is the Therapy Destroying the Science? *Journal of the American Psychoanalytic Association*, 33: 725–770.

Körner, J. (2009). Personal Communication.

Levy, S.T. (2009). Psychoanalytic Education Then and Now. *Journal of the American Psychoanalytic Association*, 57(6): 1295–1309.

Michels, R. (2007). Optimal Education Requires an Academic Context: Commentary on Wallerstein. *Journal of the American Psychoanalytic Association*, 55(3): 985–989.

Paul, R.A. (2007). Optimal Education Requires an Academic Context: Commentary on Wallerstein, *Journal of the American Psychoanalytic Association*, 55(3): 991–997.

Thomä, H. (2010). Remarks on the First Century of the International Psychoanalytic Association (IPA) and a Utopian Vision of Its Future (unpublished manuscript).

Wallerstein, R.S. (1972). The Futures of Psychoanalytic Education. *Journal of the American Psychoanalytic Association* 20: 591–606.

_____ (1980). Psychoanalysis and Academic Psychiatry-Bridges. *Psychoanalytic Study of the Child*, 35: 419–448.

_____ (2007). The Optimal Structure for Psychoanalytic Education Today: A Feasible Proposal? *Journal of the American Psychoanalytic Association*, 55(3): 953–984.

_____ (2009). Psychoanalysis in the University: A Full-Time Vision. *International Journal of Psychoanalysis*, 90: 1107–1121.

---

# 12

## SUICIDE PREVENTION FOR PSYCHOANALYTIC INSTITUTES AND SOCIETIES[1]

---

What follows are guidelines for rescue teams dedicated to suicide prevention for psychoanalytic institutes and societies. They provide a general orientation, and presuppose intensive individual and organizational training by the rescue teams. Some general notes of caution: suicide prevention is a complex, delicate effort that requires specific training, experience, knowledge, patience, and courage! It is a well-known fact that drowning persons may resist rescue efforts, thereby posing the danger of drowning the rescuer along with themselves. Similarly, expect desperate, blind resistances to your efforts, particularly when the suicidal temptation is urgent and overwhelming.

Any effort to change the present condition of a failing psychoanalytic society is likely to generate intense anxiety, frequently expressed as a desperate clinging to "standards." "Standards," in theory, should refer to criteria of competence; but here they are a simple set of criteria for training, primarily formulated by "bean counting" numbers of hours, and, at the bottom, a quiescent maintenance of the comfortable way things have been done (or seemed to have been done) in the past. The effort to teach survival skills, implying the learning of new ways to deal with a threatening reality, typically provokes worries about the victim's "identity," the existential doubt whether one still is what he/she does ("Am I still a psychoanalyst?"). The introduction of new knowledge and ways of dealing with reality tend to provoke desperate claims for the assumed purity of the past (Chapters 9 and 10).

242

Yet, don't despair! Keep your confidence. Remember Abba Eban's statement at the United Nations, in 1967, expressing his profound conviction that, "after everything else fails, nations as well as individuals become reasonable . . . "

## Suicide prevention guidelines

### 1. Establish a life line with local universities

In the long run, psychoanalytic institutions floating alone in the uncertainties of cultural seas are at risk of becoming drifting ideological islands. Psychoanalysis as a science needs the firm hand of the scientific world. To thrive, psychoanalysis needs to be connected to the sciences at its boundaries. To counteract stultifying professional, scientific and social isolation, the teaching faculty of your institute and society should lecture, supervise, lead psychotherapy seminars, and participate in the academic activities of departments of psychiatry and psychology of your local region. Invite chairpersons of university departments in the behavioral sciences and humanities to lecture and teach at your psychoanalytic institute and society, as part of an effort to relate psychoanalysis to its boundary disciplines and sciences. Establish working relationships both with academics who are sympathetic to psychoanalysis, as well as those who are sharply critical, inviting the latter for lectures, informal discussions, and joint seminars. Be prepared to listen to critiques of psychoanalysis. We have acted in a superior way at times, and have been demeaning of biological psychiatry not too long ago . . . and we still have our own gurus with supposed unique access to ultimate truths . . . (Auchincloss & Michels, 2003; Garza Guerrero, 2006; Michels, 2007; Paul, 2007; Levy, 2009; Wallerstein, 2007, 2009).

Offer collaboration of your faculty, and of carefully selected patient derived research material as a contribution for potential collaborative research projects with university departments. Consider establishing or re-establishing a close affiliation with a university school or department, under varying administrative arrangements, and explore the possibility of establishing joint programs leading to master and/ or doctoral degrees. Accept students from university departments with which your institute has established a liaison, to attend selected psychoanalytic classes.

## 2. Develop psychoanalytically derived
### psychotherapy programs

Stimulate your institution to develop psychoanalytic psychotherapies for the severe, non-psychotic and non-organic patients for whom standard psychoanalysis is not indicated, and for whom empirical evidence confirms the effectiveness of psychoanalytically derived therapies. Embrace the demonstrated value and effectiveness of psychoanalytically derived treatments (Fonagy, 2002). Free your institute from the grandiose idealization of standard psychoanalysis as the only truly worthwhile treatment method. Develop specialized seminars, at the highest level (not simplified "introductory courses" for the "great unwashed"), studying recent progress in psychoanalytic psychotherapies, particularly specialized psychoanalytic psychotherapies for severe personality disorders, brief psychoanalytic psychotherapies for specific symptomatic disorders, psychoanalytic couples therapy, psychoanalytic family therapy, psychoanalytic group psychotherapy, and psychoanalytic approaches to hospitalized patients with severe behavioral problems and personality disorders.

Provide counseling for faculty who believe that seriously engaging in psychoanalytic psychotherapy—or even exposure to the corresponding training—threatens their identity as psychoanalysts. By expanding your training into these directions, you will prepare your candidates for the treatment challenges, and the patient populations they will face in their practice, in the real world. (And you will contribute to their financial survival as well!)

You may have to "import" psychoanalysts who are experts in evidence-based, empirically researched types of psychoanalytic psychotherapy for inclusion in your basic curriculum, as well as to develop specialized tracks for a broader group of professionals. Be friendly to analysts who wish to have an exclusive psychoanalytic practice, but provide counseling for those who believe that the exclusive objective of psychoanalytic training is to produce analysts like themselves. Develop a diversity of psychoanalytic psychotherapy treatment programs in your low cost clinics, and expertise regarding indications, contraindications, prognosis, and differential techniques that sharpen and actualize these criteria for psychoanalysis proper as well as the broader therapeutic spectrum.

Offer specialized courses on standard psychoanalytic technique as well as on the other modalities, with differentiated educational tracks for psychoanalytic candidates as well as for professionals in the boundary fields of psychiatry, psychology, social work, with both joint and separate courses for alternative training programs. Offer individual and group supervisions, seminars and round tables where alternative models of technique can be discussed and corresponding research questions raised. Compete effectively with local institutions offering simplified, unsophisticated therapy training programs. Free your institute from remnants of derogatory attitudes to all therapies other than standard psychoanalysis. Put an end to the destructive attitude of considering psychodynamic psychotherapy as second-rate treatment. It demeans the corresponding training of candidates, and the treatment of patients and the patients themselves who do have an indication for psychotherapy. Above all, prepare your graduates to provide optimal treatment methods to the broad spectrum of patients they will encounter in their clinical practice.

### 3. Inject a research orientation into your organizational life

Indoctrination with monopolistic theories, once common in psychoanalytic education, should be abandoned for a contemporary tolerance of multiple, potentially contradictory theories, conveying an openness to new ideas. Consolidation of psychoanalysis as a science requires the ongoing testing of new theories, their confrontation with alternative theories, and the exploration of relations to boundary sciences. This means ongoing research (Cooper, 1987, 1995; Fonagy, 2002; Chapter 6 of this volume). You must help your society and institute to create and develop a research thrust as a major institutional goal. Import, if necessary, outside research experts in the behavioral sciences, even non-analysts who are interested in psychoanalytic principles, and support a research focused group that helps to raise questions, studies methods for exploring them, and motivates students, faculty and analysts at large to participate. Explore the boundaries of psychoanalysis: keep in mind the importance of developing new knowledge, not just clarifying the old! Develop specific research projects, and avoid endless byzantine discussions about "what is research."

Give high priority to investment in a research director, an expert in up to date methodology of research in the behavioral sciences, who, ideally, should be a psychoanalyst himself (there still are, thank God, such individuals in our international community, in spite of many years of suicidal behavior of our institutes to chase them away), or a behavioral scientist interested in and sympathetic to psychoanalysis. Develop a department of research in your institute with the task of fostering the development of significant, researchable questions throughout all the subject matters taught at the institute, and providing methodological support to candidates, faculty and society members interested in carrying out concrete research projects. The research department should interact with teaching faculty to develop these interests, organize conferences and debates to sharpen hypotheses that may be tested through formal research endeavors. A small psychoanalytic society may have difficulties in setting up such an initiative and may benefit from a general relationship with a university setting.

Organize a few basic research projects throughout your institute, including, particularly, joint projects with university departments, wherever possible. Combine the faculty and patient material resources of the psychoanalytic institute with the basic research support system and expert research organization of university settings. Provide ongoing seminars and forums on research methodology relevant to psychoanalysis and related mental health sciences. Help teachers of specific subjects in the institute to formulate controversial questions in their field, and to transform them into clinically researchable projects, including, particularly, the scientific methodology for single subject research. Give highest priority to research involving the evaluation of efficacy and effectiveness of psychoanalysis and derived treatment methods, and attempt to link up with other psychoanalytic institutions in generating an adequate research base for that purpose.

Reward candidates and faculty engaged in significant research efforts with leading administrative positions and honor roles in the psychoanalytic institution. Develop a hierarchical ladder for promotion and institutional appreciation for researchers and gifted educators, in contrast to a hierarchical structure reserved for training analysts without further meritorious contributions. Give preference of admission to academically active and interested candidates. Avoid the temptation to give preference exclusively to candidates who only wish to learn standard psychoanalytic technique, and, if possible, do only psychoanalysis as professional work: don't reject them, but make it clear where your priorities lie!

## 4. Present a realistic public image of your scientific achievement and concerns and your clinical and professional contributions

Inform your cultural community what psychoanalysis has to offer in terms of new treatment possibilities in addition to the standard analysis that most people can't afford. Communicate new findings that have relevance for cultural problems and concerns, such as drug addiction, alcoholism, sexual difficulties, education, adolescent rebelliousness, crime prevention, fundamentalist ideologies, child rearing, psychodynamics and neurobiology, etc. Expose your ideas and findings to serious public scrutiny in interdisciplinary conferences and public lectures and discussions. Make it an essential responsibility for your leading faculty to participate in these programs. Abolish "Extension Divisions" as consolation prizes for non-training analysts! Your university connections and research development are your major assets to bridge our field with the public. Organize public lecture series on prevalent mental health problems with presentation of psychoanalytic contributions to that field. Organize interdisciplinary conferences with psychoanalysts and other respected public figures in academia, university departments, cultural institutions, religious organizations, the humanities, the arts, and, even politics. Develop a network of distinguished psychoanalytic theoreticians, academics, and researchers in your region, able to carry out such public activities at a high level.

Keep the psychoanalytic society meetings open to the general public, with the exception, of course, of confidential clinical meetings. Foster the participation of knowledgeable, responsible psychoanalysts in public debates on controversial mental health issues: substance use, sexual education, gun control, terrorism, censorship, television. Provide information about your training programs to all mental health professionals. Offer consultations and information services for specialists in the behavioral sciences regarding clinical problems of your expertise.

Foster publications by faculty and candidates, particularly regarding research efforts and findings. Stimulate faculty and candidates to publish in academically prestigious journals, in addition, of course, to specialized psychoanalytic journals proper. Help candidates to develop their curriculum vitae appropriately and effectively for competing for academic positions. Make it possible for psychoanalysts of a future generation to compete effectively for university

247

professorships, in contrast to the self destructive past tendency to discourage the academic developments of psychoanalytic candidates outside their institutes. Re-educate faculty who discourage candidates from all aspects of their professional careers other than psychoanalytic work in a restricted sense. Stimulate candidates to graduate as soon as possible, and provide them with advice and counsel regarding their future academic careers, both helping their professional development and the significant presence of psychoanalysis in universities and academic life.

Rigorously extirpate all bureaucratic devices that slow the progression of candidates, such as regulations that only permit child analysts to graduate when they no longer can bend to play with children on the floor, or graduates from adult programs to celebrate their graduation with their adult grandchildren. Faculty who believe training should be lengthened to make it more effective need counseling!

## 5. Innovate psychoanalytic education

*A note of warning*: This will be the most difficult aspect of your rescue efforts, when a frightened, sometimes almost moribund psychoanalytic society and institute will desperately fight off the rescuers. You will have to protect yourself from being drawn into a self destructive struggle; combine courage with patience, firmness with concern and empathy, and be prepared to be experienced as a shocking, dangerous adversary by those to whom you extend a helping hand. You may be labeled as "non-analytic," "anti-analytic," or both, and in some countries as "psychiatrist," representing the "medical model"; and, certainly, insufficiently analyzed!

a. *Abolish the training analysis system.* By now, it is quite widely known that the hierarchical organization of psychoanalytic training has contributed to the petrification of faculty and candidates, and has become a major source of self-destructive, isolating, infantilizing, authoritarian organizational structures (Balint, 1948; Berman, 2004; Bergfeld, 1962; Germain, 1986; Garza Guerrero, 2004; Kirsner, 2003; Meyer, 2003; Reader, 2004; Roustang, 1982; Thomä & Kaechle, 1999; Chapter 3 of this volume). The positive features of the training analysis system represented the attempt to assure a high quality of the personal psychoanalytic experience of candidates. That, of course, needs to be maintained, but not the elitist, arbitrary gathering of administrative powers and non-functional authority that evolved with this system. You need to help the institution develop methods for a functional evaluation of psychoanalytic competence of all graduates, leading to a certification in psychoanalysis based on realistic criteria of competence, after a post-graduate period of three to five years (of exclusive or non-exclusive) psychoanalytic practice. Offer this certification to all interested graduates, and develop a transparent, functional system of carrying out a corresponding examination that assures its objectivity, and that includes mechanisms of assurance of institutional responsibility. Then, authorize all certified psychoanalysts to treat psychoanalytic candidates, as part of their specialty certification. This approach, by the way, will assure that the general public will receive as high quality psychoanalytic treatment as the candidates. Keep the personal psychoanalysis completely separate from all other aspects of psychoanalytic education, with the exception of information to the psychoanalytic institute, with authorization from the candidate, that the candidate is in or has terminated a personal psychoanalysis. The analytic treatment of the candidate should not make the certified psychoanalyst who treats him automatically a member of the psychoanalytic institute, nor, in any way, related to the educational administration of the institute. These arrangements will assure the complete privacy of the personal analysis, operate against the unresolvable transferential idealization of the training analyst as the highest possible carrier of psychoanalytic knowledge, and decrease the fearful submission to the training analyst as a member of an elite minority that rules over the ultimate destiny of the entire candidate body. These arrangements also will protect the certified psychoanalyst from the corrupting narcissistic grandiosity induced by the privileged status currently conveyed upon the "training analyst" as superior psychoanalyst, expert supervisor, gifted seminar teacher, and wisely experienced administrator.

These arrangements should reduce the protective ambience of the training analyst body against threats to their ivory tower atmosphere of an institution that ignores, as much as possible, the external world.

b. *Select faculty for the psychoanalytic institute* on the basis of their demonstrated capacity for excellent teaching, intellectual interests, and specialized knowledge in a significant area, tested by their participation in the scientific activities of the psychoanalytic institution, as well as in other academic institutions in which they participate.

This selection process should be the basis for your cadre of seminar leaders, and the quality of their teaching tested by the product, the knowledge development of the trainees, and the assessment by students and colleagues of these seminar leaders. Select supervisors from among psychoanalysts who have demonstrated their particular interest in, knowledge of, and potential contribution to psychoanalytic technique, demonstrated their capacity for integration and clarity in their technical approach, and the capacity to contribute significantly to the clinical gatherings, conferences and seminars of the psychoanalytic society. Such individually selected supervisors and seminar leaders should constitute the faculty, together with the specialized researchers developed by or "imported" into the institute, both psychoanalysts and non-psychoanalysts interested in contributing to the teaching of research methodology and the development of research efforts of the psychoanalytic institution. They, and other distinguished professionals from boundary disciplines with psychoanalysis would constitute the psychoanalyst and non-psychoanalyst members of the faculty.

c. *Integrate the traditional psychoanalytic institute* with the psychoanalytic society's "extension division" or "outreach division," the "psychotherapy division," the "post-graduate education" division, and the administrative structure of the psychoanalytic society at large. The concept of a *"psychoanalytic center,"* developed in some areas within the United States, is one model for such an integration. Such an integrated model should permit the organization of a large educational program that includes the various therapeutic specialties and public activities of psychoanalysis referred to above, and a combination of integrated and separate tracks of training leading to different degrees and certifications. Wherever possible, integrate all these structures within or in affiliation with a department of psychiatry or psychology within which the psychoanalytic institute may operate or with which the psychoanalytic society has become particularly related or integrated in some fashion. In the process of this overall integration as a "Center," a significant number of members of the psychoanalytic society may be activated, who, by their dedication to seminar teaching, clinical supervision, and/or research, thus become members of the faculty (Ferrari, 2009; Levy, 2009).

d. *Rotate teachers*, even very gifted ones, after some years, to avoid ossification of the curriculum. Be concerned regarding the presentation of updated knowledge in the fields of development, personality, pathology, and treatment. Avoid "introductory courses," leading to boring repetitions of educational contents; keep the seminars lively and interesting. Organize conferences on controversial issues in all fields; foster research, and report it to candidates and in society meetings; confront the candidates with the simultaneous presentation of contradictory views, rather than isolated presentation of different viewpoints with an "ecumenical" neutral tolerance and absence of critical assessments. These may be starting points for creative research.

e. *Invite outside experts* to teach in areas were you don't have your own expertise; invite university professors of boundary sciences to teach in the psychoanalytic seminars. Bring up to date information regarding social psychology and neuroscience developments into the institute curriculum.

f. *Promote a candidates' organization* represented at all levels of the institute's committees, particularly regarding the curriculum, and faculty evaluation.

g. *Be actively involved in ongoing development of professional standards and the corresponding standards for training*, in terms of what knowledge is expected, how knowledge and analytic attitude may be evaluated, how honest feedback regarding performance may be provided to candidates (in contrast to "compassionate graduation"). The lack of development of professional standards in psychoanalysis, that is, criteria of competence, in contrast to criteria for training, is a shocking fact, derived from approximately 80 years of a basically unchanging educational method. The prevalent criteria for training, such as, the consideration of number of hours of personal analysis, of supervised control analyses, and of attendance at seminars, plus a vaguely formulated "analytic attitude," are symptoms of a dysfunctional psychoanalytic training methodology, and an urgent question your institution should consider. What theoretical knowledge, technical expertise, and analytic attitude should we expect, how do we teach them, and what objective method of evaluation of the corresponding competence do we need to develop?

Your ultimate goal should be to make the institute and the psychoanalytic society exciting intellectual centers that can effectively compete with and are open to the behavioral science institutions of your area. Strive for the opposite of the classical definition of education as the "inculcation of the incomprehensible by the incompetent into the ignorant."

## 6. *"Don't worry, leave me alone, I just want to sleep!"*

As mentioned before, drowning victims often put up strong resistance against their rescuers. And mental health professionals treating severely ill patients with chronic, characterological dispositions to suicidal actions are familiar with the patients' sophisticated denials when resisting treatment efforts. The rescue teams for psychoanalytic societies need to be aware of similar opposition to their rescuing efforts. Familiarize yourselves with the expression of this opposition to rescuing efforts. A few typical expressions of resistance:

"Psychoanalysis is a science that cannot be compared to other scientific fields. In contrast to all psychotherapies it explores the unconscious in a specific approach, that requires a complex, lengthy exploration of the candidate's own unconscious in a unique inter-personal situation, the evolving psychoanalytic relationship with the training analyst. Psychoanalytic competence depends largely on this learning experience with a particularly skilled, experienced, and motivated training psychoanalyst who reflects the highest level of achievement in the exploration of the unconscious. This level of achievement cannot be assured to be reached by all psycho-analytic institute graduates, because a candidate's particular talents, his intense and long-term commitment to psychoanalysis, and his training experience with an equally motivated and highly experienced training psychoanalyst constitute a rare combination of talent, motivation, commitment and experience."

"Such a learning experience requires the careful selection of the most capable graduates as training analysts, while accepting that a broader range of adequately trained graduates may treat patients in the general population for whom such a particular training capability as required to train analysts is not necessary. Therefore, we have to maintain and protect the present training analysis system, and carefully protect, differentiate and isolate the psychoanalytic process from contamination or dilution by other procedures."

"This unique setting of training requires a sheltered, protected atmosphere, a psychoanalytic institute that clearly and consistently provides this highly specialized experience for the candidates, and protects them from the risk of dilution of their evolving expertise by focusing on merely psychotherapeutic methods. Particularly problematic may be psychotherapy methods that appear to imitate, or derive their techniques from psychoanalysis proper, but stimulate the trainee into interventionist behavior that runs counter to the psychoanalytic attitude. The attunement to the patient, the listening to the unconscious in the context of the analytic process is a highly specialized, subtle and unique method, and the combination of this learning with that of psychotherapeutic orientation and behavior are confusing and counterproductive."

"The profession of psychoanalysis requires a lengthy immersion in psychoanalytic work, time for reflection and maturation in the exploration of the unconscious that is negatively affected by competing professional goals that require commitments to other behavioral, academic, administrative and scientific fields. Under such distracting circumstances, psychoanalytic immersion in the unconscious tends to be reduced to a sporadic, increasingly less familiar and discrepant endeavor, which cannot but decrease the competence in analytic work. Analytic identity becomes eroded under such circumstances."

"Research on the nature of the unconscious and on its many influences in human life, culture and society cannot be based on the usual quantitative, objective source of data that lend themselves to standard empirical research. Psychoanalysis is a personally unique inter–subjective experience that constitutes an irreducible, essential and incomparable field of knowledge. Therefore, efforts to acquire acceptability by boundary sciences has to be based on sharing with them the unique nature of psychoanalytic findings, and not on efforts to imitate their methods as a way to promote acceptance of psychoanalysis."

Rescue teams study these manifestations of resistance to your efforts and confront them serenely, empathically, patiently, but firmly. You may point out that there is no reason why seminars on psychoanalytic theory and technique and on psychotherapy theory and technique cannot be taught in the same institute. On the contrary: candidates exposed to both fields may become more sharply aware of differentiation of techniques, indications, contraindications, and prognosis, and be better prepared to treat the patients they are going to see in their professional practice. You may also point out that the certification of psychoanalysis proposed here may, to begin, use the same criteria for selection now employed in the most functional and least authoritarian and politicized psychoanalytic institutes, while progress is made in developing authentic criteria of professional competence and methods of their evaluation. In addition, you may tactfully refer to the growing body of empirical research in psychoanalysis and psychoanalytic psychotherapies, and that empirical research and conceptual developments are complementary, not antinomic. But, finally, remember, reasonableness prevails only after everything else fails . . . Vigorously and enthusiastically, work to rescue your patient!

These, then, are your basic suicide prevention guidelines. Once again, keep calm, improvise when necessary, and remember to assure drowning victims that survival will also mean survival of their professional identity.

## Note

1 Originally published in the *Journal of the American Psychoanalytic Association*, 60:4, 707–719, 2012.

## References

Auchincloss, E.L. & Michels, R. (2003). A Reassessment of Psychoanalytic Education: Controversies and Changes. *International Journal of Psychoanalysis*, 84: 387–403.

Balint, M. (1948). On the Psychoanalytic Training System. *International Journal of Psycho-Analyst*, 29: 163–173.

Berman, E. (2004). *Impossible Training: A Relational View of Psychoanalytic Education*. New York: Analytic Press, p. 288.

Bernfeld, S. (1962). On Psychoanalytic Training. *Psychoanalytic Quarterly*, 31: 453–482.

Cooper, A. (1987). Changes in Psychoanalytic Ideas. *J Am Psychoanal Assoc.*, 35: 77–98.

_____ (1995). Discussion: On Empirical Research. In *Research in Psychoanalysis: Process, Development, Outcome*. Edited by Shapiro, T. & Emde, R.N. Madison, CT, International Universities Press, pp. 381–391.

Cremerius, J. (1986). Spurensicherung. Die "Psychoanalytische Bewegung" und das Elend der psychoanalytischen Institution. *Psyche* 40: 1063–1091.

Ferrari, H. (2009). IUSAM-APdeBA: A Higher Education Institute for Psychoanalytic Training. *International Journal of Psychoanalysis*, 90: 1139–1154.

Fonagy, P. ed. (2002). *An Open Door Review of Outcome Studies in Psychoanalysis*: London: International Psychoanalytic Association.

Garza Guerrero, C. (2004). Reorganizational and Educational Demands of Psychoanalytic Training Today: Our Long and Marasmic Night of One Century (With a Rejoinder by Eglé Laufer). *International Journal of Psychoanalysis*, 85: 3–25.

_____ (2006). Crisis del psicoanálisis: desafíos organizativos y educativos contemporaneos [Crisis of Psychoanalysis: Contemporary Organizational and Educational Challenges]. Mexico City, Mexico: Editores de Textos Mexicanos.

Kirsner, D. (2004). Psychoanalysis and Its Discontents. *Psychoanalytic Psychology*, 21(3): 339–352.

Levy, S.T. (2009). Psychoanalytic Education Then and Now. *Journal of the American Psychoanalytic Association*, 57(6): 1295–1309.

Meyer, L. (2003). Subservient Analysis. *International Journal of Psychoanalysis*, 84: 1241–1262.

Michaels, R. (2007). Optimal Education Requires an Academic Context: Commentary on Wallerstein. *Journal of the American Psychoanalytic Association*, 55(3): 985–989.

Paul, R.A. (2007). Optimal Education Requires an Academic Context: Commentary on Wallerstein. *Journal of the American Psychoanalytic Association*, 55(3): 991–997.

Reeder, J. (2004). *Hate and Love in Psychoanalytical Institutions: The Dilemma of a Profession*. New York: Other Press.

Roustang, F. (1982). *Dire Mastery: Discipleship from Freud to Lacan*. Baltimore, MD: Johns Hopkins University Press.

Thomä, H. & Kächele, H. (1999). Memorandum on a Reform of Psychoanalytic Education. *International Journal of Psychoanalysis*, 8: 33–35.

Wallerstein, R.S. (2007). The Optimal Structure for Psychoanalytic Education Today: A Feasible Proposal? *Journal of the American Psychoanalytic Association*, 55(3): 953–984.

_____ (2009). Psychoanalysis in the University: A Full-Time Vision. *International Journal of Psychoanalysis*, 90: 1107–1121.

# THE TWILIGHT OF THE TRAINING
# ANALYSIS SYSTEM[1]

What follows is the outline of a proposal for a fundamental renovation of the educational task of psychoanalytic education. I apply this proposal to the particular situation of the American Psychoanalytic Association (APsaA), but I believe that the general analysis that follows applies to the International Psychoanalytic Association (IPA) community as well. Given the complexity of APsaA, many aspects of this proposal may be illustrated with this focus. I shall focus specifically on the application of the proposed model to APsaA.

## The challenges to psychoanalysis at this time

I believe there exists, nowadays, general agreement in our psychoanalytic community regarding major external challenges to psychoanalysis. There is serious skepticism of psychoanalysis in the realms of the biological and psychological science: in neurobiology, where rapid development of knowledge impinges on the psychoanalytic theories of motivation, development, and psychopathology; in the area of psychiatric treatment, where psychopharmacology has become de rigeur for a number of conditions earlier treated by psychoanalysis; in the area of psychological treatment, where cognitive behavioral psychotherapy has achieved mainstream acceptance for a broad array of disorders, and, more fundamentally, throughout the entire scientific community there prevails a critique of the lack of empirical research on the part of the psychoanalytic profession. Further, there has been a growing critique coming from federal funding sources and private insurance companies of psychoanalysis as a too long term, too expensive, non-empirically validated treatment, creating a cultural shift away from psychoanalysis as an elitist pursuit for the wealthy. The cultural critique of psychoanalysis at this time is also related to the dominance of anti-individualistic and anti-subjectivistic currents that reflect a societal trend toward pragmatic problem solving and quick fixes. Psychoanalysis has been diminished by psychiatry through psychopharmacology, and by psychology through reliance on cognitive behavioral approaches as a panacea for all problems. Aside from the Humanities, one might say that psychoanalysis is regarded as an elitist cult.

As a consequence of all these well-known developments, we do have fewer patients, fewer candidates, a loss of professorships by psychoanalysts in the behavioral sciences, and a dramatic incapacity to compete for leading academic positions in psychiatry and psychology in Europe, North America and South America. Psychoanalysis has experienced a loss of stature in psychiatry, clinical psychology, and within graduate social work departments. Competition for candidates and patients among psychoanalytically derived psychotherapy societies and institutes has been diluting basic psychoanalytic practice, and raises the question of where the professional boundary of psychoanalysis actually lies. Our profession is aging, and shows an alarming lack of growth on all continents, except Eastern Europe and China, where there is a nascent endeavor to import psychoanalysis via internet education and training, mostly from American analysts. I believe it is fair to state that, while psychoanalysis has assured its place as a major contribution to the culture in the twentieth century, its future as a profession and a science in the twenty-first century cannot be assumed.

## Internal problems of the psychoanalytic community

While there may exist less than optimal agreement within our community as to what exactly our internal problems are, it seems reasonable to state that we have serious conflicts around psychoanalytic training; around alternative, contradictory and in part incompatible theories and technical approaches, and a related lack of clear understanding and realistic approaches to resolving differences in theory and technique, with their implications for the development of psychoanalytic practice (Berman, 2004; Garza Guerrero, 2006;

Meyer, 2003; Reeder, 2004; Thomä, 2004). A general "ecumenical" arrangement of coexistence of such different approaches reflects a reassuring growth of mutual tolerance, but mitigates the resolution of such conflicts and the pursuit of empirical validation of clinical approaches that would stimulate the development and improvement of psychoanalytic treatment and its applications. In earlier contributions to the analysis of the internal problems of our profession I have suggested that psychoanalysis suffers from fears of organizational renovation, a generally accepted lack of a scientific approach to differences in theory and technique, fear of exploring psychoanalytic approaches to severe psychopathologies that may require significant technical modifications, and a general self-protective isolation from the sciences at the boundaries of our field (Chapter 9). I have suggested in earlier work that all these reasons for lack of progress relate to a comfortable, but rigid and self-destructive educational system that centers around the training analysis system. I also have suggested that while, obviously, many of the problems experienced in relation with the external environment, as well as within the internal life of the psychoanalytic community cannot be resolved by a simple change in our educational methodology, nonetheless, a fundamental reorganization of our educational system may contribute significantly to create a dynamic of organizational strength, intellectual excitement, and professional and scientific impact. It may facilitate progress in the science, in the profession and its applications, and increase the impact of psychoanalysis on its surrounding culture.

I proposed, in a plenary lecture of the 1984 Annual Meeting of the American Psychoanalytic Association, the existence of four models of training: the university college, the professional technical school, the art academy, and the religious retreat (Chapter 3). I proposed that, while the psychoanalytic aim, in carrying out psychoanalytic education, was that of combining the model of a university college and an art academy, in practice the structure of psychoanalytic institutes combined the characteristics of a professional technical school and a religious seminary. In later work, I suggested that the fact that the appointment of training analysts carried with it the implicit designation of an "expert" in supervision, teaching, and administrative leadership, it thus generated a non-functional accumulation of power, and transformed the group of training analysts into an authoritarian social structure (Kernberg, 2000). The availability of power appropriate to the task characterizes functional authority; the appropriation of power beyond functional needs characterizes authoritarianism, the exercise of power that is not functionally justified. This development was rewarding psychologically, politically, socially, and even economically to the training analysis social structure's membership. The foundation for the appointment of training analysts was kept without clear, objective, reliable and transparent criteria. This facilitated the process of the controlled reproduction of such a power structure, geared to maintain its cohesion, kept aspirants in a position of uncertainty and submissiveness, and, adding to the fact that candidates must be analyzed by these training analysts, complemented a vicious cycle of the establishment of a class structure. In this structure the training analyst stratum, the stratum of graduates aspiring training analysis status, and the stratum of candidates jointly represent the order of a political system. This structure, I proposed, fosters idealization, submissiveness, a paranoid atmosphere which fosters splitting mechanisms, rebelliousness, and, above all, an atmosphere of infantilization of candidates, monopoly of theory and technique, and the combination of dogmatism and fearfulness regarding scientific questioning of accepted principles.

While this general situation has much improved in recent years, in the sense of the tolerance of multiple theoretical and technical approaches in the same institute under the influence of the unavoidable increase of generally shared information and teaching assignments to non-training analysts, the major problems remain unchanged. They include the general isolation from the external scientific world, the dogmatic affirmation of basic truths within the different approaches, the loss of relationship to the university and academia. The fearful, and even paranoid atmosphere within particular institutes is matched by the splits and chronic conflicts in others. Harold Blum (2012) has suggested that the wish to retain the exclusive power for appointing training analysts has been the leading motive for splits in many institutes. A widely shared fear of empirical research is sustained by the fantasy that such research implies denial or even rejection of long cherished beliefs and the uniqueness of the psychoanalytic frame (Kernberg, 2000).

The consequences of this state of affairs include a general fear of change, fear of challenges to what is the accustomed ways of doing things. The present system of psychoanalytic education exists since the 1920s, and the fear of resolving conflicts between alternative theories by means of objective testing of alternative hypotheses, scientific elaboration and exploration of findings, in general, the resolution of open questions by empirical methods of research is only recently and timidly developing. In contrast, pseudo-problems and pseudo-solutions have been ideologically circulating, such as the "uniqueness" of analytic science that cannot be related to any scientific methodology of any other science, the unique nature of every individual case that cannot be compared with any other case, the preoccupation with the "identity" of the psychoanalyst, as if such an identity could be separated from the nature of the habitual professional work, the pseudo-opposition of "hermeneutic" and "quantitative" empirical research. All these illustrate, I believe, the phobic attitude toward a scientific approach to psychoanalytic research.

At the same time, the complexity of the clinical situation and, of course, at the bottom, the complexity of unconscious psychological functioning that has been discovered by psychoanalysis defy simple explanations. This has fostered a tendency toward "guruism," that is, the idealization of some theoreticians whose originality and depth is then misused in the development of an overgeneralized understanding that implicitly should clarify all the boundaries of psychic reality at the same time: this has happened to the very important contributions of Melanie Klein, Hartmann, Lacan, Bion, Green, Kohut, etc. A simplification and overgeneralization of the respective theories conveys the impression of definite new developments and simultaneous resolutions of all the complexities of the clinical situation. When these competing and, at least, practically incompatible theories are complemented by a reassuring mutual tolerance, this leads to a dispersal or fragmentation of psychoanalytic understanding that makes the study of the relationship between psychoanalysis and the surrounding sciences even more difficult. On one extreme, Freud may be read as if it were bible reading, and on the other, one is reminded of Max Gittleson's statement "there are many people who believe in psychoanalysis, except sex, aggression, and transference."

Part of the effort to avoid scientific clarity and its related empirical approach to research can be observed in the mystification of psychoanalytic technique: to this date, we do not have a single, generally agreed upon, comprehensive textbook of technique, not even one agreed upon by part of the psychoanalytic community. Time does not permit me to illustrate this fact here: histories of psychoanalytic technique, simplified introductions, collected texts of members of a particular orientation do exist, but their very partial and simplified nature remains true. There is, on the one hand, a powerful stress, and on the other, a remarkable vagueness around concepts such as the "analytic attitude," "analytic process," "analytic identity." The over-generalization of particular concepts seems to reach the same degree of vagueness as the "ultimate reality O" in Bionian thinking, the over-generalization of human conflicts as relating to "trauma," the overextension of important concepts related to fundamental findings, such as the present emphasis on "attachment," etc. A reductionistic restriction to one or a few areas of Freudian concepts regarding motivation, development, and psychopathology fails to relate them to the contemporary understandings of the mutual relationships of constitution, temperament, somatization, character, primitive aggression and sexuality as played out in infancy and early childhood, and their impact in present reality on all the components of the personality activated in the relation with the analyst, in the transference.

Obviously, these are extremely complex dimensions, all of them touched in the psychoanalytic approach to psychic reality, that require clarity of definitions, analysis of their mutual relationships, incorporation of findings derived from psychoanalytic exploration as well as from the development in other scientific fields. All of that rich material has been languishing largely unexplored because of the dominant uninspired atmosphere in psychoanalytic education. Thus, for example, the important relation between drives and affects remains largely unexplored; as does the relationship between psychodynamics and neurobiology of depression; and, of course, the problems of the organizational aspects of psychoanalysis, that might be explored with the very findings of applications of psychoanalysis to understanding of group processes, remains underdeveloped.

One further consequence of authoritarianism in psychoanalytic education is the painful and too frequent development of corruption of power in our institutions. In my tenure as President of the International Psychoanalytic Association, where many such conflicts came to my attention, I was impressed by serious problems of boundary violation, sexual abuse, financial exploitation, arbitrariness, and antisocial behavior in all three regions, Europe, Latin America, and North America. Very often, these incidents involved leading training analysts, whose problems were knowledgeably tolerated over many years, leading to traumatization of candidates, general unhappiness, and disillusion with psychoanalysis as a profession.

A major area that has suffered because of the atmosphere of conservatism, fearfulness, and dogmatism in psychoanalytic education has been the application of psychoanalysis to the treatment of patients who cannot tolerate psychoanalysis or where psychoanalysis is not indicated, particularly the very severe psychopathologies, the frequency of which has been increasing throughout the Western world. The development of psychoanalytic psychotherapy has been neglected, often rejected, left to other organizations, empirical research in this area has been ignored, and frequently there has been an attitude, not only of fearfulness but direct hostility and opposition to psychotherapy as a competing modality of treatment that supposedly denies the uniqueness of psychoanalysis. Between the discovery of narcissistic pathology as a consequence of psychoanalytic experience from the early papers of Karl Abraham, to the development of a systematic technical approach to these patients in the 1960s, be it within the opposing theories of self-psychology and object relations approaches, the significant development of psychoanalytic technique based on those understandings only became generalized in the 1980s. This illustrates that, even in areas of significant theoretical and clinical progress, the stultified scientific atmosphere within psychoanalytic education and related professional exchanges has caused an impressive slowdown of development.

A lack of clarity and precision in concepts, in the formulation of the objectives of psychoanalytic education, in the very criteria for evaluating professional competence, have contributed to the arbitrary nature of the fate and advancement of candidates and the appointment of training psychoanalysts, where the subjectivity of the corresponding criteria, as mentioned before, also served important political purposes.

In this context, the observation of Francois Roustang (1982) that the purpose of psychoanalysis is the resolution of the transference, while the purpose of the training analysis includes the identification with one's training analyst is a radical contradiction that raises serious questions about the very nature of training analysis that was not seriously explored at that time. Its awareness never reached the table of open discussion and evaluation until the work of Luz Meyer (2003) in Brazil and others in the 1980s and later. Above all, the growth of psychoanalysis in the second half of the twentieth century, the increase in the number of training analysts that replicated, at international conferences, the division between analysts and training analysts in specialized meetings reserved for the latter, made painfully clear the existence of two levels of competence fostered by the training analysis system. Can we imagine in another profession, say, in cardiology, the existence of two levels of cardiologists, the regular ones, and the training cardiologists, with the understanding that the training cardiologists would be reserving their clinical work to treat ill cardiologists while the general population would have to make do with the ordinary cardiologists. In other words, many cardiologists would never be able to reach the highest level of their profession, they would not be eligible to become training cardiologists because the election of training cardiologists would depend on subjective criteria in the hands of those making the decisions, without any objective criteria for what it would take to ascend to a training cardiologist. And would the educated public, once it was informed of this stratification, seek out the "second string" cardiologists?

I am referring here, of course, to the lack of reflection on the consequences of the fact that subjective criteria determine the organizational differentiation of levels of competence and, of course, within psychoanalytic education, of authority and power as well. A parallel process involves candidates' evaluation, which takes place in the absence of clear standards of professional competence. In earlier work, I pointed to the fact that our so called professional standards essentially amounted to "bean counting." Criteria for competence becoming a matter of compliance, in terms of number of hours of personal analysis, of supervision, of attendance at analytic seminars, etc. (Kernberg, 2010). The absence of objective criteria to determine professional competence is, I believe, a truly shocking fact affecting the psychoanalytic profession. It certainly represents a major unfilled task of psychoanalysis as a profession to define the standards of competence in ways that would generate the development of a corresponding methodology of education, the objectives of which would be to achieve the desired level of competence, and a corresponding mechanism of evaluation of the progression toward, and the achievement of that competence. Objective criteria of competence would allow realistic quality control and realistic assessment of the competence of candidates at various stages of their development, objectively informing and confronting them with their progress, as well as with their shortcomings, and eliminating the atmosphere of uncertainty that presently prevails in psychoanalytic institutes around the world.

## Brief summary of advantages and disadvantages of the training analysis system

The training analysis system started 90 years ago in Berlin, and was later adopted by the International Training Committee. Its purpose, as Harold Blum observed (2005) was originally to "protect" proper psychoanalytic education, to promote group adhesion around Freud, and to select the best and brightest to ensure a high caliber product. The training analyst at first functioned as supervisor as well, in order to facilitate the candidates' countertransference analysis, but it was later recognized that the supervisory function should be separated, so that the training analyst, as such, in its present functions, became defined. Again, in Blum's overview these were positive intentions, and it needs to be said that the training analysis system, and its representative Board of Professional Standards (BOPS), in this country had a very positive function in the development of a high level of psychoanalytic education, that has been maintained uniformly throughout the many institutes of this country. At the international level, the education committees have, in general, been able to carry out similar work in producing a relatively uniform and high level of analytic training throughout the three regions. These positive features of the system were dominant in the early stages of psychoanalytic educational development, and it has been only the analysis of its long-range effects that have been creating the awareness of the problems created by it.

To begin, the training analysis system operated on naïve assumptions concerning intra-familiar conflicts in analytic organizations. It looked at its regressive consequences, observable in the institute in toto, as a replication of individual oedipal conflicts and family romance, and ignored the institutional dynamics related to regressive group processes, and the formation of a class system in terms of power distribution. Initially, the absolute control by the training analysts was reflected in the barbarian "reporting system" that, by now, has been mostly abolished. I am proud to have been one of the first to vehemently protest against this severe distortion of the psychoanalytic process. Older members of this readership may remember the frequently heard statement in earlier times, "the first analysis is for the institute, and the second one for myself."

The critique of Francois Roustang (1982) about the unanalyzable idealization of the training analyst only touched one aspect of the problem. It did not analyze the consequences of unrealistic idealization, nor the projection of split off negative reactions onto other aspects of the institute, other analysts, colleagues or theoretical orientations. The institute-wide hyper idealization of "training analyst" status, as the penultimate of professional achievement, served, therefore, as a restriction of intellectual and professional growth, if not granted by one's institute. The institutional contamination of this idealization of "training analyst" status is reflected, for example, in the frequent devaluation of academic careers, the devaluation of other professional interests, the disconnection from the university, and the discouragement of psychoanalytic candidates for obtaining the professional boards within the profession they were trained in originally, for example, obtaining Board Certification in Psychiatry and Neurology.

In addition, the idealization of psychoanalysis as carried out by training analysts interfered, more than the analysis of ordinary citizens outside any institutional context, with the recognition of the reality of limitations of psychoanalysis in particular cases, denial of disappointments with the effects of psychoanalysis leading to an ever lengthening process of treatment, particularly of training analyses, and an idealization of this extension of personal analysis. Not only were candidates, in many places, obliged to continue their personal psychoanalysis until graduation, but encouraged to continue many years beyond that, such that length (read longevity) of personal analysis became a positive element in the selection of training analysts.

This psychology has persisted to the present day: as one illustration, in a recent site visit to a leading university connected psychoanalytic institute in this country, the site visitors expressed their general positive impression of the institute, but had three critical formulations: (1) there was too much focus on descriptive research which may have caused, they believed, a lack of depth of interpretation of the transference on the part of candidates; (2) it seemed a problem that many of the graduates of the institute were dedicating themselves to be leaders of psychiatric institutions, clinics, and engaged in other professional endeavors in the behavior sciences, rather than dedicating themselves fully to carrying out psychoanalysis; (3) the institute graduated people too early, and they should probably remain in training longer. I trust there is no need for further comments about these recommendations, but I must add, out of personal knowledge, that the committee was constituted of very knowledgeable, intelligent, senior members of our profession.

The political dimension of the appointment of training analysts, generally speaking, has been reduced in an effort to make the process more public and accountable, but the subjectivity of the criteria, and the implied personal favoritism and unfavorable personal biases continue to haunt this system, as before. The privileging of training analysts to carry out supervision, seminars, and leadership of institute committees, regardless of personal capabilities, continues unchanged. Research, carried out in recent years at the Columbia Psychoanalytic Institute, regarding the knowledge that candidates have regarding what it takes to graduate showed an impressive lack of realistic information as to what was required by their own institute, by many of the interviewed candidates throughout the country (Cabaniss *et al.*, 2003).

The fantasy that candidates learn the technique of carrying out psychoanalysis by the experience of their own training analysis has continued unchanged, I believe, until this day. This, in spite of the massive evidence that it is precisely candidates with significant narcissistic psychopathology, and a profound difficulty in authentically depending on their own analysts, who "learn" best the style and procedures of their analysts, in a defensive process against the *emotional recognition* of their own unconscious fantasies and conflicts. Obviously, in any analysis the patient gradually internalizes his analyst's analytic attitude, with increasing curiosity about his own unconscious processes. In fact, the more effectively in his own analysis the candidate is exploring his own unconscious, with the help but not an imitation of the analyst, the more effectively may he learn about the vicissitudes of a personal psychoanalytic experience. And, of course, as mentioned before, the ideological effects of the training analysis system in the creation of an anti-research atmosphere, the infantilization of the candidates, the splitting of idealized and persecutory relationships, the professional and scientific isolation that it induces are effects that transcend those that affect the individual candidate. Finally, the consequences of this system include what might be called the psychological and professional deterioration that training analysts may suffer when too many of their patients are candidates. This situation fosters narcissistic self-aggrandizement of the analyst who is privileged to know and control the lives of their candidate/patients who are, by definition, subservient, non-questioning trainees who are expressing their experience of the authoritarian structure of the institution during their analytic hours in a shared blindness to the institutional dynamics. Wilson (2010) has explored other aspects of the narcissistic temptations of the training analyst.

## The institutional conflict in the American Psychoanalytic Association: the struggle between Executive Council and Board of Professional Standards

I assume that the membership of the American Psychoanalytic Association is well informed about the ongoing discussions involving the Executive Council and the Board of Professional Standards, and I wish to restrict myself to what I see as some essential dynamics of this situation relevant for the proposal that I shall present here. What is most striking is the amount of energy, time, and financial investment that our national organization is dedicating to this struggle between two leading components of the administrative structure of the American Psychoanalytic Association that, in fact, functions as if it were a bicameral organization, regardless of its legal structure. An enormous amount of energy and dedication is consumed by an internal struggle, while significant challenges at the boundaries of psychoanalysis with the external world would require much more of our total energy and resource expenditure. I am suggesting that this struggle, at the bottom, again reflects the self-destructive features of our present educational system. On the surface, the demand from the Executive Council that the Board of Professional Standard establish criteria for objectivity, reliability and transparency for appointment of training analysts is objectively fair and necessary. It reflects the organizational frustration with the lack of progress in developing professional standards of competence in contrast to the present criteria for compliance, and represents an effort to reduce the level of subjectivity and related arbitrariness in the appointment of training analysts.

The reluctance of the BOPS to fulfill this mandate is understandable. This mandate implicitly criticizes the striking lack of progress on the establishment of standards of professional competence, and, at a deeper level, threatens the power base of the training analysis system. In fact, if and when the BOPS were to develop such objective criteria, they would, by the same token, reflect the objective criteria of professional competence that have been so remarkably absent to this point. The question then becomes, why not consider these as the standards of professional competence valid for the entire analytic profession, applicable for certification to all graduates, with a certain level of professional experience, willing to be examined on the basis of these criteria? It would become a true, honest, objective certification of psychoanalysts, and end the elevation of a privileged class, and the training analysis system in the process.

As my proposal will deal with the abolishment of the training analysis system, I refer to this present controversy in the sense that it reflects an important aspect of the general problem under review, although, in my view, it does not yet involve a systematic, radical innovation of psychoanalytic education. The psychodynamics of this struggle, however, are of interest. I believe that the BOPS, as a body, is honestly concerned with maintaining standards, and it has to be kept in mind that generations of analysts have been instructed to misinterpret the criteria of compliance as professional standards, and that standards of professional competence is a concept with which the BOPS had not really been concerned over many years of its existence. So the wish to maintain what is presently called standards, and the related fear that these standards are at risk of being diluted by the claims of objectivity, reliability and transparency that come from the membership of the organization, can be understood as a concern of the BOPS. At the same time, from the viewpoint of the Executive Council, the obvious reluctance and anxiety of the BOPS to proceed with this request reflects the fear of reduction in their authority, and that of the training analysis system to maintain decision-making power, and the authoritarian wish to maintain control over the educational system and, at the bottom, over the total organization in the assumption of political assertion throughout all administrative levels. Robert Michels (2012) has suggested that in all professional organizations operates a dynamic of conflict between the educational establishment that tries to raise and maintain professional standards, and the membership at large that attempts to minimize the corresponding bureaucratic burden.

I believe that, in the case under review, these organizational dynamics are powerfully reinforced by implicit, regressive features of this process, that do not correspond to consciously attempted goals, but to the natural fact that as a social class the training analysis system jealously attempts to maintain its power. At the same time, I think that, in so far as Executive Council represents the membership of the organization that has implicitly suffered under the authoritarian distortion of the power of the educational system, it wants to "loosen" the present bureaucratically expressed criteria based on the subjective judgment of the power structure, and that, in that regard, it may wish, indeed, to "reduce" the supposed standards. I believe that the authoritarian distortion of power in psychoanalytic organizations generates a rebelliousness against it that may take the form of seemingly reducing standards, and that such impulses are definitely not or much reduced present when such an authoritarian structure is not in place. The proof for my argument is the observation that newly founded psychoanalytic societies under the sponsorship of the International Psychoanalytic Associations have had a strong motivation for high professional standards, shared by the entire organization, and led to a non-controversial generation of psychoanalytic institutes geared to obtain such standards of training in its educational methodology. The conflict between the BOPS and Executive Council, I believe, reflects the chronic distortion of the organizational functioning by the historically regressive development of the present authoritarian structure of psychoanalytic education. In designating the present system of psychoanalytic education as authoritarian and, therefore, non-functional, this does not mean that it has not been able, in spite of this organizational distortion, to train professional psychoanalysts at an acceptable level of competence, even if the criteria are not present and there are no reliable ways of assuring level of competence. I believe that the present training analysis system, in practice, goes from effective to benignly arbitrary to malignantly arbitrary, and that the participants in this system, as individuals, are unaware of the dynamic of the system that they are generating and perpetuating. The fact that over so many years, and in spite of numerous critics of the system, criteria of compliance should remain a proxy for standards of competence is not due to any individual incompetence or dishonesty, but is a consequence of the dynamics of a social system. The Latin proverb *Senatus mala bestia, senatores probi viri*, translated as *the senate is a nasty beast, but the senators are honest men* applies to the BOPS as well, and that all its members, in fact, all the training analysts, or the immense majority of them, would be functioning very effectively within a different organizational structure that solves the problem of the authoritarian implications of the present educational system. I am convinced that, once an educational system is truly functional, the dialectic between those who want to maintain control arbitrarily, and those who want to rebel against it would largely disappear.

## A proposal for fundamental reorganization
## of our educational system

I am proposing to completely abolish the training analysis system. The designation of "training analyst" should be replaced by an objective, reliable, and transparent set of criteria of competence, assessed in a certification process with these characteristics, open to all graduates of all psychoanalytic institutes within a certain number of years of experience after graduation, say, five years. This certification would be equivalent to the board certification in medical specialties, and be carried out by an external certifying board established by the national organization, in this case, the American Psychoanalytic Association, with a rotating membership nominated by the membership at large and elected by the Executive Council. This Certifying Board, which could also serve as committee for the accreditation of institutes, would function completely autonomously and carry out the certification process on the basis of established standards of competence corresponding to the educational objectives specified by the organization, to which I shall return. All certified analysts may analyze candidates. The certified analyst who analyzes candidates would not, by this function, become part of the psychoanalytic institute, and the personal analysis would function completely independently from all the psychoanalytic institute's educational functions. The only responsibility of the analyst would be, with the agreement of the candidate, to convey information to the institute regarding beginning, end, or suspension of that analysis.

The present BOPS would be abolished, and replaced by an Education Committee with a small number of highly expert, nationally and internationally recognized educational experts nominated by the membership, and elected by Executive Council. This Education Committee would carry out the task of defining the criteria of professional competence, the major objectives of psychoanalytic education, developing the methodology for achieving those objectives, and the criteria for assessing, step by step, the achievement of the corresponding competency by psychoanalytic candidates. It is understood that this work would take a significant amount of time, involve significant resources, and the conclusions of the Education Committee would be submitted for approval to the Executive Council and then become the guidelines for the Certifying Board.

Simultaneously, I am proposing an active participation of a Conference of Institute Directors in terms of generating information and proposals to be presented to the Education Committee for its consideration, and there would take place an active interchange of new initiatives by the Education Committee and the Conference of Institute Directors, leading to an ongoing revision and renovation of educational methodology elaborated by the Education Committee and proposed for action to the Executive Council. The Conference of Institute Directors may, themselves, suggest nominations for members of the Education Committee. It seems reasonable to consider the possibility that the nomination of part of the Education Committee come from the membership, and part of it from the Institute Directors, with final approval by Executive Council. As mentioned before, the Certifying Board would function completely autonomously, applying the approved standards of competence for the certification of psychoanalysts, and applying these same criteria for the assessment of the methodology of education of individual institutes, their achievements, and their educational success in terms of the proportion of their graduates that apply for certification and are successfully certified.

The certification examination would include the assessment of the following three major components of professional competence suggested by Körner (2002): knowledge, technical skill, and analytic attitude. It is assumed that knowledge is relatively easy to assess by standard tests, once the decision of what basic knowledge should be incorporated by all candidates has been established. Technical skills may be assessed by a combination of specific instruments, already available for the assessment of competence in psychoanalytic psychotherapies (Muller & Rieder, 2004), as well as clinical situations presented to the applicants, as, for example, videotapes of actual sessions and/or typewritten reproduction of them with a corresponding examination regarding relevant alternative technical interventions. Psychoanalytic attitude may be evaluated by the candidate presenting cases he/she has treated, his/her understanding of them, and, in many ways, would follow that similar aspect of the present selection of training analysts, reflecting the inclusion of subjective criteria as part of an examination that is, however, framed by objective, verifiable, and transparent criteria. Appropriate mechanisms for redress of grievances would complement this process.

At this point, I may mention a more radical proposal formulated recently by Robert Wallerstein, one of our most distinguished and experienced psychoanalytic educators:

What I am suggesting, and I trust not rashly, is a trial by at least some established psychoanalytic training entity, of such a system as I propose—the voluntary psychoanalytic treatment, as desired or felt needed by the candidate, combined with the strengthened, more rigorous educational program of theoretical and clinical seminars, together with intensive, properly long psychoanalytic supervisions of an adequately diverse set of control cases—together with an intensive, many year-long (at least ten) monitoring and research study of achieved outcomes in terms of the demonstrated clinical competence of the graduates. (Wallerstein, 2010).

While not endorsing this proposal, I believe it deserves our attention, illustrating the wide spectrum of concern over the present training analysis system.

Obviously, the development of criteria of professional competence, methodologies for evaluating the acquisition of competence, the development of curriculi in the realm of psychoanalytic theory of personality development, pathology, treatment, and applications, would require significant time and research. This is the task that the BOPS should have been engaged in for many years, yet did not pursue. A new educational system could not be implemented from one day to the next, and would require a long period of time in which the present system would continue functioning while the proposed Education Committee carries out its tasks. Upon the completion of these tasks by the Education Committee, the Certifying Board may be appointed, again, with members proposed by the membership of the organization and the Conference of Institutes to Executive Council. After the selection and appointment of the Certifying Board, the certifying process may take place autonomously, independently from both Executive Council and Education Committee, while the Education Committee continues its work on educational renovation, on an ongoing basis. Any changes in certification criteria, or, in general, of the working criteria for the Certification Board would have to be proposed by the combined action of the Education Committee and the Conference of Institute Directors, and proposed to the Executive Council for approval. The complexity of the process of carrying out changes in the certifying process should assure the educational authorities of the organization against regressive efforts for reducing requirements or adding requirements not justified by educational needs, while the ultimate authority of the Executive Council, supported by the innovative work of the Education Committee, should prevent educational petrification.

In parallel to this overall administrative structure, institute faculty would be constituted by the body of supervisors, seminar leaders, researchers, and candidate representatives. Ongoing group seminars studying psychoanalytic cases, involving candidates as well as society members, would permit the selection of expert supervisors; the presentations, panels, and conferences of the psychoanalytic society would facilitate the selection of seminar leaders who may provide original and stimulating contributions to the various areas of the curriculum; a department of research should combine a group of experts to help candidates and faculty, as well as members of the society, raise questions and develop scholarly research as well as empirical methods for controlled investigations of such questions. The leadership of the institute would be selected by these faculty groups, and the Institute Directors be responsible either to the psychoanalytic society, of which this institute is a component, or to the head of the administrative department of a university setting of which that institute forms a part. The analysis of the corresponding administrative problems, checks and balances, and assurance of functional organization are beyond the scope of this particular presentation.

I need to stress that, as may already have emerged from the proposed structures and governance involved in psychoanalytic education, the simple abolishment of the training analysis system and its corollary, BOPS, would not solve by itself the problem of rigidification, authoritarian structure, and absence of present-day educational objectives, methodology, and functional methods of certification and the accreditation of institutes. The preliminary work carried out by the proposed Education Committee following the mandate of the Executive Council to develop standards of competence, generally acceptable objectives of psychoanalytic education, the corresponding methods of education, and methods and instruments of quality control and evaluation of the development and achievement of professional competence will require careful and lengthy work that, while it is proceeding, will require the maintenance of the present structure during the transitional time until the new structure can take its place. The automatic certification of training analysts may consolidate the period of transition to the new system. The selection of an institute faculty based upon the corresponding specific supervisory, teaching, or research skills may proceed gradually and may be supported by a methodology developed by the Education Committee. The point where clear objectives of psychoanalytic education and objective, verifiable, reliable and transparent criteria of competence have been achieved, may mark a crucial point at which the Certification Committee may be appointed, the Conference of Institute Directors organize itself and begin its function in relation to the Education Committee, and the Board of Professional Standards pass into oblivion together with the entire training analysis system.

At that point, work on the criteria for selection, progression, and graduation of psychoanalytic candidates may proceed in the light of the educational objectives and the methodology for their evaluation.

## Summarizing overview

This proposal contemplates abolishing the Board of Professional Standards and replacing it with a high level Education Committee selected by Executive Council, in charge of defining objectives and methods of psychoanalytic education and corresponding quality control, and methodology of certification. A certifying board, in charge of implementation of Executive Council's decision regarding criteria for certification and accreditation upon the recommendation of the Education Committee and advisory functions of the Conference of Institute Directors complements this arrangement. A permanent Conference of Directors of Institutes would carry out the task generating proposals to the Education Committee and react to the Education Committee's proposals, and, together with the Education Committee, may suggest changes in the criteria for certification. The autonomy of the Certification Board would be limited by such new proposals stemming from an Executive Council's decision based on joint recommendation of the Education Committee and Institute Directors. The Institute Directors Conference would be elected by institute faculties constituted by seminar leaders, supervisors, research representatives and students' representation.

This structure, in short, abolishes the category of training analyst and the training analyst system in total, replacing it by a process of certification available to all graduates after a period of post-graduate experience, with the explicit authority for all certified psychoanalysts to carry out analysis of the general public as well as of psychoanalytic candidates, without that activity implying that they are a member of the faculty of a psychoanalytic institute. Such certified analysts who are analyzing candidates may, of course, be eligible as members of institute faculty if, and when, their specific talents in the area of supervision, seminar leadership, or research would warrant it.

I believe that this proposal may provide the possibility of a high level quality control without the related risk of stifling the freedom of development in psychoanalytic education. It would eliminate to a large extent the authoritarian consequences of the training analysis system, and provide psychoanalysts with a high level of education and the potential excitement of the intellectual world of the institute, eliminate the odious class division presently existing in our profession, and provide alternative career ladders for psycho-analysts, involving both their activities in psychoanalytic institutes and societies, as well as academic enterprises linked to identification with psychoanalytic theory and knowledge. It would attempt to put psychoanalysis at the forefront of the development of contemporary psychotherapies, foster academic and university recognition by the commitment to a significant research enterprise, and, to conclude, assure the future of psychoanalytic science and profession for the present century.

## Note

1 Published in *The Psychoanalytic Review.*

## Bibliography

Berman, E. (2004). *Impossible Training: A Relational View of Psychoanalytic Education.* New York: Analytic Press, p. 288.

Blum, H. (2005). Discussion of O. Kernberg's Paper: "The Coming Changes in Psychoanalytic Education." Professional meeting of the Association for Psychoanalytic Medicine, New York, March 2005.

Cabaniss, D.L., Schein, J.W., Rosen, P. & Roose S.P. (2003). Candidate Progression in Analytic Institutes: A Multicenter Study. *Int. J. Psychoanal.,* 84: 77–94.

Garza-Guerrero, C. (2004). Reorganizational and Educational Demands of Psychoanalytic Training Today: Our Long and Marasmic Night of One Century (With a Rejoinder by Eglé Laufer). *Int. J. Psychoanal.,* 85: 3–25.

Körner, J. (2002). The didactics of psychoanalytic education. *Int. J. Psychoanal.,* 83: 1395–1405.

Meyer, L. (2003). Subservient Analysis. *Int. J. Psychoanal.,* 84: 1241–1262.

Michels, R. (2012). Personal Communication.

Mullen, L.S. & Rieder, R.O. (2004). The Psychodynamic Psychotherapy Contemporary Test, 2004 version (unpublished manuscript).

Kernberg, O. (2010). A New Organization of Psychoanalytic Education. *Psychoanalytic Review*, 97(6): 1–24.

_____ (2000). A Concerned Critique of Psychoanalytic Education. *The International Journal of Psycho-Analysis*, 81: 97–120.

Reeder, J. (2004). *Hate and Love in Psychoanalytic Institutions: The Dilemmas of a Profession*. New York: Other Press, p. 808.

Roustang, F. (1982). *Dire Mastery: Discipleship from Freud to Lacan*. Baltimore, MD: Johns Hopkins University Press, p 160.

Thomä, H. (2004). Psychoanalysis without a Specific Professional Identity: A Utopian Dream? *Int. Forum Psychoanal.*, 13: 213–236.

Wallerstein, R.S. (2010). The Training Analysis: Psychoanalysis' Perennial Problem. *Psychoanalytic Review*, 97: 903–936.

Wilson, M. (2010). Putting Practice into Theory: Making the Training Analyst System Coherent. *Journal of the American Psychoanalytic Association*, 58(2): 287–311.

# Index

Made in the USA
Middletown, DE
24 February 2018